BELIEF IN MEDIA

To our partners, families and friends who, even through long absences of extended travel and meetings, encouraged us to pursue this new direction.

Belief in Media

Cultural Perspectives on Media and Christianity

Edited by

Peter Horsfield
Mary E. Hess
Adán M. Medrano

ASHGATE

Peter Horsfield, Mary E. Hess and Adán M. Medrano have asserted their moral right under the Copyright, Designs and Patents Act, 1988, to be identified as the editors of this work.

Published by
Ashgate Publishing Limited
Gower House
Croft Road
Aldershot
Hants GU11 3HR
England

Ashgate Publishing Company
Suite 420
101 Cherry Street
Burlington, VT, 05401–4405 USA

Ashgate website: http://www.ashgate.com

British Library Cataloguing in Publication Data
Belief in Media: Cultural Perspectives on Media and Christianity
  1. Technology – Religious aspects – Christianity. 2. Mass media – Religious aspects –
  Christianity. 3. Progress – Religious aspects – Christianity. 4. Christianity and culture.
  5. Spirituality – Social aspects. I. Horsfield, Peter. II. Hess Manry E. III. Medrano, Adán M.
  261.5'2

Library of Congress Cataloging in Publication Data
Belief in Media: Cultural Perspectives on Media and Christianity / edited by Peter Horsfield,
  Mary E. Hess and Adán M. Medrano.
    p. cm.
  Includes bibliographical references and index.
  1. Mass media – Religious aspects – Christianity. 2. Christianity and culture. 3. Mass media
  and culture. I. Horsfield, Peter G. II. Hess Manry E. III. Medrano, Adán M.
  P94.B45 2004
  261.5'2–dc22

2004006141

ISBN 0 7546 3830 8

Typeset by IML Typographers, Birkenhead, Merseyside
Printed and bound in Great Britain by MPG Books Ltd, Bodmin, Cornwall

Contents

List of Figures

Contributors

J. Kwabena Asamoah-Gyadu did postgraduate studies in religion at the University of Ghana and holds a Ph.D. in Theology from the University of Birmingham, UK. He is Lecturer in the Study of Religion; Pentecostal/Charismatic Theology; and Theology, Media and Culture at the Trinity Theological Seminary, Legon, Ghana. Dr Asamoah-Gyadu was elected to serve as Senior Research Fellow at the Center for the Study of World Religions, Harvard University (2004). His works include: 'Blowing the Cover': Religious Functionaries in African Films', *Legon Journal of Humanities* (2003); and *African Charismatics* (Leiden: E. J. Brill, forthcoming). He is currrently researching into the appropriation of modern media technologies by Pentecostal/charismatic movements in West Africa focusing on the handbills, posters, and banners through which they advertise their programs.

Lynn Schofield Clark is Assistant Research Professor on the faculty of the School of Journalism and Mass Communication at the University of Colorado, where she is also Director of the Teens and the New Media @ Home Research Project. A former television producer and marketing professional who has spent years as a volunteer with young people, Clark is author of *From Angels to Aliens: Teenagers, the Media, and the Supernatural* (Oxford University Press, 2003), co-author of *Media, Home, and Family* (Routledge, 2003), and co-editor of *Practicing Religion in the Age of the Media: Explorations in Media, Religion and Culture* (Columbia University Press, 2001). A member of the Academic Advisory Board for the Pew Internet & American Life Project, Clark was a 1997–98 Louisville Institute Dissertation Fellow and a 1998 nominee to the Harvard Society of Fellows. She currently serves as the Secretary to the Popular Communication Division of the International Communication Association and is on the editorial board for the journal, *Popular Communication*.

Roberto S. Goizueta is Professor of Theology at Boston College. He is President-Elect of the Catholic Theological Society of America and a past President of the Academy of Catholic Hispanic Theologians of the United States. Dr Goizueta has a B.A. degree in Political Science from Yale University, M.A. and Ph.D. degrees in Religious Studies from Marquette University, and an honorary doctorate from the University of San Francisco. The *National Catholic Reporter* has named him one of the ten most influential Hispanic American educators, pastors and theologians.

Dr Goizueta's book *Caminemos con Jesus: Toward a Hispanic/Latino Theology of Accompaniment* has received a Catholic Press Association Book Award. He is married and has three children.

Juan Carlos Henríquez is Research Professor in the Department of Communications of the Universidad Iberoamericana in México City, where he teaches Communication Theories and Communication and Cultural Problematic. He is director of the Design of the Research Project on 'Media Religion' de la Universidad Iberoamericana. He is a member of the Society of Jesus. He has been a video maker, and his production *Ciudad Apocalipsis* (1995) is a seven-chapter work in two volumes that explores new video expressions to teach about biblical themes. He was the Director of the Production Department of the Centro de Comunicación Javier in México City. Involved in grassroots communications processes, he was the director of the community radio station, Radio Pueblo, in Guadalajara and program director of Radio Teocelo XEYT and Radio XEJN in Huayacocotla, Veracruz. Until August 2003 he was the director of the College Radio XHUIA Ibero 90.9 Radio in México City.

Mary E. Hess is Assistant Professor of Educational Leadership at Luther Seminary, an ELCA seminary in St Paul, MN. She is a Roman Catholic layperson whose research focuses on the challenges posed to religious education within media culture contexts. She is a member of the executive committee of the Association of Professors and Researchers in Religious Education. Her recent publications include: 'Practicing Attention in Media Culture', in *Mediating Religion: Conversations in Media, Religion and Culture*, edited by Jolyon Mitchell and Sophia Marriage, T&T Clark/Continuum, 2003; 'Marriage on TV,' *Word & World*, Vol. XXIII, No. 1, Winter 2003; and 'Rich Treasure in Jars of Clay,' in *The Conviction of Things Not Seen: Worship and Ministry in the 21st Century*, edited by Todd E. Johnson, Brazos Press, 2002. She also contributes regularly to the journal *Religious Education*, and she maintains a web site at http://www.luthersem.edu/mhess.

Stewart M. Hoover is Professor in the School of Journalism and Mass Communication at the University of Colorado. He is Adjoint Professor in the Department of Religious Studies and in the Program in American Studies. He is an internationally known scholar of media and religion, media audiences and media practice, and is co-editor of a book series on media and religion published by Routledge in London. His own books include *Mass Media Religion: The Social Sources of the Electronic Church* (1988); *Religion in the News: Faith and Journalism in American Public Discourse* (1998); *Media, Home, and Family* (2003), of which he was a co-author, and the forthcoming *Religion in the Media Age*. In addition, he has co-edited three books, the most recent of which is *Practicing Religion in the Age of the Media* (with Lynn Schofield Clark).

Peter Horsfield teaches and is the Program Manager for the Bachelor of Communication at RMIT University in Melbourne, Australia. He has published widely in the area of Christian uses of media and the social and theological impact of media developments. His earlier work, *Religious Television: The American Experience* (1994), is recognized as one of the early classics in studies on televangelism. From 1987 to 1996 he was Dean of the Uniting Church Theological Hall in Melbourne and from 1997 to 1999 headed the Electronic Culture Research Project for the Uniting Church in Australia. He chairs the Executive Committee of International Catholic Fellowships for Research in Media, Religion and Culture. His most recent publication is *The Mediated Spirit*, a CD-Rom on the influence of media in the historical development of Christianity (http://www.mediatedspirit. com).

Adán M. Medrano is President of JM Communications and an award-winning producer of religious digital media. In 1981 he was the founding President of Hispanic Telecommunications Network and executive producer of the national Spanish-language TV series, *Nuestra Familia*, broadcast on Univisión TV Network in the USA. In 1976 he founded *San Antonio CineFestival*, the first and longest-running exhibition venue for Latino film and video in the USA. Among his recent productions are: *The Catechism of the Catholic Church*, a five part Spanish-language series produced for the US Conference of Catholic Bishops, *Hope In A Time of AIDS* produced for National Catholic Charities USA, and the interactive web site of the Catholic Migrant Farmworker Network. Among the awards that have honored his productions are the Gabriel Awards, Telly Awards and the Chicago International Film Festival. In 2001 he served as a juror in the Ecumenical Jury of the Cannes Film Festival.

Jolyon Mitchell is Senior Lecturer at New College, Edinburgh University, where he is also director of the Media and Theology Project. He teaches both postgraduates and undergraduates in fields related to media, religion and culture, as well as film and theology. He is also a life member of Clare Hall, Cambridge University. He is author of *Visually Speaking: Radio and the Renaissance of Preaching* (Edinburgh: T&T Clark, 1999), and co-editor of *Mediating Religion: Conversations in Media, Religion and Culture* (London: Continuum, 2003). He was formerly a producer and journalist with BBC World Service. Programs produced include *Garrison Keillor's Radio Preachers* for BBC Radio 4 and a BBC World Service *Omnibus* documentary on Western African video films. He is currently working on *Media and Christian Ethics* (Cambridge University Press, forthcoming).

David Morgan is the Phyllis and Richard Duesenberg Professor of Christianity and the Arts in Christ College, Valparaiso University (Indiana). Morgan has chaired the ISCMRC for several years and published several books on the history of religious visual culture. These include *Visual Piety: A History and Theory of Popular Religious Images* (1998) and *Protestants and Pictures: Religion, Visual Culture, and The Age of American Mass Production* (1999). His latest book is *Religious Visual Culture in Theory and Practice* (2005). Morgan is also co-founder and co-editor of the international journal, *Material Religion: The Journal of Objects, Art, and Belief.*

Jin Kyu Park is a doctoral student and research assistant for the Symbolism, Meaning and New Media @ Home Project at the School of Journalism and Mass Communication, the University of Colorado at Boulder. As a nationality holder of Republic of Korea, he has a B.A. degree in Mass Communication from Yonsei University, Seoul, Korea and a M.A. degree in Journalism from the University of Texas at Austin. His research interests focus on: religion as a component for audiences' cultural text reading; religious and ethnic identity construction and media use; Japanese *Anime*'s intercultural popularity and its religious implications; the Internet as a medium for religious expression and meaning making.

Frances Forde Plude is Professor of Communications at Notre Dame College, Cleveland, Ohio. She completed doctoral studies in telecommunications and public policy at Harvard University and MIT and has taught at Syracuse University, John Carroll University and Emerson College. She has served as consultant to the US Congress, the US Conference of Catholic Bishops and the telecommunications ministers of the European Union. Her work in conceptualizing the new field of Communications Theology has led to publications and seminars in this field. She is a co-author of the Longman book, *Communications Ethics and Global Change.*

Germán Rey is Professor in the Department of Communications of the Pontifical Javeriana University in Bogotá, Colombia and also Vice President of the Fundación Social. He is a regular presenter at the Latin American *Creators of Christian Images* seminars. He has been advisor to the Ministry of Communications of Colombia and is a regular media columnist in the daily newspaper, *El Tiempo*. He has also been an expert of the Department of Communications of CELAM (Latin American Council of Catholic Bishops). He is co-author of three books, *La Imagen Nuestra de Cada Día*, *La Realidad Imaginada* and *Imagens da América Latina* dealing with church ministry and video culture in Latin America. His other books include: *Las Industrias Culturales* (México) and *Escenografías Para el Diálogo* (Lima). He is on the editorial board of the journal, *Revista de Estudios Sociales* and is director of the book series, *Conversaciones.*

Siriwan Santisakultarm holds a Bachelor's degree in journalism and a Master's degree in social welfare from the Thammasart University of Thailand. She has 15 years of working experience as a producer for children's programming and news reporter on the nationwide wide Thai TV Channel 9. While working as a TV reporter, she specialized in children's and women's stories and on social issues that emphasized social concern for human values, peace and justice. A number of her broadcasting productions received awards both nationally and internationally. In 1990 she was recognized by the department of National Youth Bureau under the office of Prime Minister as the first and best reporter for children's stories in Thailand. In November 2001 she received the Agnellus Andrew Award, an award for lifetime achievement in the field of Catholic communications. She is currently the President of Signis-Asia, serves on the Bishop's Conference of the Catholic Church of Thailand in the Department of Social Communication and has been instrumental in the establishment of Signis in Cambodia.

Robert A. White has recently retired as Director of the Centre for Interdisciplinary Studies in Communication of the Gregorian University, Rome, Italy and continues to teach there in communication ethics, interreligious dialogue, communication for development, and seminars in media religion and culture. He is editor of the book series, *Communication and Human Values* and Associate Member of the Publications Committee of the International Association for Mass Communication Research. He was Research Director of the Centre for the Study of Communications and Culture in London throughout the 1980s and in the early 1970s was Associate, the Institute of Socio-Economic Studies in Tegucigalpa, Honduras. He is a member of the Society of Jesus. He initiated the book series in Latin America, *Comunicación* and was founding editor of *Communication, Culture and Theology* published by Sheed and Ward. He is the author of numerous articles in the area of communication ethics, communication and development, theology and communication and media and religious development.

All but Jin Kyu Park are core group members of the International Study Commission on Media, Religion and Culture.

Media, Culture and Religion: An Introduction

Peter Horsfield

In his book *Cosmopolis*, Stephen Toulmin suggests that the issue of religion is pivotal in understanding the rise and influence of the scientific rationalist movement in the modern period. Even though science and rationalism claim to be rigorously secular and 'objective' in their interests and not concerned with matters of religion, the question of religion stands at the center of the major shifts that have taken place in the modern period (Toulmin, 1990).

Toulmin's work provides an analysis of the emergence of scientific rationalism out of Renaissance humanism in the seventeenth century and how its influence spread into every arena of western life: through Galileo into astronomy and mechanics, through Descartes into logic and epistemology, and through Hobbes into political and social organization.[1] The irony for Toulmin is that this major social revolution whose emphasis has been on building a universe of unconditioned, objective knowledge and practice arose as a solution to a specific historical situation. That situation was the practical need to find a solution to the religious wars of the seventeenth century.

The deep trauma and chaos of these long-running wars between Roman Catholics and Protestants in Central Europe created a longing for a basis of certainty by which the apparent arbitrariness and differences in religious doctrines and knowledge could be managed politically. It led to a search for a practical intellectual basis for a secular nation-state or what Toulmin calls 'a new cosmopolis', a view of the world (cosmos) as a basis for the ordering of society ('polis').

In this context the work of René Descartes opened up for people in his generation the hope of reasoning their way out of political and theological chaos and uncertainty. The alternative basis he proposed was human cognition deriving from the fundamental certainty, 'I think, therefore I am', a genuine alternative to the previous humanistic skepticism of Montaigne and the uncontestable dogma of revelation.

Initially the intent of modern thinkers was neither anti-religious nor to do away with religion, but to find a more harmonious way of being Christian citizens. As it developed, however, scientific rationalism came into conflict with the approach of faith because of its alternative way of knowing and the different world and political views that emerged from this. If its major historical impulse was to find a basis for greater certainty then, as Graham Murdock has noted, as it developed the scientific rationalist movement took on characteristics of a 'totalizing project', a quest not just to explain, but also to predict, manipulate and control, to create a cosmos in which there was no room left for any mysterious incalculable forces.

> Its aim was to calibrate the messiness of the world so that Nature could be tamed, workers made more docile, books balanced, and complexity contained. To this end the champions of modernity waged an unceasing war to defend the sovereignty of reason against mystery, magic, and faith ... To win the stakes, to win all of them and to win them for good, the world had to be *de-spiritualized*. (Murdock, 1997, p. 86)

Changes in media were fundamental in these social and religious changes. The development and expansion of the printing press was essential to development of the western scientific movement. Among the first texts printed were early classic Hellenistic works that had codified and systematized scientific knowledge into well-organized textbooks in mathematics, geography, astronomy, medical science and grammar. These became the foundation of Western European scientific inquiry. Printing as a medium allowed for the reproduction in textual form the linear logic, structural order and subdivision that was fundamental to scientific logical positivism. It enabled the accurate reproduction in large volumes of newly developed charts and tables, allowing for much wider distribution of emerging scientific discoveries and the opportunity for a wider body of people to improve on them. As Burns notes,

> Almost all the books which provided Copernicus with his conceptual tools came off the presses during his lifetime, most of them precisely during Copernicus' formative study years. In contrast to Peurbach and Regiomantanus, who had to work from a single medieval translation of the *Almagest* (Ptolemy's text in Arabic) and to travel from one manuscript source to another, Copernicus working alone in his study in Frombork, 'in the remotest corner of the earth', as he described it, had a whole library of recent scholarly editions of ancient and contemporary sources right at his fingertips. (Burns, 1989, p. 239)

One of the major impacts of the spread of the printing press on religious thinking and practice was that it provided the means for development of alternative centers of power based on ideological argument rather than military, political or ecclesiastical power. One of those significant alternative centers of power was the commercial printers, who through the processes of the commercial market serviced people's desire for alternative viewpoints and popular reading material (Febvre and Martin, 1957). Mark Edwards notes how the success of Martin Luther's religious reformation was due in no small measure to his ability to muster support through his dominance of print publications and his ability to write in a way that earned profit for and therefore the support of the commercial printers (Edwards, 1994). Burns quotes the example of Galileo in 1630 who, when censored by the Catholic Church, turned to the people through the printed word in his masterpiece, *Dialogue Concerning the Two Chief World Systems*. In order to reach the largest possible audience, as with other of his books, he wrote in Italian rather than the more scholarly Latin.

Because the book treated a contemporary controversy in Italian in an extremely readable satirical fashion, it was an immediate success. By the time the book was banned all copies had been sold and had become hot black market items. A Latin translation was published shortly thereafter by a group of Protestant scholars. (Burns, 1989, p. 263)

The 'disenchantment' that scientific and technological rationalism required – the questioning of the reality of faith, mystery, or the supernatural and rejection of these as satisfactory explanations for the cause of events – created tensions with those social perspectives and institutions that promoted or depended on them. A significant part of the history of the modern period is a history of the contests that occurred intellectually, politically and culturally to negotiate and reconcile the various approaches and interests of parties along the secular and metaphysical continuum.

To a significant extent, the secular scientific–technological approach to social development and problem-solving became acceptable in a large measure because the scientific technology world brought its own enchantment: it provided a seemingly all-encompassing framework of interpretation and control that continually generated new discoveries and solutions to age-old problems and mysteries, as well as generating substantial material benefits. Murdock notes that there was a conviction, widely held, that

the application of scientific rationality would lead to cumulative and irreversible gains, an aspiration that found attractive expression in the idea of 'progress,' modernity's master narrative. People wanted to believe, and many did ... They saw steady improvements in the physical and material conditions of everyday life – sanitation, street lighting, vaccination against disease – and new opportunity for mobility and choice – the railway system, mass education, department stores. (Murdock, 1997: pp. 86–87)

While 'the totalizing project' of modernity was never fully total, the scientific–technological–rationalist approach to the development of social and public life was influential across all strata of society. Of course movements across societies cannot be reduced to simplistic generalizations. But the desirability of being seen to be rational, objective and scientific in one's public life became the trademark of the élite in intellect, industry and commerce and set ideals or norms of thought and aspiration against which other social frameworks needed to justify themselves and on the basis of which public resources were allocated. I recall that the first lecture given in my first undergraduate course in psychology in the mid-1960s was entitled, 'Why psychology is a science', a lecture justifying the seemingly nebulous study of the human mind and behavior against scientific principles. This *rapprochement* is illustrated by the significantly different ways in which the study and teaching of religion takes place in public universities compared to church seminaries.

During the twentieth century, however, the progress that was promised and anticipated began to show cracks, cracks some say have reached the scale of chasms. These have surfaced in a number of critical outlooks:

- **Loss of faith in progress** The 1914–18 and 1939–45 wars, the horrors of the German and Russian holocausts, mass publicized wars in Vietnam, Bosnia and Kuwait, the failure of economic and social development to resolve endemic problems of poverty, the recent of terrorism on a world scale, and the perception that world political and economic systems are not robust but profoundly vulnerable, have all contributed to a crisis of confidence in political and social goal-setting and a growing cynicism about the idea of progress.

- **A growing suspicion about modern institutions** Weber observed that one of the consequences of the demands of modernity for certainty and rational structure was an 'iron cage of bureaucracy and routine based around an incessant drive to eliminate the haphazard and annihilate the spontaneous'. The growth of bureaucracy in recent decades, however, and personal experiences of frustration with it, have led to widespread suspicion about the effectiveness of government institutions and cynicism about the capacity of leaders to reform them.

- **The questioning of consumerism** The enjoyment brought by the attainment and consumption of goods and services takes place within a total nexus of relationships and meaning. When that nexus is removed, the goods and services in themselves can quickly become empty and meaningless. The unreserved promotion of goods and services on a global basis through mass advertising, and the appropriation of social activities through commodification as a foundation of economic transaction raises questions on a broad scale about the emptiness of consumption. Murdock suggests that consumerism has diminishing value as a sustaining social philosophy.

> People have been exhorted to behave as consumers rather than as citizens. They have been discouraged from thinking of themselves as members of moral and political communities, and invited instead to assert their rights to choice in the marketplace. But as the underpinnings provided by public goods are dismantled, the pleasures of possession are left to bear a greater and greater responsibility for delivering contentment and confirming personal identity and self-worth ... As David Harvey has argued, 'The moral crisis of our time is a crisis of Enlightenment thought ... The affirmation of 'self without God' in the end negated itself because reason, a means, was left, in the absence of God's truth, without any spiritual or moral goal. The secular theology of consumption was increasingly unable to address this lack. Consumerism had always promised 'something which it can't deliver'. (Murdock, 1997, p. 94)

● **An intensified sense of social meaninglessness**   The advance of scientific technologism has resulted in a stripping of human values and loss of a foundation for human meaning. In its drive to eliminate uncertainty, scientific positivism emphasized and overvalued those aspects of our experience about which we could be certain. But it failed at the same time to provide other essential aspects of the human situation, a coherent system of meaning that incorporated goals and values as well as mechanisms.

Initially science's disenchantment of the world was of little account, since it brought with it its own faith assurances and its own experiences of enchantment. In recent decades this faith and enchantment have worn off and we find ourselves in what Bar Haim calls a state of 'historical exhaustion of ideologies and social utopias'.

> In summary, the social ideals that once defined and focused political energies, inspired new challenges for reform, paved the way to a more flexible stratification, and gave legitimization to a secular morality have reached a point of ineffectiveness, incapable of mobilizing and fulfilling expectations. A perpetual search for leadership on both sides of the Atlantic has yielded an acute sense that the present malaise of Western society requires the remedy of altogether new and different kinds of leaders who have yet to make their appearance. (Bar-Haim, 1997, p. 141)

In the latter part of the twentieth century, therefore, one can argue that there is evidence of a renewed desire and search for a basis of re-enchantment. Murdock suggests:

> The two strands in the growing disillusionment with modernity – the confrontation with the dark side of progress and the evacuation of meaning – left a gap in popular structures of feeling through which religion could re-enter people's lives. Weber understood this very well and argued strongly that the old gods were about to 'ascend from their graves' and resume their struggle 'to gain power over our lives'. The time was ripe for a re-enchantment of the world. (Murdock, 1997, p. 88)

This does not mean a rejection of science or technology – the desire for products and gadgets is as strong as ever. Rather one can see in the use of technologies a rejection of pure rationalism or empiricism and a re-emergence of those aspects of human experience and society that modernity had displaced: religion, mystery, myth and magic. The technologies of media have become central to this. Media have become the practical marketplace where individuals gather, converse, gain information, communalize their concerns, and build meaning, identity and world-views.

Jesus Martín-Barbero, writing from the perspective of the growth of popular religiosity in South America, comments:

Despite all the promise of modernity to make religion disappear, what has really
happened is that religion has modernized itself ... What we are witnessing, then, is not the
conflict of religion and modernity, but the transformation of modernity into enchantment
by linking new communication technologies to the logic of popular religiosity. (Martín-
Barbero, 1997, p. 112)

In many ways the media have become the dominant governing institution of the
emergent global culture. This applies not just in terms of the growth of a number of
multinational media organizations that have acquired a global reach, but also in
terms of the expanding accessibility and adaptability of new media technologies
that are shifting the control of construction of meaning out of the hands of
centralized bodies into the hands of individual media users.

Writers such as Febvre (Febvre and Martin, 1957), Edwards (Edwards, 1994) and
Eisenstein (Eisenstein, 1983) have identified in their work how the processes of
print technologies, production, distribution, commercial interest and market forces
interacted with individuals and complex cultural movements to influence the nature
of the religious changes that occurred during the sixteenth and seventeenth century
European Reformation. In the same way, new and more complex processes of
media technologies, production, distribution, commercial interest and market
forces are interacting with complex cultural movements in shaping new patterns of
social and institutional religiosity and spirituality at the beginning of this new
millennium.

This book explores different aspects of these changes in the interaction between
media and Christianity. In difference from earlier work in this area, which has
tended to be positivist in its frameworks and methodologies and perpetuate
scientific distinctions between inner meaning and overt practice, this work explores
the interfaces of these from within a cultural methodology and framework.

The work arises from a seven-year international and interdisciplinary
collaboration within the International Study Commission on Media, Religion and
Culture, a group formed by an initiative of Stichting Porticus, which also
coordinated the funding. Following the first International Conference on Media,
Religion and Culture in Uppsala in 1995, the Commission focused its work on
developing new directions for theorizing the interaction of media and religion and
fostering new research in the area.

Early in its life, the Commission identified four core issues that have informed
and guided its work:

1. **In what ways can we say that the media have come to occupy the spaces
    traditionally occupied by religion?** What religious functions do media
    fulfill? What are the new forms of spirituality that are emerging? Where/how is
    transcendence found or experienced? What are the means of meaning-making?
2. **What is the relationship of religious authority to modes of symbolic
    practice?** Is there a necessary or historic relationship between authority and

certain modes of symbolic practice, such as the linear modes? Are the visual modes inherently threatening to authority? If so, what kinds of authority? Where? Whose? What are the prospects of religious authority and its practices of legitimation as a consequence of these conditions?

3. **How must we re-think the relationship between religion and the media?** How does the new situation call into question former dichotomies of sacred and profane spheres, 'good' vs 'bad' media, etc? How does the new situation call into question the traditional 'instrumental' understanding of media which has been supported: many media production activities of the churches; media reform activism of various kinds; and the so-called 'media literacy' movement?

4. **What does this new situation imply about epistemology?** Does it call for new epistemologies in order to account for it? Is the new situation indicative of changed epistemologies in general, that is, that the whole way we think about reality has now been altered? What is the relation of media practice to epistemology (i.e., are the postmodernists right in claiming that the changed epistemology of the postmodern is a consequence of the media)?

In recognition of the cross-disciplinary nature of this new approach, the Commission has comprised a mix of scholars and media practitioners from different disciplines, with different professional interests and from different continents (details of members of the Commission can be seen in the List of Contributors). In its seven years it has supported three more international conferences and held ten consultations in eight countries on five continents, each of them engaging local scholars, activists and practitioners in discussions, debates and explorations on dimensions of research and theory in the interaction of media, religion and culture in global and local contexts. These perspectives are reflected in different ways through these chapters.

We recognize that one of the major developments in the area of media and religion in the late twentieth and early twenty-first centuries has been the growing awareness in the West of the presence and difference of Islam as a religious, cultural and political presence. The various ways in which the different manifestations of Islam relate to and interact with western media and cultural products, and to their own media, is a huge and complex area and well worthy of a similar study to what we have done here. We have not been able to address that here because of the size and complexity of the task, but see it, and developing a conversation between scholars looking at the two religions, as a crucial and fruitful future task.

Using this Book

This book is organized in three sections. The first gives an introduction and overview of some of the approaches and issues in seeing media and Christianity from a cultural perspective. The second presents a number of case studies of mediated Christianity that illustrate either particular aspects of study or the complexity of factors that contribute to the shaping of religious belief and practice. The third section explores the impact that the new mediation of Christianity is having for the traditional embodiment of Christianity, the Christian institutions. A final chapter surveys the developments and study that have taken place by looking at ten key issues that have emerged as a basis for future development and research.

The book is a rich resource for teaching and study in a variety of contexts. It can be used effectively in a number of ways depending on that context. If you are an undergraduate student in a communication program who is new to the field of media or religion, or a teacher working with these students, it may be helpful to begin with Clark's chapter (Chapter 1) and then White's chapter (Chapter 14), which provide overviews of some of the theoretical issues, and then select other chapters as case studies illustrating the theory. The most theologically complex of the chapters is that of Goizueta (Chapter 3), which may require some preparation or discussion.

If you are a student or teacher working from within a primarily theological or pastoral context, the chapters by Goizueta (Chapter 3) and Horsfield (Chapter 2) will give a better introduction to the theological and pastoral issues raised by media. The chapters by Plude, Hess and Santiskultarm (Chapters 13, 11 and 12 respectively) will serve as good case explorations before moving on to the case studies from Africa and Latin America or the more theoretical chapters by Clark and White (Chapters 1 and 14).

Those whose focus or interest is in the area of media production or media arts will likely find Medrano's chapter (Chapter 10) the best entry point, moving from there to those by Morgan, Mitchell, Asamoah-Gyadu and White (Chapters 7, 8, 5 and 14). Yet another possibility is to ask groups of students to prepare reflections on the material in the book in relation to the specific geographical areas that the authors represent.

There are several concepts that thread through all of the essays in the book. One is the shift in methodology away from focusing on institutions and traditional religious behavior towards looking at the cultural nature of religion and spirituality and its foundations in common search for and construction of meaning. Highlighting actual practice rather than authorized behaviors, and the processes by which meaning is created by the individual, will often provide a scaffold that can give students access to the ideas under discussion and some grasp of the particular discourses in use.

Additional resources may be found on the Study Commission web site, www.iscmrc.org. The web site also has information about the media.faith listserv and the International Catholic Fellowship program for doctoral research in the area. Many of the authors represented in this volume maintain extensive web sites that can provide resources and additional reading material to further study. Clark and Hoover's research work at the University of Colorado can be found at www.Colorado.EDU/Journalism/mcm/mrc/. Hess's work in media and religious education can be found at www.luthersem.edu/mhess. Horsfield's site www.mediatedspirit.com introduces a CD-ROM on media and Christianity that is an excellent adjunct to this volume. Medrano's web site provides videos, resources and links in both English and Spanish: www.jmcommunications.com.

Acknowledgements

While the various authors would acknowledge individuals who have contributed to their individual pieces of work, we want to acknowledge a number of individuals who have contributed to the production of this volume, for example, the many individuals in the different countries we have visited who have stimulated our thinking about media and religion as much as we hope we have stimulated theirs. The hospitality and friendship we have experienced has greatly enriched the intellectual exchanges that have taken place.

Diane Alters has provided extensive help in reviewing and editing individual chapters and in ensuring that the chapters have a common voice and pitch.

Note

1 Toulmin argues that there have been several stages of modernity: the literary or humanistic phase in the fifteenth century, the scientific and philosophical phase from 1630 on, and the current phase, which he prefers to call a third stage of modernity rather than postmodernity. In this third phase, he argues for recovery of many of the positive aspects of the earlier humanistic phase.

References

Bar-Haim, G. (1997), 'The dispersed sacred: anomie and the crisis of ritual', in S. M. Hoover and K. Lundby (eds), *Rethinking Media, Religion and Culture*, Thousand Oaks, CA: Sage.

Burns, A. (1989), *The Power of the Written Word: The Role of Literacy in the History of Western Civilization*, New York: Peter Lang.

Edwards, M. U., Jr (1994), *Printing, Propaganda and Martin Luther*, Berkeley, CA: University of California Press.

Eisenstein, E. L. (1983), *The Printing Revolution in Early Modern Europe*, Cambridge and New York: Cambridge University Press.

Febvre, L. and H.-J. Martin (1957), *The Coming of the Book: The Impact of Printing, 1450–1800* (D. Gerard, trans.), London: NLB.

Martín-Barbero, J. (1997), 'Mass media as a site of resacralisation of contemporary culture', in S. M. Hoover and K. Lundby (eds), *Rethinking Media, Religion and Culture*. Thousand Oaks, CA: Sage.

Murdock, G. (1997), 'The re-enchantment of the world: religion and the transformations of modernity' in S. M. Hoover and K. Lundby (eds), *Rethinking Media, Religion and Culture*, Thousand Oaks, CA: Sage.

Toulmin, S. (1990), *Cosmopolis: The Hidden Agenda of Modernity*, New York: The Free Press.

PART I
THE CULTURAL PERSPECTIVE

Introduction

It is reasonable to say that until recently the relationship between media and religion has not been a large area of research concern. In the modernist sacred-secular dichotomy, media have not been seen as very significant by those whose primary interest has been in the world of the sacred and religious, and issues of religion have not been considered important for those who have been involved in research in the largely secular field of media studies.

What studies there have been of media and religion have tended to be defined by and oriented around the actions and interests of religious institutions or individuals. As Horsfield points out in this section (Chapter 2), these studies operated out of a largely unquestioned modernist framework that conceptualized religion and culture as separate entities, with studies focusing on aspects of their interaction rather than their interdependence. Using largely instrumentalist or narrowly focused theological methodologies, traditional studies of media and religion have concentrated on such things as analysis and critique of (secular) media contents from religious perspectives, media activities of particular religious institutions, and the effectiveness of media uses for achieving particular religious outcomes in areas such as evangelism, propaganda, church growth or education.

That situation has been changing over the past several decades as a result of a number of convergences in theory and research. One has been the growing influence in the latter part of the twentieth century of the European cultural studies approach to media research in the United States. The cultural approach to the study of media has challenged and gradually been assimilated into what has been a much more instrumentalist approach to media research in the US. This approach to culture as belonging to all people rather than just a social élite has broken down some of the singularity of modernist definitions and demarcations and opened the way to study the characteristics of all groups from a perspective of greater complexity of individuals, power relationships, diversity of cultural positions, and various stances of acceptance, resistance, negotiation and subversion of the dominant order. Applying a cultural perspective within the much more 'religious' popular culture of the United States has begun to open up new considerations of media and religion from a cultural perspective.

A number of characteristics of the cultural perspective have thrown new light and created new collaborations in the study of media and religion. Those new perspectives and collaborations are reflected in these chapters.

One is the cultural focus on the construction of meaning as central to understanding and researching media and communication. In a production-centered or effects approach to media study, it is assumed that meaning is created by the person or institution producing the message. The study of media then largely involves researching the extent and effectiveness with which that meaning is generated and transferred to those receiving it, and the effects that are brought about as a result. In a cultural perspective meaning is seen as a joint enterprise: a negotiated outcome that comes about through an interaction of the person generating the text, the text itself, the person engaging with the text, and the contextual circumstances in which these occur.

This culturalist concern with meaning has lead to a breakdown in the modernist attempt to separate 'fact' and 'opinion', the objective and subjective, and created new convergences between the field of media studies and that of religious studies. From an institutional point of view, it could well be argued, as Steve Bruce does, that religion is of declining importance and interest today. Steve Bruce, for example, suggests:

> As I shall show below, the religious cultures of different societies have developed in very different ways. However, as a starting-point, we may note that, with the partial exception of the USA … the pattern of decline in the social significance and popularity of religion sketched above is common to most industrial societies and there is widespread agreement that such evolution is driven by common social forces and hence that a general explanation of secularization is possible (Bruce, 1996).

It's unknown whether Bruce would argue the same thing since the events of 11 September 2001 and the impact in western countries of Islamic political fundamentalism. The perspective of this book is not necessarily to challenge Bruce's argument in relation to the decline of religious institutional practices, but rather to explore the fact that the character of religion and religious practice in western countries has significantly changed. One of those major changes has been a shift in religious exploration and practice away from traditional religious institutions into the institutions of the commercial media marketplace.

A second major theoretical shift that has influenced the study of media and religion has been away from the concept of the truths of religion being unconditioned revelations or cognitions towards the realization that understandings and concepts of truth, even religious truths, are constructed and in the process of construction they reflect a power struggle between competing positions and interests. When the element of vested power is introduced into the analysis of religion, it challenges existing religious hegemonies (the claim by some religious groups or institutions that they alone are concerned for the preservation of the integrity of the religion) and opens up new dimensions of questioning, conceptualization and research about how particular religious phenomena have been constructed, how they are perpetuated, and the changes that occur as power relationships change. One of the concerns of this book is to explore in what ways the social structures and practices of religion are changing as a result of the different power relationships created by the development of new electronic, visual and digital media.

The chapters in this section explore the theoretical dimensions of the cultural approach to media and religion in different ways. Lynn Schofield Clark (Chapter 1) from her perspective as a media scholar explores some of the theoretical issues in removing the traditional research boundaries between secular media and religious practice. Peter Horsfield (Chapter 2) follows a historical biographical approach to trace the theoretical shift that occurred during the later part of the twentieth century and issues within it. Roberto Gozuieta (Chapter 3) from a theological perspective examines the implications of taking media and symbolization seriously in theological analysis, with a case study on the practical differences in religious practice that emerge from different symbolic practices. Juan Carlos Henríquez, a film-maker, media producer and academic researcher (Chapter 4), explores questions of epistemology, one of the initial four core issues of the Commission, using science fiction narratives as an example.

Reference

Bruce, S. (1996), *Religion in the Modern World: From Cathedrals to Cults*, Oxford: Oxford University Press.

Chapter 1

Reconceptualizing Religion and Media in a Post-National, Postmodern World: A Critical Historical Introduction

Lynn Schofield Clark

Zimbabwean author Yvonne Vera's (1993) book *Nehanda* tells the story of a missionary priest attempting to convert Kaguvi, a leader of the Chimurenga, to Christianity (Landow, 2002). The exchange between the priest and the Shona spiritual leader occurs at the end of the novel, as nineteenth-century colonization has wrought devastation and loss to the Zimbabweans. Kaguvi, rooted in an oral culture, first expresses puzzlement at the priest's insistence on the importance of the Bible. Yours is a 'strange' god who is 'inside your book', he tells the priest. In contrast to this book-bound god, Kaguvi says: 'My god lives up above. He is a pool of water in the sky. My god is a rain-giver. I approach my god through my ancestors and my mudzimu ... My mudzimu is always with me, and I pay tribute to my protective spirit.' The priest then tells Kaguvi that his Christian god is also 'in the sky' but adds that his is 'the true God. He is the way to eternal happiness.' Kaguvi is further confused by this claim, as he has never considered the possibility that happiness could be eternal. 'If a man harvests his crops, that is happiness. If a man marries and has children, that is happiness. If a man talks to his neighbors and they respect him, that too is happiness' (p. 105). Misconceptions define the encounter between the priest and Kaguvi, highlighting the inextricable relationship between cultural context and religious understanding. Yet Kaguvi is confused rather than offended by the missionary's words, for despite the priest's arrogance, he appears to Kaguvi to be sincere in his desire to help him, and Kaguvi finds it hard to believe that the priest is lying or that he is foolish (Grundy, 1999). Ultimately in Vera's story, Kaguvi is not so much converted to Christianity as he is dissociated from his traditional ancestral spirituality, a loss that comes to symbolize, as Vera's conversion story itself does, the tragic losses that occurred through Zimbabwe's encounter with colonization.

The first decades of the second millennium seem destined to be defined by such important reconsiderations of the encounters between cultures and religions around the world as fictionalized in Vera's story. Nation-states and the relationships between them have been reorganized throughout the twentieth century, with the end of colonial control, the reordering of a global capital market, and the subsequent transformation of the global/local relationship. Meanwhile, the 'next Christianity' is emerging in Africa, Asia, and Latin America, with sweeping implications for worldwide practices of faith and the looming possibility of a schism between the liberal North and the conservative South (Jenkins, 2002).

Today we see evidence of what Castells (1989) has termed the 'dual city', embodied on the one hand by the cosmopolitanism of information producers, and by the localism of laborers on the other (see also Appadurai, 1996). Nations and the political and economic élite that rule in them have not disappeared but remain powerful entities, of course. As David Harvey (1990) has pointed out, capital accumulation remains the primary organizing principle that influences how nation-states interact with one another, and how people within various locations are situated in relation to labor and capital. While much of the celebratory literature on globalization has hailed the developments of a transnational identity and the benefits accrued to those of privilege (as VISA, McDonald's, Microsoft and other western products are now truly 'everywhere you want to be'), poverty has been restructured and exacerbated by a globally networked society as well, and along very familiar lines (Beasley-Murray, 2002). Our world may now be post-colonial, but, as Williams and Chrisman (1996) have reminded us, it is not post-imperial.

Religion often becomes a point of connection and distinction in this context, providing comfort and familiarity among immigrant communities, but at the same time exacerbating tensions. Identification with religion is often viewed by the majority as a disruptive threat to the nation-state. Colonialist approaches to mission work like those of the missionary priest in Vera's story have been largely delegitimated in this new context, but this is not to say that such drives to conversion no longer exist; they simply play out on different stages. While twentieth-century technologies such as radio broadcasts and satellite television serve as less personally disruptive and more efficient evangelization tools as used by celebrity televangelists from the West, the formerly colonized countries in Africa, the Pacific and Latin America now have their own home-grown versions of such luminaries, as Kwabena Asamoah-Gyadu demonstrates in Chapter 5 of this volume. These areas have witnessed the rise of Pentecostalism, Christian fundamentalisms and Islamicist movements in the past few decades, as relocated and restructured communities are motivated to embrace traditions of their homeland more fervently. In addition to the highly visible and costly uses of television and film, leaders of such movements have employed low-cost audiocassettes and radio broadcasts, reproduced photographs and press coverage to mobilize constituents for both religious and political ends, thereby creating new interactions between politics, religion and identity.

This is the context, then, in which we must begin to reflect on the intersection of media and religion in the world today. In this chapter, I review the history of the study of media and religion, offering a critical review of the field's development and attempting to highlight how this book represents a step in new directions that reflect the learnings from the new global context of religion and media. I then consider the status of religion and media in the contemporary context, offering a challenge to the secularist view that religion is merely a marginal interest of the minority. We begin with a consideration of the origins of the study of religion and its historical relation to ideas of the nation-state.

Religion and National Identity

Scholars studying the role of media in society have long been concerned with how developments in the mass media have played a central role in the creation and maintenance of political communities such as those of the nation-state (Braman and Sreberny-Mohammadi, 1996; Calabrese and Burgelman, 1999; Morley and Robins, 1996). These cultural and political identities, in turn, play key roles as individuals seek to create a sense of belonging and community within the fragmented practices of everyday life. Benedict Anderson's (1991) concept of 'imagined communities' has been particularly influential in coming to understand the role of the media in the restructuring of such communities of identification.

Anderson suggested that print media such as newspapers and novels allowed readers to imagine themselves as part of a broad community not based on geography or personal involvement in governance, but on shared sentiments about the nation. This nation, understood in relation to both ancestry and destiny, is thus capable of evoking and demanding a moral commitment on the part of its individual citizens. Thanks to developments in industry, international trade policy, communication and transportation, persons and their labor have been relocated at a quickening pace, enabling – and indeed, necessitating – the construction of transnational identities within certain locations and diasporas around the world. Media therefore play a key role in cementing loyalties in the post-colonial situation, providing resources both for shared sentiments among distinctive communities and for the 'invention of new scripts for their members' lives', as Meyer (2001) has argued.

As Peter van der Veer (1993) has reminded us, the idea of religion as a phenomenon to be studied emerged simultaneously with the ideology of nationalism in the nineteenth-century discourses of modernity. Thus, ideas of the nation have always been centrally related to how the religious and the secular have been understood.

There are historical reasons for this relationship between religion and nation. In the medieval period, a common religion created bonds across Western and Central Europe that facilitated exchanges of power and capital, such as through marriage of an English prince to a member of a Spanish royal family, for example. But in the centuries following the Reformation, confessional differences became a source of political division in Europe. As Gorski (2000) points out, the sixteenth and seventeenth centuries were marked by a politicization of religion, a context in which confessional loyalty could be a mark of political identity and belonging, or a cause for violent persecution and mass exodus:

> As Catholics and Protestants squared off against one another in the Schmalkaldean
> conflict, the French Wars of Religion, the Dutch Revolt and, finally, the Thirty Years' War,
> confession became a critical marker of political loyalty, and vice versa ... The
> consequence, in most cases, was political polarization, manifested in the formation of
> competing 'religious parties' (e.g., the Huguenots and the Catholic League in France, the
> patriots and the Malcontents in the Netherlands, the Loyalists and the Covenanters in
> Scotland etc.). (p. 158)

While the Reformation was assisting in a redrawing of the European map, other
forces were at work in the redrawing of the global map, and these had much to do
with religion and nation, as well. As commercial leadership was shifting to
Northern Europe – first with Dutch merchants and then the English and French – the
Catholic states to the South, including Spain, Portugal and France, were launching
missionary ventures into Africa, Asia, North and South America (Jenkins, 2002).
Thus, as Jenkins points out, by early in the seventeenth century, 'the Catholic
church had become the first religious body – indeed, the first institution of any sort –
to operate on a global scale' (p. 55). These colonialist ventures were sources of
capital for the European nation-states, of course, and thus missionaries, as they
introduced literacy as well as European worldviews, worked in allegiance with the
nation-state, albeit sometimes inadvertently (Comaroff and Comaroff, 1991).

Gorski argues that although the alignment of political and confessional identity in
early modernity had been overlooked, historians now see this period as a key
turning point in the differentiation of religion and the state. It was during the
seventeenth and eighteenth centuries that severe tensions between religious and
state authorities emerged over such issues as education, social welfare and
discipline, ultimately resulting in the sharpening of boundaries between what we
now think of as the separate spheres of the religious and the secular. Thus by the
nineteenth century, as a consequence of transformations in the world system,
political loyalty would rest on citizenship rather than on membership in the state
church, and nationhood would hinge on the establishment of a national market
rather than on a relation with the church. As van der Veer has argued:

> [Western] societies assumed the nation form in the historical transformation that we refer
> to as 'modernity' and it is this form that determines what is understood as the religious or
> the secular. This assertion is not a re-phrasing of the secularization thesis since there is not
> much evidence for the disappearance of religion or its marginalization in public life in
> most societies. Rather, it emphasizes the importance of the nation-state for the location
> and nature of religion. (p. 2)

Studies of the Media

Studies of the media stretch back to the nineteenth century as well, and were, like
concerns of religion, intimately bound up with ideas of the nation. In his
observations of the large and increasingly diversified society of the US, French

historian and political theorist Alexis de Tocqueville (1835) first noted the ability of the press to inform public opinion. With the waves of immigrants arriving on US shores at the turn of the twentieth century at the height of industrialization, political philosopher John Dewey (1927) took up the same theme. He observed that newspapers might enable people to form a 'great community' of common interests and purposes. Thus, in these early analyses, media studies shared with studies of religion a concern for how these phenomena might facilitate or undermine relations within the nation-state.

Not all were as optimistic about the role of the media in society as Dewey and Tocqueville, however. This was especially true when it came to media that were produced for entertainment purposes. By the end of the nineteenth century, the fictional novel had found a secure spot in the domestic lives of much of the middle and upper classes in the US and in Europe. Industrialization had regulated the hours of the workday and electricity had made it possible to extend leisure activities into the evenings. Thus, changes in society had allowed for both leisure-time reading as well as the pursuit of other more communal – and commercial – entertainment such as dance halls and theater-going. These and other factors contributed to two themes that occurred in the early scholarship on the entertainment media in particular. First, linking concerns of entertainment with more latent concerns about an emergent working class largely comprised of immigrants, many social critics of the day decried the so-called 'immorality' of such pursuits (Arnold, 1869). Religious leaders, whose flocks had experienced some decline even then, were among those often voicing such critiques (Thompson, 1963). But in media studies, a different critique was emerging. Some scholars, such as the German economist and historian Karl von Bucher (1893), came to question the commercial role of the newspaper that had been so highly regarded by Dewey and others. Taking up this issue of why people turn to the newspaper and the commercial interest inherent in producing a product for widespread sale, Robert Park and others at what is known as the Chicago School of Sociology took to the streets to conduct interviews with newsreaders (Park, 1925). These two approaches to the media thus informed two concerns still central in studies of the media today: the study of 'media effects' that has been concerned with the effects of fictional novels, film, and later television, on populations considered to be particularly vulnerable, and the political/economic conundrum of a medium held up as a resource of the public interest while based firmly in private, commercial interests.

It is worth noting that in what might be called the foundational writings of US media scholarship of Dewey, Park and others, religion was not seen to be directly related to these goals of community-building. If anything, religion was related to what social theorist Ferdinand Tonnies (1935) had called 'Gemeinschaft' – the pre-modern, often-idealized vision of what life had been like before industrialization. While some social theorists might have felt nostalgic for such a life presumed lost, therefore, Weber's (1919) view of a world 'disenchanted' held a great deal of sway in social scholarship in both the US and in Europe. Religion was simply not on the agenda for these scholars, and certainly not connected with the media. In fact, this theme of a presumed 'secular' society in which religion is marginalized, rather than seen as an aspect of many people's everyday lives, continued to inform media scholarship until very recently (Hoover and Venturelli, 1996).

While religious leaders may have been concerned with the negative 'effects' of the media on their constituencies, decrying what they perceived as the lack of religious values and representation in the mass media, therefore, scholars in media studies continued to have little interest in studying religion. In fact, by mid-twentieth century even studies into the effects of the media, that common ground of social critics from both fields, were within media studies moving in directions at some distance from the concerns of religious leaders. What is called the 'limited effects' model had replaced the presumed 'magic bullet' approach in the US, while what is known as the 'critical tradition' was taking root in Europe in the years before the Second World War (Lang, 1964). Coalesced around a group of scholars in Frankfurt who emigrated to the USA at the time of the Second World War, the founders of the critical tradition were less interested in the psychological effects of the media on individuals than on the values and ideological images communicated to society through media content. Theorists associated with the critical tradition explored popular magazines, radio soap operas, popular art and popular music, considering how popular tastes were cultivated through the commercialization of media (Lowenthal, 1961; Marcuse, 1941; Herzog, 1941; Adorno, 1972; Benjamin, 1969). In the context of the horrors and devastation of the war and its aftermath, this group of scholars was understandably pessimistic about social and ideological domination and the fast-growing 'culture industries' that seemed to facilitate it.

Mainstream research in the US, meanwhile, continued to be influenced by the social-psychological traditions of behavior research, thus exploring the relationship between overt media content and individual interpretative strategies. Looking at the sophisticated political campaigns of the day in the US, Harold Lasswell (1938) had argued that propaganda did not create facts, but rather reinterpreted existing ideas. Scholars in the US following in Lasswell's footsteps affirmed the importance of interpersonal relationships in the persuasive power of the media, noting the limited effects of media messages alone. Thus, studies of 'personal influence' emerged as a theme in media interpretation that remains important within media research today (Lazarsfeld and Katz, 1964; Blumler and Katz, 1974).

At mid-century, other developments further contributed to the direction of inquiry for media studies. The commercialization of radio and the evolution of advertising agencies sparked a need in those industries for research into the habits of media consumption. Thus other research, notably led by Paul Lazarsfeld, delineated relationships between personal attributes and such behaviors as voting and product purchasing. The positivist model of survey-based research like this predominated in the US social sciences in the 1950s and beyond, and provided important legitimacy and funding for mass media research. Its practical and market-oriented approach to research guided the first major twentieth-century study of religion and media (Parker, Barry and Smythe, 1955). Research into religion was still marginalized at the time, but this kind of research and the way it was done shaped how research into religion was first explored in the later twentieth-century media studies in the US. Religion, like political affiliation or other demographic information, was viewed as one personal attribute or 'variable'. Some contemporary research still approaches religion in this way, examining how religious affiliations affect viewing selections or how religious symbols appear in conjunction with other images in mass-mediated contexts (Buddenbaum and Stout, 1996; Hamilton and Rubin, 1992; Pardun and McKee, 1995).

By the 1970s, however, the critical tradition, with its emphases upon historical contextualization and critical evaluation of the media's role in society, was beginning to reemerge in the US, Europe and Australia, as well as in Latin America and Asia. In large part this was fueled by the rise of higher education and its increased availability to disadvantaged members of society throughout the US, postwar Britain, Latin America, Australia, and Asia. These 'scholarship students', as they were known in Britain, brought to their studies a high level of participation in popular culture and in the everyday lives of the working class that had not been encountered at the élite university cultures of earlier centuries. Moreover, Marxist and other ideologically based critiques of dominant society were on the rise throughout the 1960s, both in universities and in the revolutions that had been overturning colonialist ventures since the early part of the twentieth century. In the UK, scholars turned to explorations of the relationship between media and power (Collins, Garnham and Lockley, 1987). Even the positivist tradition of research in the US was influenced by this turn of events, with the development of empirical and historical studies that critically explored media in relation to social events, and examined the inner workings of the media industries themselves (Gans, 1979; Gitlin, 1980; 1983; Tuchman, 1978; Hallin, 1986).

By the 1970s, the ease of transnational travel for scholars had increased interaction between researchers in various parts of the world, institutionalizing academic conferences as an important aspect of intellectual development. The tradition of Marxism, so vibrant in places outside the US, challenged the scientific commitments of US-based mass communication survey research while also rejecting the moralist and elitist tone of the mass culture debates from both continents. This approach to mass communication and in particular its popular culture forms may have been particularly appealing at the time to younger scholars, as they were members of that same large population of young people who had fostered the development of a 'youth culture' and had provided the economic basis for the development of popular culture in the US and Europe twenty years earlier. Popular culture became an important topic of study at the Birmingham Centre for Contemporary Cultural Studies at the University of Birmingham in the 1970s, viewed not so much as a threat to a perceived 'better' culture as an expression of ideology that was found to be meaningful in the everyday lives of citizens (Turner, 1990). Similarly in Latin America, popular culture came to be viewed as a form of expression in which individuals could find and construct meaning, complicating the earlier view of media as a form of imperialistic manipulation (Romero, 1982; Martín-Barbero, 1987). Building upon Gramsci, Althusser and other neo-Marxists, cultural studies came to see within popular culture possible seeds for social change, a topic of great interest in the wake of the turbulent era of the 1960s and afterwards. Because cultural studies had divided the field between high and low culture and had placed 'religion' on the side of 'high' culture, religion was deemed a subject of little interest to those within cultural studies, many of whom came from or were educated in the universities of Northern Europe and the US.

Exploring Religion in Media Studies

In the late 1970s and early 1980s, however, the emergence of televangelism and its corollary in the political realm, the Religious Right, led to a significant turning of attention to religion within media studies in the US (Clark and Hoover, 1997). Studies by Stewart Hoover (1985), Peter Horsfield (1984), Quentin Schultze (1990, 1991), Jeffrey Hadden and Anson Shupe (1988), Steve Bruce (1990), and Janice Peck (1993), among others, all contributed to this work, challenging simplistic notions of media influence while also affirming that the process of televangelism provided its practitioners with celebrity and a claim to legitimacy in the public and political realms.

As the scandals of televangelism waned in the latter years of the 1980s, interest in the intersection of media and religion seemed to take a new course. With the rise of religiously based militia movements such as that of the Branch Davidians, scholarly interest turned to the coverage of religion and religious organizations by news organizations and journalists (Dart and Allen, 1993; Buddenbaum, 1988, 1990, 1998; Silk, 1995; Hoover, 1998; Schmalzbauer, 2003). Meanwhile, with the rise of interest in cultural history throughout the 1970s and 1980s, historians had been establishing a significant body of literature examining such things as the decline of religious authority with the introduction of the printing press (Eisenstein, 1979), the connections between early periodicals and the religious motivations to publish (Nord, 1984; Lippy, 1986; Sweet, 1993), the use of media by religious organizations and persons in their efforts to convert and encourage others (Blumhofer, 1993; Winston, 1999; Hangen, 2002), and the linkages between literacy, missionary efforts, and colonialism (Comaroff and Comaroff, 1991). In the 1980s and 1990s, US theologians and scholars of religion began to contribute to the interdisciplinary dialogue as well, turning their attention first to the role of the media in ritual (Goethals, 1981) and the intersection of theological reflection and film (May and Bird, 1982; Martin and Ostwalt, 1995; Marsh and Ortiz, 1998; Bergeson and Greeley, 2000), and eventually locating popular culture more broadly as an important area of religious study (Hoover, Clark and Alters, 2004; McDannell, 1995; Forbes and Mahan, 2000; Mazur and McCarthy, 2001).

While televangelism itself has faded from its once-central position to studies of media and religion, studies of the religious right, such as the fine edited volume by Marcia Kintz and Victoria Lesage (1998), offer deeper understandings of the sophisticated use of the media by members of the Religious Right. Additionally, conservative Christian subcultures and their relation to entertainment media continue to be an area of interest, such as in Hillary Warren's (1998, 2001) analysis of the Southern Baptist boycott of Disney and Michael Roth's (1999) study of constraints and creativity within the contemporary Christian music industry.

Televangelism does remain an important concern for those scholars outside the US. Knut Lundby (2002) and Keyan Tomaselli and Arnold Shepperson (2002) are all looking at televangelism's role in African societies. Alongside these studies in western culture's incursions into other cultures around the world, scholars related to parts of the world beyond the US and Europe have looked to the role that religious media play in the construction and maintenance of geographically specific diasporic communities of Iran and India (Naficy, 1993; Gillespie, 1995; Cieko, 2001) and in geographically dispersed religious communities, as well (Eickelman and Anderson, 1999). These, I believe, are important clues for the future directions of the study of media and religion in the US and around the world.

The Study of the Media and Religion in a Post-national Context: A Challenge to Castells

The 'secularist' idea that religion had no place within media studies was forever shattered with the events of 11 September 2001. On that day, as Carey (2002) has observed, 'religion, media, and politics dramatically merged, not only in carnage but in remembrance, mourning, and the search for mutual understanding and tolerance' (p. 3). Those who are interested in the role that the media play in the construction and maintenance of religion and of the nation have new questions to ask that are suddenly of significant international import.

What is the future role of the church and other religious organizations? Most western reviews of such matters have been rather bleak, such as Giddens's (1991) argument for what he calls the emergence of the 'post-traditional self', and Castells's (1997) observation that what he terms the *legitimizing identities* of churches, political parties and civic associations are all in decline. Castells argues that these traditional sources of authority are being replaced with, or at least challenged by, two different types of identities. The first consists of what he terms *resistance identities*, which are built on the basis of shared identifiers among groups excluded from dominant society, and are largely the products of alienation and resentment. The second he terms *project identities*, which he argues coalesce around desire to undermine an existing worldview and replace it with some other worldview, such as in the case of feminists working for post-patriarchal societies, activists in the environmental movement, and, I would add, the anti-globalization movement that is exemplified by the protests against global capital's incursion into all aspects of everyday life.

For all of his insights into changes in the information age, Castells misses some of the nuances of the changes that are occurring in the relationships between these legitimizing, resistant and project identities, which can be highlighted by an examination of the intersection of media and religion. As Lawrence Moore (1994) has argued, the 'legitimizing identities' of religion have remained important in society and in individual practices to the extent that they have been able to locate themselves within the marketplace of culture. With this in mind, it is possible to argue that Castells's theory overlooks the ways in which savvy leaders in religious movements independent of traditionally legitimated organizations have sought to employ the media to enhance their own power in relation to groups that may be mobilized around these resistance and project identities. An example is the German evangelist Reinhard Bonnke, who is able to command a certain legitimacy as a cosmopolitan leader through highly mediated 'crusades' in Africa (Hackett, 1998).

Similarly, it is important to note that the 'legitimizing identities' have themselves been changed by their attempts to harness the media for their own purposes, as in the case of the Salvation Army in the US – an organization that, as Winston (1999) has argued, ultimately and inevitably lost control over how its work and mission would be portrayed in popular media. Religion's entrance into the mediated realm can also result in a 'spectacle of difference', a term McLagan (2000) employs to highlight such phenomena as coverage of 'celebrity Buddhists' such as Richard Gere and accompanying oversimplified and westernized coverage of Tibet and the Dalai Lama. Religious organizations have themselves been altered by this media coverage, as practitioners' expectations and meanings are informed by such texts. This results in changes in worship styles and rituals, as discussed by Kaur (2000) in relation to the Anapati Festival in India and its media-inspired spectacles.

Castells's typology also does not offer a way to address the interest in spirits and occult forces that take center stage in many of the fantasies in Ghanaian, Nigerian, Latin American and even US films, many of which depict such forces within stories that give expression to broader, popularly accepted views about money and power in society (Meyer, 2001, 1998; Clark, 2003; see Mitchell and Henríquez, Chapters 8 and 4 in this volume). These images, as Meyer (2003) has pointed out, are an important aspect of the new 'image-economy' that draws upon and reflects the rise of Pentecostalism and conservative Protestantism around the world, and they highlight the fact that the realm of popular culture, fantasy and the imagination must be considered as a part of the political public sphere. These genres, as Juan Carlos Henríquez points out in this volume, allow for reflexive and transcendental meaning-making as viewers may employ metaphor and metonym to make meanings. In this way, such films are able to reflect 'what is of concern to everybody and only realizes itself in peoples' heads' (Negt and Kluge, cited in Meyer, 2003).

Another interesting media practice that does not seem to fit with Castells's typology yet is worthy of consideration includes the ways in which audiences approach media as individualized spiritual experiences that relate to a presumed larger, historically and geographically specific collective, a phenomenon observed in relation to the popularity of Ghanaian films (Meyer, 1998), the use of televised versions of the Mahabharata in relation to devotional practices in the UK (Gillespie, 1995), and the spiritual and identity quests of young people as reflected in the youth culture of the US (Clark, 2003; Beaudoin, 1998). In this volume, Germán Rey (Chapter 6) similarly argues that Latin American soap operas communicate views about the vast social changes in that continent and serve as 'reference points' for religious beliefs, value systems and human relations in general. Additionally, migrant groups, as van der Veer (2001) has observed, tend to be more traditional, or more 'reactionary', because they become more aware of their religion and culture 'due to their constant interpellation by "established" communities.' Yet even this changes the nature of religion and its relationship to nation, as he argues: 'When Hindus and Muslims in the Netherlands begin to speak about their religious specialists and their religious services by using Protestant Christian vocabulary they are already in a process of transformation, in which pundits and imams provide guidance in spiritual matters and become not-yet secularized social workers' (p. 12).

As suggested in these writings, such practices may alternately serve to reinforce or to undermine individuals' connections to a wider societal and political field and to historical institutions of religion.

Conclusion

We began with a story of the encounter between the colonial powers of the West and the traditional beliefs of the South in the collusion of missionary and colonial projects. Thus, it is fitting to conclude with a story of a reverse encounter between differing religions and their cultures. In the early 1990s, Moses Tay, the Anglican Archbishop of Southeast Asia, traveled to Vancouver. Archbishop Tay was horrified to encounter the totem poles that are common tourist attractions in that city. He immediately set out to address the evil spirits he believed resided in these idols through prayer and exorcism. The local Anglican church, intent on building positive relations with local Native American communities, was in turn horrified by his actions, which they viewed through liberal northern eyes as the workings of an absurd and ill-informed superstition. Yet as Jenkins (2002b) points out, the Archbishop was correct in his understanding of the totems as authentic religious symbols, and was drawing upon a long tradition within Christianity of concern about exorcism and possession: 'on that occasion Tay personified the global Christian confrontation', Jenkins notes (p. 64).

In this era of globalization, revolution and capital have reshuffled the relationships between formerly colonial societies and the 'super nation-states' such as the European Union and the US. Emerging global institutions like the UN Security Council, the International Monetary Fund and the World Trade

Organization have further reordered the world map and the relationships between its peoples. Religion, with its long connections to national identity, has come to play an important role in the securing or disturbing of commitments at the local and global levels. The chapters that follow aim to explore how the mass media facilitate the strategies in which people engage in their efforts to understand themselves as both wholly human and simultaneously connected to others, and how both religion and media, in their myriad forms and intersections, play a role in the formation and maintenance of these imagined communities and self-identities.

References

Adorno, T. (1972/1991), *The Culture Industry*, London: Routledge.
Anderson, B. (1991), *Imagined Communities: Reflections on the Origins and Spread of Nationalism* (rev. edn), London: Verso.
Appadurai, A. (1996), *Modernity at Large: Cultural Dimensions of Globalization*, Minneapolis, MN and London: University of Minnesota Press.
Arnold, M. (1869/1994), *Culture and Anarchy*, New Haven, CT: Yale University Press.
Beasley-Murray, J. (2002), 'Introduction to the Conference, The New Latin Americanism: Cultural Studies Beyond Borders', Centre for Latin American Studies, University of Manchester, June.
Beaudoin, T. (1998), *Virtual Faith: The Irreverent Spiritual Quest of Generation X*, San Francisco: Jossey-Bass.
Benjamin, W. (1969), *Illuminations*, New York: Shocken.
Bergeson, A. and A. Greeley (2000), *God in the Movies*, New Brunswick, NJ: Transaction Press.
Blumhofer, E. (1993), *Aimee Semple McPherson: Everybody's Sister*, Grand Rapids, MI: William B. Eerdmans.
Blumler, J. G. and E. Katz (1974), *The Uses of Mass Communication: Current Perspectives on Gratifications Research*, Beverly Hills, CA: Sage.
Braman, S. and A. Sreberny-Mohammadi (1996), *Globalization, Communication, and Transnational Civil Society*, Cresskill, NJ: Hampton Press.
Bruce, S. (1990), *Pray TV: Televangelism in America*, London: Routledge.
Bucher, K. von (1893), *Die Entstehung der Volkswirtschaft: Vorträge und Versuche*, Tübingen: Verlag der H. Laupp'shen Buchhandlung.
Buddenbaum, J. (1998), *Reporting News about Religion: An Introduction for Journalists*, Ames, IA: Iowa State University Press.
Buddenbaum, J. (1990), 'Religion News Coverage in Commercial Network Newscasts', in R. Abelman and S. M. Hoover (eds), *Religious Television: Controversies and Conclusions*, Norwood, NJ: Ablex, pp. 249–63.
Buddenbaum, J. (1988), 'The Religion Beat at Daily Newspapers', *Newspaper Research Journal* 9(4), 57–69.
Buddenbaum, J. and D. Stout (1996), *Religion and Mass Media: Audiences and Adaptation*, Thousand Oaks, CA: Sage.
Calabrese, A. and J. Burgelman (eds) (1999), *Communication, Citizenship, and Social Policy: Rethinking the Limits of the Welfare State*, Lanham, MD: Rowman & Littlefield.

Carey, J. (2002), Preface to the First Edition of the *Journal of Media and Religion*, *Journal of Media and Religion* **1**(1), 1–3.

Castells, M. (1997), *The Information Age: Economy, Society, and Culture*, Vol. 2: *The Power of Identity*, Oxford: Blackwell.

Castells, M. (1989), *The Informational City: Information Technology, Economic Restructuring, and the Urban–Regional Process*, Oxford, UK: Blackwell.

Ciecko, A. (2001), 'Superhit Hunk Heroes for Sale: Globalization and Bollywood's Gender Politics', *Asian Journal of Communication* **11**(2), 121–43.

Clark, L. S. (2003), *From Angels to Aliens: Teenagers, the Media, and the Supernatural*, New York: Oxford University Press.

Clark, L. S. and S. M. Hoover (1997), 'At the Intersection of Media, Culture, and Religion: A Bibliographic Essay', in S. M. Hoover and K. Lundby (eds), *Rethinking Media, Religion, and Culture*, Thousand Oaks, CA: Sage, pp. 15–36.

Collins, R., N. Garnham and G. Lockley (1987), *The Economics of Television: The UK Case*, London: Sage.

Comaroff, J. and Comaroff, J. (1991), *Of Revelation and Revolution: Christianity, Colonialism, and Consciousness in South Africa*, Vol. I, Chicago: University of Chicago Press.

Dart, J. and Allen, J. (1993), *Bridging the Gap: Religion and the News Media*, Nashville, TN: Freedom Forum First Amendment Center at Vanderbilt University.

Dewey, J. (1927/1957), *The Public and its Problems*, New York: H. Holt.

Eickelman, D. F. and J. W. Anderson (1999), *New Media in the Muslim World*, Bloomington, IN: Indiana University Press.

Eisenstein, E. (1979), *The Printing Press as an Agent of Change*, Cambridge and New York: Cambridge University Press.

Forbes, B. and J. Mahan (2000), *Religion and Popular Culture in America*, Berkeley, CA: University of California Press.

Gans, H. (1979), *Deciding What's News: A Study of CBS Evening News, NBC Nightly News, Newsweek, and Time*, New York: Pantheon Books.

Giddens, A. (1991), *Modernity and Self-Identity: Self and Society in the Late Modern Age*, Stanford, CA: Stanford University Press.

Gillespie, M. (1995), *Television, Ethnicity and Cultural Change*, London and New York: Routledge.

Gitlin, T. (1983), *Inside Prime Time*, New York: Pantheon Books.

Gitlin, T. (1980), *The Whole World is Watching*, Berkeley, CA: University of California Press.

Goethals, G. (1981), *The TV Ritual: Worship at the Video Altar*, Boston, MA: Beacon Press.

Gorski, P. (2000), 'Historicizing the Secularization Debate: Church, State, and Society in Late Medieval and Early Modern Europe, CA. 1300 to 1700', *American Sociological Review* **65** (1), 138–67.

Grundy, M. (1999), 'Colonization and Christianity in Zimbabwe', *The Literature and Culture of Zimbabwe*, available online at: http://www.scholars.nus.edu.sg/landow/post/ zimbabwe/religion/grundy2.html.

Hackett, R. (1998), 'Charismatic/Pentecostal Appropriation of Media Technologies in Nigeria and Ghana', *Journal of Religion in Africa* **28** (3), 1–19.

Hadden, J. and A. Shupe (1988), *Televangelism, Power, and the Politics of God's Frontier*, New York: H. Holt.

Hallin, D. (1986), *The Uncensored War: The Media and Vietnam*, New York: Oxford University Press.

Hamilton, N. and A. Rubin (1992), 'The Influence of Religiosity on Television Viewing', *Journalism Quarterly* **69** (3): 667–78.

Hangen, T. (2002), *Redeeming the Dial: Radio, Religion, and Popular Culture in America*, Chapel Hill, NC: University of North Carolina Press.

Harvey, D. (1990), *The Condition of Postmodernity*, Cambridge: Blackwell.

Herzog, H. (1941), 'On Borrowed Experience. An Analysis of Listening to Daytime Sketches', *Studies in Philosophy and Social Science*, **IX** (1), 65–95.

Hoover, S. M. (1998), *Religion and the News*, Thousand Oaks, CA: Sage.

Hoover, S. M. (1985), *Mass Media Religion*, Thousand Oaks, CA: Sage.

Hoover, S. M., L. S. Clark, and D. F. Alters, with J. G. Champ and L. Hood (2004), *Media, Home and Family*, New York and London: Routledge.

Hoover, S. M. and S. Venturelli (1996), 'The Category of "The Religious": The Blind Spot of Contemporary Media Theory', *Critical Studies in Mass Communication* **13** (September), 251–65.

Horsfield, P. (1984), *Religious Television: The American Experience*, New York: Longman.

Jenkins, P. (2002), *The Next Christendom*, New York: Oxford University Press.

Jenkins, P. (2002), 'The Next Christianity', *Atlantic Monthly* (October), 53–68.

Kaur, R. (2000), 'Rethinking the Public Sphere: The Ganapait Festival and Media Competitions in Mumbai', *Polygraph* **12**. Available online at http://www.lehigh.edu/~amsp/poly12.htm.

Kintz, L. and J. Lesage (1998), *Media, Culture, and the Religious Right*, Minneapolis, MN: University of Minnesota Press.

Landow, G. P. (2002), 'A Clash of Religions: Kaguvi Encounters the Christian Conception of the Afterlife', *The Literature and Culture of Zimbabwe*, available online at: http://www.scholars.nus.edu.sg/landow/post/zimbabwe/vera/afterlife.html.

Lang, K. (1964), Communications Research: Origins and Development, *International Encyclopedia of Communication*, 369–74.

Lasswell, H. (1938), *Propaganda Technique in the World War*, New York: P. Smith.

Lazarsfeld, P. and E. Katz (1964), *Personal Influence*, Glencoe, IL: Free Press.

Lippy, C. (1986), *Religious Periodicals of the United States*, Westport, CT: Greenwood Press.

Lowenthal, L. (1961), *Literature, Popular Culture and Society*, Englewood Cliffs, NJ: Prentice-Hall.

Lundby, K. (2002), 'Between American Evangelicalism and African Anglicanism', in S. M. Hoover and L. S. Clark (eds), *Practicing Religion in the Age of the Media*, New York: Columbia University Press.

Marcuse, H. (1941), 'Some Social Implications of Modern Technology', *Studies in Philosophy and Social Science*, **IX** (1), 414–39.

Martin, J. and C. Ostwalt (1995), *Screening the Sacred: Religion, Myth, and Ideology in Popular American Film*, Boulder, CO: Westview Press.

Martín-Barbero, J. (1987/1993), *Communication, Culture, and Hegemony: From the Media to Mediations*, trans. E. Fox and R. A. White, London: Sage (originally published as *De los medios a las mediaciones: comunicación, cultura y hegemonia*).

Marsh, C. and G. Ortiz (1998), *Explorations in Theology and Film: Movies and Meaning*, Oxford: Blackwell.

May, J. and M. Bird (1982), *Religion in Film*, Knoxville, TN: University of Tennessee Press.

Mazur, E. and K. McCarthy (eds), (2001), *God in the Details: American Religion in Popular Culture*, New York: Routledge.

McDannell, C. (1995), *Material Christianity*, New Haven, CT: Yale University Press.

McLagan, M. (2000), 'Spectacles of Difference: Buddhism, Media Management, and Contemporary Tibet Activism', *Polygraph* **12**. Available online at http://www.lehigh.edu/~amsp/poly12.htm.

Meyer, B. (2003), 'Impossible Representations: Pentecostalism, Vision and Video Technology in Ghana', presented to the annual meeting of the Society for the Anthropology of Religion, Providence, RI, April.

Meyer, B. (2001), *Modern Mass Media, Religion and the Imagination of Communities: Different Postcolonial Trajectories in West Africa, Brazil and India*, Research Proposal for NWO-PIONIER (grant received), available online at: http://www.pscw.uva.nl.media-religion.

Meyer, B. (1998), 'The Power of Money, Politics, Occult Forces, and Pentecostalism in Ghana', *African Studies Review* **41** (3), 15–38.

Moore, R. L. (1994), *Selling God: American Religion in the Marketplace of Culture*, New York: Oxford University Press.

Morley, D. and K. Robins (1996), *Spaces of Identity*, London and New York: Routledge.

Naficy, H. (1993), *The Making of Exile Cultures: Iranian Television in Los Angeles*. Minneapolis, MN: University of Minnesota Press.

Negt, O. and A. Kluge (1974), *Öffentlichkeit und Erfahrung. Zur Organisationsanalyse von burgerlicher und proletarischer Öffentlichkeit*, Frankfurt am Main: Suhrkamp. Cited in Meyer, B. (2003), 'Impossible Representations: Pentecostalism, Vision and Video Technology in Ghana', presented to the annual meeting of the Society for the Anthropology of Religion, Providence, RI, April.

Nord, D. (1984), 'The Evangelical Origins of Mass Media in America, 1815–1835', *Journalism Monographs* **88**, 1–30.

Pardun, C. and K. McKee (1995), 'Strange Bedfellows: Symbols of Religion and Sexuality on MTV', *Youth and Society* **26** (4), 438–49.

Park, R. E. (1925), 'Immigrant Community and Immigrant Press', *American Review* **3**, 143–52.

Parker, E., D. Barry and D. Smythe (1955), *The Television–Radio Audience and Religion*, New York: Harper & Brothers.

Peck, J. (1993), *The Gods of Televangelism*, Cresskill, NJ: Hampton Press.

Romero, J. L. (1982), *Las Ideologias de la Cultural Nacional*, Buenos Aires: CEDAL. Cited in Martín-Barbero, J. (1993), *Communication, Culture, and Hegemony: From the Media to Mediations*, trans. E. Fox and R. A. White, London: Sage.

Roth, M. (1999), 'That's Where the Power is: Identification and Ideology in the Construction of Contemporary Christian Music', unpublished thesis, University of New Mexico.

Schmalzbauer, J. (2003), *People of Faith: Religious Conviction in American Journalism and Higher Education*, Ithaca, NY: Cornell University Press.

Schultze, Q. (1990), 'Television Drama as Sacred Text', in John P. Ferre (ed.), *Channels of Belief: Religion and American Commercial Television*, Ames, IA: Iowa State University Press, pp. 3–28.

Schultze, Q. (1991), *Televangelism and American Culture: The Business of Popular Religion*, Grand Rapids, MI: Baker Book House.

Silk, M. (1995), *Unsecular Media*, Urbana, IL: University of Illinois Press.

Singh, A. (2000), 'Preface to the Special Issue on World Religions and Media Culture', *Polygraph* **12**. Available online at http://www.lehigh.edu/~amsp/poly12.htm.

Sweet, L. (1993), *Communication and Change in American Religious History*, Grand Rapids, MI: William B. Eerdmans.

Thompson, E. P. (1963), *The Making of the English Working Class*, New York: Vintage Books.

Tocqueville, A. de (1835/2000), *Democracy in America*, trans. S. D. Grant, Indianapolis, IN: Hackett Publishing.

Tomaselli, K. and A. Shepperson (2002), 'Speaking in Tongues, Writing in Vision: Orality and Literacy in Televangelistic Communication', in S. M. Hoover and L. S. Clark (eds), *Practicing Religion in the Age of the Media*, New York: Columbia University Press.

Tonnies, F. (1935/1957), *Gemeinschaft und Gesellschaft (Community and Society)*, trans. C. P. Loomis (ed.), East Lansing, MI: Michigan State University Press.

Tuchman, G. (1978), *Making News: A Study in the Construction of Reality*, New York: Free Press.

Turner, G. (1990), *British Cultural Studies: An Introduction*, London and New York: Routledge.

Veer, P. van der (2001), 'Transnational Religion', paper presented at the Conference on Transnational Migration: Comparative Perspectives, Princeton, NJ.

Veer, P. van der (1993), *Orientalism and the Postcolonial Predicament: Perspectives on Southeast Asia*, Philadelphia, PA: University of Pennsylvania Press.

Vera, Y. (1993), *Nehanda,* Harare: Baobab Books.

Warren, H. (2001), 'Southern Baptists and Disney', in D. A. Stout and J. M. Buddenbaum (eds), *Religion and Popular Culture: Studies on the Interaction of Worldviews,* Ames, IA: Iowa State University Press.

Warren, H. (1998), 'Standing Against the Tide: Conservative Protestant Families, Mainstream and Christian Media', unpublished Ph.D. dissertation, University of Texas at Austin.

Weber, M. (1919/1947), 'Science as a Vocation' (Wissenschaft als Beruf), in Weber, M., *From Max Weber: Essays in Sociology*, trans. H. H. Gerth and C. W. Mills (eds), London: Kegan Paul.

Williams, P. and L. Chrisman (1996), 'Introduction', *Colonial Discourse and Post-Colonial Theory*, New York: Columbia University Press, pp. 1–20.

Winston, D. (1999), *Red Hot and Righteous: The Urban Religion of the Salvation Army*, Cambridge, MA: Harvard University Press.

Additional Resources

Meyer, B. (1999), *Translating the Devil: Religion and Modernity Among the Ewe in Ghana*, Edinburgh: Edinburgh University Press.

Meyer, B. (1995), '"Delivered from the Powers of Darkness", Confessions about Satanic Riches in Christian Ghana', *Africa* **65** (2), 236–55.

Miles, M. (1996), *Seeing and Believing: Religion and Values in the Movies*, Boston, MA: Beacon Press.

Veer, P. van der (1994), *Religious Nationalism: Hindus and Muslims in India*, Berkeley, CA: University of California Press.

Chapter 2

Theology, Church and Media – Contours in a Changing Cultural Terrain

Peter Horsfield

The shifts that have taken place in thinking about the relationship between media and religion, from a primarily instrumentalist approach to a more cultural approach, have major implications not only for media research and understanding but also for religious institutions. For this change in thinking shifts the focus away from religious institutions as the primary definers and guardians of religious reality, who use media to disseminate that reality, towards seeing religion as a broader mediated cultural phenomenon within which religious institutions have a place, but along with a variety of other powerful cultural factors.

This is more than a change produced by change in theory. The approach that looks at the study of media and religion from a cultural rather than instrumental perspective is part of the broad range of intellectual, cultural and technological changes that took place through the latter part of the twentieth century.

My research and involvement in media and religion have spanned the last quarter of the twentieth century, when many of these key changes were taking place. Because much of my professional career has been spent working at the interface of media and the churches – as a theologian, church pastor, media producer, theological educator and media scholar – the changes in my work reflect an attempt to understand and interpret the implications that the contours of this changing media cultural terrain have had on western Christianity in the latter part of the twentieth century.

In this chapter I want to explore some of the implications that changes in media thinking, research and practice have for religious institutions by tracing aspects of my own intellectual and professional journey, a journey that characteristically for the time is marked by significant changes in thinking and approach.

Churches and Media in the 1970s

I became involved in the media field in the early 1970s on the advice of a perceptive colleague who told me that mass communication was going to be one of the crucial issues for churches in the future. The colleague also advised me to do more than study simply media production, but to include theological study as well. This was easier said than done – there were few places in the world where one could study both media and theology at an advanced level. When I enrolled in the Ph.D. program at Boston University, I had to set up my own program, taking courses from both the School of Theology and the School of Public Communication. For supervision of my doctoral dissertation I had to organize a committee comprising faculty members from both schools and introduce them to each other.

This life on the margins of two disciplines arises from the disciplinary structure of modern thought and has characterized most of my professional life and generally characterizes the experience of those who seek to take seriously both media and theology.

My original intention in studying media was to understand how media worked in order to use them as tools for religious communication. The School of Public Communication was a good site for this. The School was strong in research and production within what had been the dominant theoretical perspective of US media research for almost half a century: an empirically based instrumentalist approach. This empirical, social science based approach to theorizing and studying media was largely unquestioned at the time. Like other scientific disciplines, it was seen simply as objectively describing things the way they are. Today the 'scientific' approach is subject to significant criticism for using the concept of objectivity to hide the particular political, ideological and administrative interests that are served by the presumption of objectivity.

From this critical perspective, it is possible now to see that there is a lot about this instrumentalist, empirical approach to thinking about media that makes it attractive as a communication model for church communicators (as well as others such as politicians, public relations professionals and marketers). As David Morgan illustrates in his chapter in this volume (Chapter 7), texts such as James F. Engel's *How to Communicate the Gospel Effectively* (Engel, 1988), which use an instrumentalist model of media, are still common in theological and ministerial education.

One reason for this is that the instrumentalist approach is relatively simple to understand and maps onto our developing understanding of who we are – as we grow our tacit, subjective, experiential world generates within us an innate link between action and consequences. This simplicity sets the mind free to direct attention to the development of strategy.

A second is that it's a theory for action. Communication is a process: learn the techniques and you can achieve the results, holding out the hope that people's minds can be changed by the power of the message.

A third is that it corresponds to the dominant proclamation concept of communication that exists within churches. This makes it relatively easy for churches simply to transfer their central practices, metaphors, and understandings of preaching and teaching into their media work. (Conversely, it also meant that when churches' work in television, for example, didn't begin to produce the results of converts and church members that were expected, its expense was considered unjustified and churches withdrew from the television environment.)

A fourth attraction is that the instrumentalist approach structurally serves church institutional interests. The approach assumes that the meaning of a message is generated and determined largely by the person who constructs and produces the message in the process of production, very attractive to church leaders who assume that it is their task to interpret what Christianity means. The approach also assumes a fairly passive audience, which reinforces the hope of church leaders that by controlling the production of Christian messages they will be able to safeguard its interpretation.

As I will note later, moving away from instrumentalist theories of how media work to more comprehensive cultural approaches changes not just thinking about media but thinking about religious institutions as cultural forms as well.

The dominant framework for thinking about culture at the time was Richard Niebuhr's formative work, *Christ and Culture* (Niebuhr, 1951). Aspects of Niebuhr's five models of *rapprochement* between Christianity and secular culture were frequently questioned and debated. What was neither questioned nor debated was Niebuhr's modernist assumption that it was possible to see religion and culture as two separate entities. There was little debate also on whether one could talk about 'Christ' without at the same time talking about culture. It was still possible with integrity to think of a single entity called Christianity or 'The Church' which was separate from the culture and what was needed to protect it from cultural contamination.

Televangelism: A Case Study of Religion and the Media

With a concern to understand how churches could best use media to communicate, in my doctoral dissertation I undertook a study of the American televangelists, who were running hot and controversial at that time. I integrated theological analysis with empirical research, defining theological issues and goals around the use of mass media for religious communication and evaluating these against what the empirical research said (Horsfield, 1981).

My research clarified a number of misconceptions about the religious broadcasters. In general, it showed that the televangelists were not as effective as they claimed to be: their audiences were not as large as was claimed; while they justified their huge fund-raising on the basis of evangelism, their programs were clustered around areas of the country that were already highly churched; and though they got a lot of responses to their programs, few of those respondents became involved in local church communities (Horsfield, 1988).

I concluded that the success of the televangelists, whatever that was, had come at the expense of theological integrity: 'in accommodating themselves to the demands of commercial television, [they] have lost the essence of the Christian message and have simply become indistinguishable facsimiles of other commercial television programs' (Horsfield, 1984, p. 39).

Leonard Sweet would later describe such distaste for televangelism as arising in effect out of Liberal snobbery.[1] He may well be right. Hoover's work on televangelism in the late 1980s (Hoover, 1988) began to articulate an alternative theoretical perspective, moving analysis away from a linear effects framework towards a more cultural analysis of how televangelism was contributing to a coalescence of evangelical culture within the mainstream of American life. That cultural shift would be developed further in the following decades.

In many ways, in my doctoral research I argued myself out of one job into another. I concluded at the end of my study that if the televangelists with their traditional evangelical concern for right doctrine could be so influenced by the ideology of television, and with the vast amounts of money that were at their disposal were doing little more than circulating Christians from one church to another, a different approach had to be found. For me that had begun to focus on an interest in the culture of media rather than in seeing how media could be used. That became the focus of my subsequent study.

Christian Critique of Media

I returned to Australia to take up a position as minister of a suburban parish and taught at a local university in mass media and society, with a critical analysis of media functions and institutions similar to that of the Frankfurt School (Boorstin, 1972; Ellul, 1985; Ewen, 1976; Postman, 1987). I wrote a guide for parents to assist them in mediating the influence of television on their children (Horsfield, 1986). This critique of media institutions and media culture left unquestioned the culture of Christianity and hence resonated with many church leaders. The perspectives and conclusions presented in my work over the course of the 1980s were quoted in various places as giving voice to an informed and scholarly theological critique on the relationship between Christianity and the media.

I now consider such an antagonistic stance to be inadequate, partly because it fails to recognize the value of different cultures, and partly because it fails to acknowledge churches' own cultural and media positioning and their associated interests. Yet this antagonistic attitude towards mass media and popular culture is still dominant among church leaders and theological teachers today (Horsfield, 1989).

In the mid 1980s I took a position as Dean at a theological faculty in Victoria, a position that involved me directly in the education and formation of men and women for ministry. This position provided more space and opportunity to explore alternative understandings of the relationship between media and religion apart from the dominant religious antagonistic one. A number of influences, both media and theological, began to converge in this exploration.

I began to revisit the work of the cultural technologists Marshall McLuhan and Walter Ong. This rereading stimulated thought about the connections between dominant systems of mediation and their cultural outcomes, and the media base of particular cultures (Ong, 1967, 1982). This reading of Ong is reflected in Tom Boomershine's work on the place of media in the historical shaping of Christianity (Boomershine, 1987, 1991).

A traditional theological college, heavy in literate discourse, policy and practice provides a good context for observing Ong's proposals on links between media and culture. As in most religious seminaries, theological teaching and research were organized in the modernist disciplinary structure that has evolved from that originally proposed by Schleiermacher. My courses on media were located in the department of applied theology, reflecting the instrumentalist perspective that media were tools you considered once the ideas had been formed in the separate disciplines of scripture, history and theology. Despite my best efforts, after ten years I had made little progress in convincing my theological colleagues that media were a constitutive factor in theological thought, not just a functional one (Horsfield, 1989). This situation is not unique. Ken Bedell's study in the US in 1990 found that courses in media at seminaries had dropped in the previous ten years, not increased (Bedell, 1993).

Seeing Media from a Cultural Perspective

I found greater stimulation in development of my thinking outside the theological college through part-time teaching in journalism and media studies in a nearby university. It began to dawn on me that there was operative in Australian media studies a quite different theoretical perspective to that which had guided my studies in the US. That was the more European-based cultural studies perspective, which sees and analyses media as cultural forms within a cultural–literacy framework rather than the instrumental–social scientific approach dominant in the US.

Many of the elements of the cultural studies approach were not totally new – concepts such as textual analysis, semiotics, culture and context were familiar to me from biblical exegesis and theology, though often in different terms. The greater challenge of this approach for thinking about media and religion lies not so much in its different concepts, but in its underlying assumptions.

In contrast to the modernist, scientific approach that conceives of 'reality' as an objective existent within a singular universe toward which all knowledge contributes, the cultural studies approach conceives of a variety of constructed 'realities', which serve particular purposes for those who hold them and which continually contest with other constructions for access to social recognition and resourcing. In place of the instrumentalist view of media as tools for communicating ideas developed elsewhere, in a cultural view media are seen as arising from within the culture through different cultural processes and with particular cultural biases, and they function both as tools for maintenance of the culture and as cultural sites within which this power contest and reality construction is continually taking place.

A shift in theoretical perspective such as this brings not only an alternative way of integrating ideas, but also a different conception of how the world and social institutions function. As mentioned earlier, seeing media primarily as instruments is attractive to churches because it reinforces the importance of the church as an institution within a structured society, while at the same time hiding the vested interests of those who hold power within the institution.

The cultural perspective challenges this institutional determination in a number of crucial ways. In place of the common religious emphasis on commonality and universality, the cultural view affirms difference and argues that one needs to be open to the diversity of realities and truths that exist, and to the exceptions that do not fit into the norm. In place of the view of knowledge as a dispassionate, rational discovery enterprise, the cultural view sees knowledge as contested constructions reflecting the vested interests of those who are doing the constructing. In place of the view that the meaning of communication is created by the originator of the message at the point of production, the cultural view sees meaning as a negotiation between the text and the receiver at the site of reception.

Theological Implications of a Cultural Perspective

Each of these perspectives has significant theological ramifications. Increased exposure to alternate theologies such as feminist and liberation theologies, visits to churches in Asia and the Pacific and the realization that standard histories of Christianity have largely excluded the history of Christianity in Asia (largely because that significant history was not preserved in written documents (Philip, no date)) have increased my awareness of the difference there is within and between churches. It is becoming increasingly problematic to refer to 'the Church' as if it is a single concept, and I find myself increasingly referring to 'churches' and 'Christian communities'.

The power dimensions of theology and the church became apparent during a lengthy involvement as one of the early advocates for women who had been subject to violence or sexual abuse by clergy in Australia. No education could teach as clearly as that experience the particular cultural stake and vested interests of church leaders and the lengths to which they will go to protect those vested interests. Insights into the dynamics of power within churches provided a good basis for re-examining how and why theology is formulated, how power is and has been used to suppress difference in order to achieve what is called Christian unity, and how communications are controlled in order to protect the interests of particular groups over others.

Kathryn Tanner's work *Theories of Culture: A New Agenda for Theology* provides a valuable re-examination of Christianity from this perspective of its plurality rather than uniformity and the power relationships that are involved in establishing coherence within this plurality (Tanner, 1997). Tanner argues that at its heart Christianity is and always has been a pluralistic, diverse and at times contradictory movement that defies any form of general summary or identification of some common 'essence.' She argues that we need to affirm this diversity in ideas and material practice rather than seek to suppress it. What it means to be distinctively Christian, for Tanner, is not some central fixed truths, but a continually changing diversity that finds coherence in relation to specific contexts and practical demands, not abstract principles:

> The insistence that there is only one right way of being a Christian is even more likely to rupture Christian fellowship, to make a mockery of the unity of peace and love of Christ, than the existing diversity of practice for which it is the supposed remedy. (p. 172)

Tanner argues that part of this realism involves a recognition that the concepts of culture and Christianity are inextricably intertwined and the artificial boundary that modern theologians such as Niebuhr have tended to erect when thinking about 'Christianity' and 'culture' are artificial:

> The distinctiveness of cultural identity is therefore not a product of isolation; it is not a matter of a culture's being simply self-generated, pure and unmixed; it is not a matter of 'us' vs. 'them.' Cultural identity becomes, instead, a hybrid, relational affair, something that lives between as much as within cultures. What is important for cultural identity is the novel way cultural elements from elsewhere are now put to work, by means of such complex and ad hoc relational processes as resistance, appropriation, subversion, and compromise (pp. 57–58)

Tanner's argument provides a valuable theological perspective for thinking about the intertwining of media and media cultures with particular constructions or historical forms of Christianity. I explore this interface between media and the shaping of Christianity in fuller detail in my CD-ROM *The Mediated Spirit* (Horsfield, 2002).

A good example of this integrated analysis can be found in Marianne Sawicki's work *Seeing the Lord: Resurrection and Early Christian Practices*. In that work, Sawicki examines the influence of different forms of mediation in the early construction of Christian thinking (Sawicki, 1994). Sawicki's is one of the first works I have read that uses a cultural understanding of media as an integral element in analysing early Christianity, to demonstrate how different media reflected and shaped different cultural positions that became crucial in contests over how Christianity was to be understood, preserved and communicated.

The other challenge posed to theological thinking by media cultural theory is in the area of reception theory. Reception theory explores the way in which meaning is constructed through the mediation of a text by the user at the point of reception, facilitated by a diversification and decentralization of media production and the extension of consumer capitalism. Reception theory addresses much of the shift in social structure away from institutional determination and control of meaning towards consumer control.

The idea that religious meaning is created not by the producers of messages but through an interaction of the text, context and user represents a significant shift of power that challenges previous understandings and power structures of Christianity as a coherent movement. Yet in many ways it recovers many aspects of how Jesus communicated and simply affirms what most preachers know: that prepare as much as you like, people will make their own meaning out of what you say.

Seeking to find a supportive intellectual community when you work in an area that crosses boundaries is not easy. While both places were friendly, the theological faculty weren't really concerned about media, and the university media faculty weren't really concerned about religion. In 1997 I was invited to join the International Study Commission on Media Religion and Culture. The group provided a fruitful and enjoyable interdisciplinary, international and intercultural context within which to develop and integrate further this continuing ferment. After years of sitting on the fringe of theology because of my interests in media, and sitting on the fringe of media because of my interests in religion, I found that the Commission has been one group to whom I haven't had to explain myself. Each meeting has been an experience of helping towards integration of new ideas, while at the same time delaying that integration by raising new dimensions to be considered.

A meeting of the Commission in Boulder in January 1999 was a fruitful one in expanding this emerging nexus between media, culture and religion. Two themes were explored at that meeting: the embodiment of faith in material culture, and the different apprehension of experience in visual culture (Morgan, 1998a, 1998b). It is fairly common to recognize that Christianity is much more than ideas and beliefs. But academic theology privileges beliefs and ideas over other aspects of faith. Work being done on the importance of visual media and material objects in popular practices of religious faith is crucial in understanding the complex ways in which religious practices are immersed in and arise out of rich beds of cultural life. Colleen McDannell's book *Material Christianity* provides a good framework and resources for exploring religious material culture further (McDannell, 1995).

Future Directions

The new perspectives between media, culture and religion that are being explored by the Commission are a crucial exploration not just of media, but of the new interfaces emerging between media, cultural studies, theology and religious practice. It is just the beginning of what I think is still a largely uncharted field.

Note

1   Sweet wrote, in his analysis of the debate around televangelism that occurred during the 1980s: 'Clearly, much of the available scholarship shows tremendous distaste for the subject, especially that which emerges from liberal Protestantism. Peter G. Horsfield's

Religious Television (1984) is a case in point, *although Horsfield is of a different mind today'* (Sweet, 1993, p. 64. Italics mine).

References

Bedell, K. (1993), Seminary study conducted for the National Council of Churches Media Education Committee – Summary of findings.

Boomershine, T. E. (1991), 'Doing Theology in the Electronic Age: The Meeting of Orality and Electricity', *Journal of Theology,* **95**, 4–14.

Boomershine, T. E. (1987), 'Biblical Megatrends: Towards a Paradigm for the Interpretation of the Bible in Electronic Media', in H. R. Kent (ed.), *Society of Biblical Literature Seminar Papers,* Atlanta, GA: Scholars Press, pp. 144–57.

Boorstin, D. (1972), *The Image: A Guide to Pseudo-events in America,* New York: Atheneum.

Ellul, J. (1985), *The Humiliation of the Word,* Grand Rapids, MI: William B. Eerdmans.

Engel, J. F. (1988), *How to Communicate the Gospel Effectively,* Achimota, Ghana: Africa Christian Press.

Ewen, S. (1976), *Captains of Consciousness: Advertising and the Social Roots of the Consumer Culture,* New York: McGraw-Hill.

Hoover, S. M. (1988), *Mass Media Religion: The Social Sources of the Electronic Church,* Newbury Park, CA: Sage.

Horsfield, P. (2002), *The Mediated Spirit,* Melbourne: Commission for Mission, Uniting Church in Australia.

Horsfield, P. (1989), 'Teaching Theology in a New Cultural Environment', *Media Development,* 6–9.

Horsfield, P. (1988), 'Evangelism by Mail: Letters from Broadcasters', *Journal of Communication,* **35** (1) (Winter), 89–97.

Horsfield, P. (1986), *Taming the Television: A Parent's Guide to Children and Television,* Sydney: Albatross.

Horsfield, P. (1984), *Religious Television: The American Experience,* New York: Longman.

Horsfield, P. (1981), 'Religious Television Broadcasting: An Analysis of the Theological Debate in Light of the Empirical Research', unpublished Ph.D., Boston University, Boston.

McDannell, C. (1995), *Material Christianity: Religion and Popular Culture in America,* New Haven. CT: Yale University Press.

Morgan, D. (1998a), 'Notes on Meaning and Medium in the Aesthetics of Visual Piety', unpublished email post to the media.faith listserve, http://monaro.adc.rmit.edu.au/mailman/listinfo/media.faith.

Morgan, D. (1998b), *Visual Piety: A History and Theory of Popular Religious Images,* Berkeley, CA: University of California Press.

Niebuhr, H. R. (1951), *Christ and Culture,* New York: Harper and Row.

Ong, W. (1982), *Orality and Literacy: The Technologising of the Word,* London: Methuen.

Ong, W. (1967), *The Presence of the Word,* New Haven, CT: Yale University Press.

Philip, T. V. (no date), 'The Missionary Impulse in the Early Asian Christian Tradition', *PTCA Bulletin,* 5–14.

Postman, N. (1987), *Amusing Ourselves to Death,* London: Methuen.

Sawicki, M. (1994), *Seeing the Lord: Resurrection and Early Christian Practice,* Minneapolis, MN: Fortress.

Sweet, L. I. (1993), 'Communication and Change in American Religious History: A Historiographical Probe', in L. I. Sweet (ed.), *Communication and Change in American Religious History*, Grand Rapids, MI: William B. Eerdmans.
Tanner, K. (1997), *Theories of Culture: A New Agenda for Theology*, Minneapolis, MN: Fortress Press.

Additional Resources

Babin, P. (1991), *The New Era in Religious Communication*, Minneapolis, MN: Fortress Press. Babin provides a provocative exploration of the implications of audio-visual culture for various aspects of religious experience and education.
Edwards, M. U., Jr (1994), *Printing, Propaganda and Martin Luther*, Berkeley, CA: University of California Press. Provides a historical context for understanding present media and religious change by examining how the Lutheran Reformation was intricately bound up with Luther's command of and adaptation to demands of the printing press and the interests of the commercial printers.
Horsfield, P. (2002), *The Mediated Spirit,* Melbourne: Commission for Mission, Uniting Church in Australia, www.mediatedspirit.com. One of the few available resources in digital form that explores the part played by media in the historical shaping of Christianity, from the oral–manuscript culture of the early church to the present electronic–digital era.
McDannell, C. (1995), *Material Christianity: Religion and Popular Culture in America*, New Haven, CT: Yale University Press. A good survey of how religious experience and practice are rooted in and expressed through 'stuff' – material objects and practices. A good corrective to the view that religion is mainly about faith as ideas.
Ong, W. (1982), *Orality and Literacy: The Technologising of the Word*, London: Methuen. Provides an extensive description of the characteristics of oral and literature cultures as they emerge from the characteristics of the technologies. A good background and framework for understanding characteristics of electronic cultures of today.
Sawicki, M. (1994), *Seeing the Lord: Resurrection and Early Christian Practice.* Minneapolis, MN: Fortress Press. Sawicki provides an insightful analysis of the early construction of Christianity and the meaning of Jesus. Incorporates the media of the early Christians, and conflicts in different mediations, as a foundational element of this construction.
Tanner, K. (1997), *Theories of Culture: A New Agenda for Theology*, Minneapolis, MN: Fortress Press. Analyzes the dominant view of culture used in much theological thinking, and proposes an alternative that takes into account much of the recent thinking of cultural analyses as a basis for exploring the coherence of the Christian movement as a diverse, complex and at times contradictory movement.

Chapter 3

Because God is Near, God is Real: Symbolic Realism in US Latino Popular Catholicism and Medieval Christianity

Roberto S. Goizueta

At the beginning of his Apostolic Exhortation *Ecclesia in America*, Pope John Paul II challenges us to 'reflect on America as a single entity' (John Paul II, Para. 5). The use of the singular is appropriate, he suggests, as 'an attempt to express not only the unity which in some way already exists, but also to point to that closer bond which the peoples of the continent seek and which the Church wishes to foster as part of her own mission, as she works to promote the communion of all in the Lord' (ibid.). As someone who has always found it rather puzzling that the United States, but one country in North America, could so innocently refer to itself as, simply, 'America', I consider the Pope's assertion much more than semantic quibbling; in itself, his inclusive use of the singular 'America' represents both an acknowledgement of historical reality and, on the basis of such historical honesty, a call to conversion. Indeed, as Cuban-American theologian Justo González has observed: 'What preposterous conceit allows the inhabitants of a single country to take for themselves the name of an entire hemisphere? What does this say about that country's view of those other nations who share the hemisphere with it?' (González, 1990, p. 37).

Pope John Paul II's challenge is today more appropriate than ever, given the recently released US Census Bureau figures reporting the dramatic growth of the US Latino population. In the Mexican War, the United States conquered and annexed almost half of the territory of Mexico; today we are witnessing the reconquest of that territory, not by the force of arms but by the sweat of the brow, by the very power of the 'American dream'.

The ongoing Latin American 'reconquest' of the United States has even more significance for the Catholic Church in this country. In ten years, a majority of all Catholics in the United States will be Spanish-speaking. In other words, Catholicism in the United States is *already* an 'American' Catholicism whose face, whether we like it or not, is dramatically different from that of the 'American Catholicism' so often portrayed in our textbooks, media, sociological studies, or theological research. In *Ecclesia in America*, Pope John Paul II challenges us to acknowledge this reality and to consciously embrace it as a source of renewal for the Church in America.

In this chapter, I want to explore some of the ways in which, if thus embraced, the Latino presence might contribute to the future of American Catholicism. That is, US Latino popular Catholicism – or the way in which Latinos concretely live their Catholicism – offers us the possibility of recovering forgotten aspects of the Catholic tradition and, more broadly, forgotten aspects of the western Christian religious tradition. More specifically, the religious practices of Latino Catholics represent the enduring, 'subversive' presence of a particular (though not unique) way of living and understanding religious faith.

In the United States, that lived faith survives even in the midst of a dominant culture whose worldview is very different. I will suggest that one important source of tension between US Latino Catholics and Euro-American Catholics is their different notions of symbol as mediating the divine, or the real. These different understandings of symbol and ritual in turn yield different notions of divine revelation (how and where God is revealed) and different notions of religious faith itself (what *defines* religious faith). Ultimately, the worldview and epistemology underlying Latino popular Catholicism reflect fundamental assumptions about the intrinsically symbolic character of reality that differ from (post)modern western epistemologies which trace their roots to late medieval nominalism.

Consequently, a renewed appreciation of the medieval Christian worldview that predated the rise of nominalism in the West could facilitate an openness to Latino popular religion which would enrich not only 'American' Catholicism but the larger US culture as well. I will suggest, moreover, that such a retrieval/ openness to 'the other' in the form of Latino popular religion as well as 'the other' in the form of *pre-modern* western traditions would call into question both the naïve realism that underlies much modern Christian fundamentalism and relativist epistemologies that underlie much (post)modern culture, with its insistence on the disjunction between the symbol (appearance, text) and the symbolized (reality).

Different Histories, Different Ways of Being Catholic

To address these issues as they impact American Catholicism specifically, we must first appreciate the different histories of the Catholic Church in Latin America and in the United States: the roots of Latin American Catholicism are found in Iberian medieval and baroque Christianity, whereas the roots of Anglo-Catholicism in the United States are found in Northern European post-Tridentine Roman Catholicism. As historian William Christian has noted, the medieval Christian worldview and faith were not seriously threatened in Spain 'until ... the late eighteenth century' (Christian, 1998, pp. 326–27). Consequently, Iberian Catholicism was not forced to develop a response to the reformers' arguments or rebut them point by point – as, also, European Catholics in the United States would later be forced to do (ibid., 1998, p. 327).

In order to defend itself against the Protestant 'threat' to orthodoxy, Northern European Catholicism would become increasingly rationalist, demanding a clarity, precision and uniformity in doctrinal formulations which were simply not necessary in areas where 'Catholic' and 'Christian' continued to be essentially interchangeable terms; in Spain, there was no urgent need to define, clarify and distinguish Catholic belief, especially in the wake of the *reconquista* and the expulsion of the Jews in 1492 (Macy, 1995, p. 27). It would be the more rationalist, Northern European Catholicism that would take hold in the English colonies – and it is this understanding of Catholicism that continues to inform the US Catholic establishment to this day, whether conservative or liberal.

The differences between Catholicism in the English and in the Spanish colonies were reinforced by the fact that, like the Iberian colonizers as a whole, Iberian Catholicism interacted – even if often violently – with an Amerindian culture that, in many ways, shared a worldview quite similar to that of medieval Christianity. Conversely, like the English colonizers as a whole, Anglo-American Catholicism in the English colonies generally rejected any such intermingling with the indigenous culture, preferring to expel and exclude rather than subjugate and subdue that culture.

If we are to understand the contemporary context of American Catholicism and address successfully the challenges and opportunities of the future, therefore, the Catholic Church in the United States must begin by recognizing the fact that Catholicism in this country did not begin in the English colonies but, rather, on the shores of what is now Florida, in the deserts of what is now New Mexico, and, indeed, in the first voyages of Columbus. Without rejecting either of these histories, or any of those that came afterward in subsequent waves of immigrants, we must begin to forge a future rooted in that polyglot, multicultural past.

In his research into the historical origins of Latino popular Catholicism, Orlando Espín observes that the Iberian Christianity brought by the Spanish to Latin America 'was medieval and pre-Tridentine, and it was planted in the Americas approximately two generations before Trent's opening session' (Espín, 1997, p. 117). He continues: 'While this faith was defined by traditional creedal beliefs as passed down through the Church's magisterium, those beliefs were expressed primarily in and through symbol and rite, through devotions and liturgical practices ... The teaching of the gospel did not usually occur through the spoken, magisterial word, but through the symbolic, 'performative' word' (ibid., p. 119). As yet, in their everyday lives, Christians did not clearly distinguish creedal traditions from liturgical and devotional traditions; both were assumed to be integral dimensions of *the* tradition. Espín avers that 'until 1546 *traditio* included, without much reflective distinction *at the everyday level*, both the contents of Scripture and the dogmatic declarations of the councils of antiquity, as well as devotional practices (that often had a more ancient history than, for example, Chalcedon's Christological definitions)' (Espín, 1995, p. 19). According to Espín, the clear distinction between dogma, that is, the *content* of tradition, and worship, that is, the *form* in which that tradition was embodied in everyday life, did not become crystallized until the Council of Trent. He goes on to suggest that, 'on this side of the Atlantic the Church was at least in its second generation, and it took approximately another century for Trent's theology and decrees to appear and become operative in our ecclesiastical scene' (ibid.).

Liturgical theologian Mark Francis observes that

> during its formative period and even after the struggle for independence from Spain, Catholicism in Latin America never underwent the systematic standardization that was brought about by the Council of Trent elsewhere in the Catholic world. North American Catholicism, for example, was largely dominated by clergy drawn from European ethnic groups who immigrated to this country along with their people in the nineteenth century and who were inspired by the norms and centralized pastoral practices of Tridentine Catholicism. In contrast, Hispanic Catholics, except perhaps those from large cities, have never been historically so influenced. The first period of evangelization of Latin America antedates the Council of Trent; and even after the decrees and norms established by the council were promulgated in Europe, their implementation was slow and sporadic, even into the nineteenth century. (Francis, 1995, pp. 165–66)

This history also helps underscore not only the similarities but also the differences between Latin American and European popular Catholicism:

> Because it adhered more strictly to the spirit of the Council of Trent, the devotional life of most of the European immigrant groups … was regulated by the clergy, who were instrumental in its revival during the nineteenth century. Latin America never had a history of such clerical oversight, both because of a lack of native clergy and a policy toward popular religion that was much more laissez-faire on the part of the Church. (Ibid., 1995, p. 166)

Thus, Euro-American popular Catholicism has a different ecclesiastical history from that of US Latino popular Catholicism, even though they share a similar emphasis on symbol and ritual as defining the way in which the faith is lived out.

As Catholicism in the United States becomes increasingly *pan*-American, the historical argument of scholars like Espín and Francis becomes increasingly relevant for understanding our context sociologically, theologically and pastorally. The Catholicism that originally came to Latin America was essentially Iberian and medieval in character; the Catholicism that came to the English colonies was Northern European and, as Jesuit historian John O'Malley has argued, essentially modern in character. This distinction has important ramifications. For instance, the distinction helps explain why US Latino Catholics, being of little real interest to either liberal or conservative 'mainstream' Catholics, are generally invisible to scholars of 'American Catholicism', whether these scholars are liberal or conservative; whether liberal or conservative, Euro-American Catholics in the United States share an essentially modern worldview that tends to view Latino Catholicism with suspicion.

Ironically, the reasons for the suspicion are similar to those that legitimated anti-Catholic, nativist sentiments *against* Euro-American Catholics not long ago. In both cases, an underlying modern prejudice against anything 'medieval' (the word itself connoting 'backwardness') has engendered violent reactions against any group perceived as embodying a worldview, values, or beliefs that in any way resemble those of medieval Christianity, which are themselves perceived as naïvely materialistic, superstitious and infantile. Thus, if today Irish-American Catholics are wary of Mexican-American Catholics, it is because these latter embody a type of Catholicism similar to that which Irish-American Catholics have long been trying mightily to live down, so as to be accepted as full-fledged members of our modern democracy. Arguing that the prejudice against medieval Christianity is based on the anachronistic assumption that medieval Christianity was identical with post-Tridentine Roman Catholicism, historian Gary Macy has perceptively diagnosed the problem facing Hispanic Catholics in the United States: 'If the Church in the Middle Ages was tyrannical, corrupt, and immoral, and the Church in the Middle Ages was (and is) Roman Catholic, then Roman Catholics are immoral, corrupt, and tyrannical. Hispanics, as mostly Roman Catholics, can therefore be expected to be devious, immoral, lazy, technologically underdeveloped, and ignorant' (Macy, 1995, p. 40). The irony lies in the fact that, whereas in the first half of the twentieth century Catholics as a whole were the objects of this modern prejudice, today it is Hispanic Catholics who are often the objects of prejudice at the hands of a thoroughly 'Americanized', thoroughly modern US Catholic establishment that has assimilated the modern prejudice against the Middle Ages.

The point here is not to suggest either that US Latino popular Catholicism can simply be equated with medieval Christianity, which it of course cannot, or to suggest that we can or should somehow 'return' to some romanticized version of medieval Christianity – which was, after all, also characterized by a great deal of horrific violence, oppression and corruption. Rather, I simply mean to suggest that, while not sufficient, an understanding of the historical influences of medieval Christianity on Latino popular Catholicism is certainly necessary in order to understand the present and future of American Catholicism. And, I submit, a *critical* retrieval of the medieval Christian worldview might offer resources for addressing the challenges confronting the US Catholic Church.

Because it is a Symbol, it is Real

As Orlando Espín and other Hispanic scholars have repeatedly observed, the faith of the Hispanic people is primarily embodied and expressed in and through symbol and ritual. Yet that statement itself begs the further question: what precisely do we *mean* by symbol and ritual or, more precisely, what do Hispanics mean by symbol and ritual? It is here, in differing *notions* of symbolic expression and mediation, that

we find the source of conflict and, it is hoped, the possibility of mutual understanding and unity.

US Latino popular Catholicism embodies an understanding of religious symbols
and, therefore, of religious faith rooted in the medieval and baroque popular
Catholicism first brought to the 'New World' by the Spanish and Portuguese in the
late fifteenth and early sixteenth centuries. Such an understanding differs radically
from the modern notion of symbol that, I will suggest, has influenced Christianity
since the late Middle Ages and became normative in the wake of the Protestant
Reformation, the Council of Trent, the Catholic Reformation, and the neo-
scholastic theologies that reached their apex in the nineteenth century. Indeed, one
might even argue that it is precisely the Latino (and medieval) 'realist' or
'materialist' notion of symbol and ritual that modern western Christians find most
distasteful among Latinos/as, dismissing such ideas as mere infantile superstition in
the face of more rationalist (read 'mature') understandings of religious symbol,
ritual and faith.

At the very heart of the historical and cultural differences between Latino
and Euro-American Catholics, therefore, are fundamentally different ways of
conceiving the relationship between symbol, or 'appearances', and the symbolized,
or 'reality'; one of the great differences between medieval and modern Catholicism
is found in their different understandings of religious symbols. As the Catholic
philosopher Louis Dupré has observed, the roots of this key difference can be traced
back to the rise of nominalism in the late Middle Ages. Medieval Christianity had a
unified, profoundly sacramental view of the cosmos; creation everywhere revealed
the abiding presence of its Creator, a living presence that infused all creation
with meaning. In turn, 'the *kosmos* included humans as an integral though unique
part of itself' (Dupré, 1993, p. 94). As the place where one encountered the living,
transcendent God, all creation was assumed to be intrinsically symbolic; that is,
creation re-presented God, made the transcendent God present in time and space for
us, here and now. That God had not made the world only to withdraw from it,
leaving it to its own devices; rather, the Creator remained intimately united to
creation. All creation was assumed to be *intrinsically* meaningful and intelligible,
therefore, inasmuch as that creation was *graced* from the beginning. The Sacred
would therefore be encountered, not 'above' or 'outside' creation, but in and
through creation.

Most systematically articulated in the writings of Thomas Aquinas, this organic,
sacramental worldview was reflected, above all, in the religious practices of
medieval Christians. To them, matter mattered. Religious life was sensually rich;
the believer encountered God in the physical environment, through the five senses.
The Christian faith of the Middle Ages was firmly anchored in the body: the body of
the cosmos, the body of the person, the Body of Christ. Contrary to the modern
stereotype of the medieval Christian as having a dualistic worldview antithetical to
the human body, the Christian of the Middle Ages 'assumed the flesh to be the
instrument of salvation' and 'the cultivation of bodily experience as a place for

encounter with meaning, a locus of redemption' (Bynum, 1999, pp. 251–52). (Of course, as in every age, the view of the body was also profoundly ambiguous and conflicted – ibid.).

This organic, intrinsically symbolic worldview also implied a particular understanding of the relationship between the individual person and the cosmos: the person was perceived to be *integrally* related to the rest of creation and its Creator. Knowledge of reality thus presupposed and implied *relationship*; it is through *inter*personal *inter*action that we could come to know God, ourselves, other persons, and creation.

According to Dupré, this organic, holistic, integral, sacramental worldview began to break down during the late Middle Ages. Afraid that too intimate a connection with material creation would compromise God's absolute transcendence, nominalist theologians such as William of Ockham

> effectively removed God from creation. Ineffable in being and inscrutable in his designs, God withdrew from the original synthesis altogether. The divine became relegated to a supernatural sphere separate from nature, with which it retained no more than a causal, external link. This removal of transcendence fundamentally affected the conveyance of meaning. Whereas previously meaning had been established in the very act of creation by a wise God, it now fell upon the human mind to interpret a cosmos, the person became its source of meaning. (Dupré, 1993, p. 3)

The nominalist coin had another side, however: such an understanding of God's autonomy and freedom implied the autonomy and freedom of creation itself. Paradoxically, then, the Christian attempt to safeguard God's transcendence laid the groundwork for the emergence of modern rationalism and secularism. In order to protect God's immutability and transcendence, nominalism posited an absolutely inscrutable God and, as a corollary, an absolutely inscrutable creation: if divine revelation were no longer to be found *in* creation, but rather *from beyond* creation, creation *per se* could have no intrinsic meaning. It was thus left up to the human subject alone to construct meaning.

Likewise, neo-scholastic theologians like Thomas Cajetan began to read Thomas Aquinas through a modern, dualistic lens. Their theology 'detach[ed] the realms of nature and faith from each other' (Dupré, 1993, p. 179). The birth of *modern* Christianity is thus characterized by the splitting, or dichotomizing, of reality: as God is severed from creation, the natural and spiritual realms are separated, and, in the end, the human person – now as an autonomous 'individual' – is severed from both God and nature: 'modern culture ... detached personhood from the other two constituents of the original ontological synthesis' (Dupré, 1993, pp. 163–64). Henceforth, the autonomous individual would stand outside God, who is far removed from everyday life, and outside nature; God's autonomy *vis-à-vis* the human person implies the person's own autonomy *vis-à-vis* God. If, eventually, secular humanists would preach a world without God, it was only because Christians had already been preaching a God without a world.

The breakdown of what Dupré calls the 'medieval synthesis' also had important consequences for the Christian understanding of symbol. Medieval Christians had looked upon creation as intrinsically symbolic, making present its Creator in our midst. In the wake of nominalism and neo-scholasticism, however, the ultimate meaning of creation could no longer be encountered *in* creation, which could exist independently of its Creator; now meaning would have to be imputed to creation, or imposed on it from without. From without, the rational *mind* would impose a meaningful order on a world that itself lacked intrinsic meaning. Physical existence no longer 'revealed' a God who lived in its very midst; now, physical existence *'pointed to'* a God who related to the world extrinsically; it was left up to the rational individual to make the connection. Creation-as-symbol became simply 'an extrinsic intermediary, something really outside the reality [i.e., God] transmitted through it, so that strictly speaking the thing [i.e., God] could be attained even without the symbol' (Rahner, 1966, p. 244). The symbol and the symbolized were no longer *really* united; they would now have to be 'mentally' united (to use Karl Rahner's phrase). If there were a relationship between God and creation, it would have to be one forged and explained by the human intellect. The locus of revelation would no longer be the cosmos (including though not reducible to human subjectivity) but the human *intellect*, which alone could impute meaning to the 'external' world. Consequently, the sacramental dimension of religious life would become increasingly superfluous: why bother communicating with God in and through sacramental practices when one could go 'directly' to God?

The medieval Christian world had been pregnant with symbolic meaning, for the world of matter was recognized as the locus of God's self-revelation. From sometime in the sixteenth century on, the world-as-symbol could only point *away* from itself to a God who remained impassible and aloof. Creation would no longer be a privileged place of encounter with the Sacred but a mere sign pointing elsewhere, to the spiritual realm where God resided transcendent and impassible.

It is important to note, however, that even as post-Tridentine Catholic theologians were making God evermore distant, the popular faith continued to reflect a stubborn insistence on God's abiding, concrete nearness to us in every aspect of life.[1] That nearness was embodied above all in the elaborate religious symbols and, especially, the explicitly *dramatic* character of communal religious life that flowered during the Baroque period. Theologian Thomas O'Meara describes Baroque Catholicism as follows:

> There was a universality in which Catholicism experienced God in a vastness, freedom, and goodness flowing through a world of diversity, movement, and order. Christ appeared in a more human way, filled with a personal love, redemptive and empowering ... The Baroque world was also a theater ... Liturgies, operas, frescos, or palatial receptions were theatrical, and Baroque Christianity was filled with visions and ecstasies, with martyrs, missionaries, and stigmatics ... The theater of the Christian life and the kingdom of God moved from the medieval cosmos and the arena of society to the interior of the Baroque church and the life of the soul. In the Baroque, light pours down through clear windows

into the church and states that God is not distant nor utterly different from creatures. God is actively present in the church and in the Christian. (O'Meara, 1999, pp. 115-16)

It is impossible for a contemporary Latino Catholic to read those descriptions without hearing resonances to the ways in which the Catholic faith is lived in our own communities. Neither the Christian medieval synthesis nor the dramatic faith of the Baroque has, in fact, been completely destroyed – at least not yet. Their enduring influence can still be witnessed in, among other places, the lived faith of the Latin American and US Latino Catholic communities.

The same deep faith in God's nearness reappears in Latino popular Catholicism, where dramatic reenactments like the *Via Crucis*, the *Posadas*, or the *Pastorela* serve as constant expressions of God's solidarity. It reappears in the polysemic ambience of our churches, where angels and demons, saints and penitents, celestial stars and spring flowers are fully incorporated into our lives even as these are drawn into the cosmic liturgy. This profound sense of the interpenetration of the spiritual and the material is not only a legacy of the Iberian Catholic heritage of Latino culture, but also of the indigenous (and African) roots that have for centuries mixed together to generate a culture characterized by *mestizaje* (racial–cultural mixture). The Mexican-American filmmaker Gregory Nava explains the significance of such an integral worldview for his own work, specifically the film *My Family/Mi Familia*:

So you have a tremendously strong and deep pre-Columbian spirituality that comes from the film, a concept of Olin [an Aztec concept/motif of cyclical movement], the movement around the center, that it is in what you do in life that you find your spirituality. The house represents that concept in a sense because it's centered yet it's always moving and changing colors, and they keep adding on to it. And of course the corn field which is regeneration and cyclical. All of these things are very powerful and form a mythic structure to the film. There is also this syncretic relationship, because this is about a Mestizo family, between the pre-Columbian and the Catholic, so I reflect that in the mythic structure of the movie. Therefore Ometeotl [the Creator Couple] and Tezcatlipocas [an Aztec God] become at the same moment José and María, which is Joseph and Mary, and Chucho is Jesus; and so there's the Catholic sacrifice of the Jesus character in the film, which forms the central traumatic moment of the family. So there is a syncretic, mythic, logical structure to the movie that is at once pre-Columbian and Catholic. (West, 1995, p. 26)[2]

Having been brought to Latin America by the Spanish, and having interacted with indigenous religions that often embodied similar beliefs in the nearness of the divine, Latino popular Catholicism is the embodied memory of this integral worldview. What sociologist David Morgan observes about medieval religious piety could just as easily be said of Latino popular religious practices: 'It was the Savior himself who greeted the devout in the icon; his image was transfigured into something more, into a corporeal gaze, into a look that touches … Simply put, visual piety in the late Middle Ages was that cultural operation whereby images were transformed into something revelatory' (Morgan, 1998, p. 66).

Because God is Near, God is Real: US Latino Popular Catholicism

The God of Latino Catholics is one whose reality is inseparable from our everyday life and struggles. It is in the very warp and weft of everyday life that God becomes known to us. For Latino Catholics, our faith is ultimately made credible by our everyday relationship with a God whom we can touch and embrace, a God with whom we can weep or laugh, a God who infuriates us and whom we infuriate, a God whose anguished countenance we can caress and whose pierced feet we can kiss. This, as Salvadoran Jesuit theologian Jon Sobrino avers, is no vague God but a very particular, incarnate God, the God of Jesus Christ:

> A vague, undifferentiated faith in God is not enough to generate hope. Not even the admission that God is mighty, or that God has made promises, will do this. Something else besides the generic or abstract attributes of the divinity is necessary in order to generate hope. This distinct element – which, furthermore, is the fundamental characteristic of the Christian God – is something the poor have discovered viscerally, and in reality itself: the nearness of God. God instills hope because God is credible, and God is credible because God is close to the poor ... Therefore when the poor hear and understand that God delivers up the Son, and that God is crucified – something that to the mind of the nonpoor will always be either a scandal or a pure anthropomorphism – then, paradoxically, their hope becomes real. The poor have no problems with God. The classic question of theodicy – the 'problem of God', the atheism of protest – so reasonably posed by the nonpoor, is no problem at all for the poor (who in good logic ought of course to be the ones to pose it). (Sobrino, 1988, pp. 166–67)

Because Jesus Christ walks with us, we know he is real. *Because* we have come to know him as our constant companion, we know that he is indeed who he says he is. 'Be the problems of the "truth" of Christ what they may', writes Sobrino, 'his credibility is assured as far as the poor are concerned, for he maintained his nearness to them to the end. In this sense the cross of Jesus is seen as the paramount symbol of Jesus' approach to the poor, and hence the guarantee of his indisputable credibility' (ibid., 1988, p. 171). This is indeed a God who stayed with us, who resides in our midst – not just 'spiritually' but concretely in every aspect of our world. That is how we know this God is real. It is not our Christian belief that makes God's nearness credible; rather, it is God's nearness that makes Christian belief credible.

The Christ of Latino Catholics encounters us through his wounded, bleeding, holy countenance, the *Divino Rostro* (Holy Countenance) seen on the walls of millions of Latino homes. He encounters us through his body, beaten and broken as it hangs lifeless from the cross. He encounters us, above all, as he accompanies us on the Way of the Cross, the innocent victim who continues to cry out to God even at the moment of deepest anguish.

In the eyes of many Hispanic Catholics, the greatest threat to true faith is not that of idolatry, the danger of mistaking a wooden statue for Jesus Christ himself, or superstition, the danger of utilizing everyday objects as a means of manipulating or controlling God. Rather, the greatest threat to true faith is the relegation of God to a distant corner of our cosmos; the greatest threat to faith is that, by insisting that God is immaterial, absolutely transcendent and inscrutable, we will indeed end up making God immaterial, that is, irrelevant to our everyday lives. The greatest threat to faith is precisely that represented by a rationalist or spiritualist Christianity that preaches a God without a world, a Christ without tears, without a body, without wounds, a cross without a corpus.

If the medieval Christian worldview posited an intrinsically symbolic cosmos, which makes present 'God for us', then that worldview posited an intrinsically *relational* cosmos insofar as the symbol makes the Other present *for us*. The same can be said about the worldview expressed in Latino popular Catholicism. If our lives have meaning, it is not because we ourselves have constructed that meaning and imposed it on creation, but because we have been empowered to cultivate a meaning that we first *received* from others, ultimately from God, but that we help shape through our creative response to that gift. Before reality can be 'constructed' it must first be received as gift, as it becomes present to us *in* creation. Indeed, the act of reception is the first truly free, constructive human *act*. (Thus I would concur with scholars such as Morgan and Catherine Bell, who reject as artificial any dichotomy between symbol and ritual, between 'seeing' a religious image or symbol and participating in a religious ritual or practice – Morgan, 1998; Bell, 1992). It is in the very act of receiving what is given us in the world that we, in turn, make the gift 'ours' thereby transforming what we have received and constructing 'our' world. Precisely as *symbolic* practice, human agency involves both a receiving and a doing; the real is revealed in our *interaction* with symbols (Morgan, 1998, pp. 50–58).

The revelation of the real occurs, then, in the very process of that interaction. Reality is what is revealed at the precise point where the blank screen interacts with the ray of light emitted by the film projector – an image appears. Neither the blank screen (the objective, 'given' empirical world) nor the projector (the subjective, human person 'projecting' him/herself into the world) is sufficient. Both are needed; more precisely, their interaction is needed to produce an image, the Real. In some sense, then, the communications media are the paradigmatic loci of revelation, the paradigmatic place where the Real is revealed precisely as self-communicating. If self-communication is the very essence of God – what *defines* the Sacred – then the human task of communication is itself a truly sacred task, a task in which the Sacred is made present, and through which the human person, the creature, participates in the very (trinitarian) life of God. It would not be an exaggeration to say, then, that persons engaged in the mass communications media enjoy a truly blessed privilege and, at the same time, shoulder an awesome responsibility.

The Possibility of an 'American' Catholicism

At its best, Latino popular Catholicism offers us a fundamentally sacramental, organic worldview which affirms an ultimate interconnectedness – ontological, if you will; Latino Catholicism reminds us that we indeed are not alone. At its best, modern Euro-American Catholicism, on the other hand, holds before us that promise which is at the heart of the gospel message but which has all too often been obscured, namely, the promise of human freedom and the creative possibilities inherent in the rational human person. After all, the modern rejection of meaning as something that is primarily 'given' but is instead 'constructed' has made possible the unleashing of incredible creative energy in every area of human endeavor, from the arts to science and technology. Yet each insight needs the other. The future of American Catholicism as both 'American' and 'Catholic' will depend on our ability and willingness, as Americans and as Catholics, to affirm the wisdom of the *whole* Catholic tradition.

American Catholics are heirs to both of these currents in the larger Catholic tradition. We can affirm the value of a world, a cosmos that reveals the God who remains with us. Against a materialism that enslaves human persons by denying the possibility of transcendence and exploits nature by denying its character as 'cosmos', as God's creation, American Catholics can affirm a genuinely Christian 'materialism', a genuinely Christian humanism.

In other words, the very possibility of realizing the promise of the Enlightenment as this was embodied in the founding documents of the United States may well depend on a retrieval of that history which, though rejected as 'pre-modern' and 'unenlightened', endures among those communities, like the Latino community and other Third World peoples, which constitute the 'underside' of modernity.

The danger of medieval sacramental, or symbolic realism was that, by locating the supernatural *within* the natural, it could lead to an *identification* of the natural with the supernatural. When symbolic truth – which is the most profoundly *real* truth – is mistaken for empirical truth, the result is idolatry. And such idolatry has had horrific, violent consequences in Europe and America when, for instance, the Church as symbol, or *sacrament* of the Kingdom of God on earth has been simply *identified with* the empirical Kingdom of God on earth. Symbolic truth is not merely empirical truth, not because the former is not 'real' but precisely because it *is* real in the deepest sense.

As a needed reaction to the idolatry that, in the Middle Ages, led to so much corruption and bloodshed, modern Christianity has attenuated if not completely severed the relationship between the symbol and what it signifies – so that, for example, we have become exceedingly uncomfortable with *any* mention of the Kingdom of God in relation to the Church, aware as we are of the patent *dis*continuity between the Reign of God and Christian history, a history that has not always been particularly Christian.

The opposite danger of idolatry, however, is a neo-gnosticism that completely severs the intrinsic connection between religious faith and its necessarily particular, concrete, historical, social embodiment. The two possible results of this fragmentation are: (1) an individualistic rationalism that identifies faith *exclusively* with individual assent to theological propositions; or (2) an individualistic, privatized and disembodied 'spirituality.' Each of these options has its 'conservative' and 'liberal' versions. Many current attacks on modern individualism have tended to place the blame for the fragmentation of the Catholic organic worldview on post-Enlightenment liberalism, with its glorification of reason and individual autonomy. However, if it is true that, as I have suggested above, modern Christian nominalism and neo-scholasticism are the handmaidens of modern atheistic secularism, then theologies that reduce Christian faith to propositional assent or that attempt to impose a preconceived uniformity on the Christian community through a standardized, centralized and bureaucratized authority are as prototypically modern as those that are criticized in so many harangues against modern liberal individualism and subjectivism. Both seek to impose meaning on symbolic reality from *outside*. Both, for instance, feel compelled to impose a 'supernatural', rational meaning on the 'faith of the people', who are assumed to be so alienated from God that they cannot be trusted to worship God without explicit directions or instructions.

As sociologist Robert Orsi notes in his analysis of the decline of Euro-American popular religion in the 1960s, liturgical reformers 'insisted that if popular devotions were to remain a feature of Catholic life, they would have to be surrounded by *words* ... the saints and the Virgin Mary were to be reimagined in the languages of friendship, morality, or mythology, deemphasizing what the reformers considered an inappropriate and extravagant emphasis on the miraculous and the material' (Orsi, 1996, pp. 33–34). That is, the saints and the Virgin Mary would have to be rationalized, *explained* to the people. The obsession with words also helps us understand the ongoing obsession with the reform of liturgical *texts* – a concern which, again, characterizes both liberals and conservatives. The implicit identification of orthodoxy with correct *texts* simply reinforces the marginalization of the people's faith, a faith lived out not primarily through texts but through embodied relationships and practices. The character or validity of religious worship cannot be reduced to the words or texts one uses. Though these are important, they are not sufficient. While symbols and rituals must indeed 'give rise to thought' and theological propositions (in the words of Paul Ricoeur), they cannot be simply reduced to such propositions without divesting the symbols and rituals of their power to make God present. As the primary expressions of religious faith, symbols and rituals demand theological explanation and critique, but theology can never forget its roots in the symbols and rituals that embody the *lived* faith.

In their need to rationalize the faith, what distinguishes conservative from liberal Catholics is often simply the identity of the person authorized to impute meaning on religious symbols and rituals from without: that person may be the ecclesiastical authority or, perhaps, the theological, liturgical, or pastoral expert (whether lay or clerical). What defines modernity is the *dichotomy* between faith and reason, between nature and supernature, between the material and the spiritual, between the individual and the collective. As Orlando Espín reminds us, post-Tridentine Catholic theology 'responded to the reformers' arguments by assuming as valid many of the latter's premises' (Espín, 1995, p. 26).

Beyond these dichotomies, then, what is called for is a truly integral understanding of religious faith, one rooted in the *life* of faith as itself the paradigmatic symbol of the divine in our midst. It is my contention that such an understanding is reflected in US Latino popular Catholicism. This latter represents an important spiritual and theological resource for American Catholicism and for American society as a whole. What is called for, then, is an American Catholicism that rejects neither its American nor its Catholic character but, instead, an American Catholicism that is *more* inclusively and thus *more* truly *both* 'American' and 'Catholic'.

More broadly, the popular religious practices and beliefs of the Third World peoples who are increasingly defining 'American' society represent a challenge to fundamental (post)modern western assumptions about the very nature of reality, and the correlative epistemological assumptions about how we come to know 'reality'. Such popular practices and beliefs just might offer an alternative to both a naïve realism that would perceive the true as, in the words of Canadian philosopher Bernard Lonergan, 'the already out there now real' and to a radical relativism that would reject a priori the very notion of reality. The former would distort the symbolic character of the cosmos by simply identifying the symbol with the real, while the latter would distort that character by positing an absolute separation between the symbol and the real. The alternative, moreover, would not demand a rejection of western Christian traditions in favor of an openness to 'the other', but would call for a retrieval of depreciated aspects of those traditions *in the light of* the contemporary encounter with 'the other', thereby making dialogue possible. As the very definition of 'America' becomes increasingly broadened, such dialogue will be demanded not only of US Catholics and Christians, but of US society as a whole.

Notes

1   For a fascinating analysis of medieval religious practices, particularly their bodily and empathic/sympathetic character, see Morgan (1998), pp. 59–73.
2   Among Nava's other films are *Selena* and *El Norte*.

References

Bell, C. (1992), *Ritual Thinking, Ritual Practice*, New York: Oxford University Press.
Bynum, C. W. (1999), 'Why All the Fuss About the Body? A Medievalist's Perspective', in V. E. Bunnell and L. A. Hunt (eds), *Beyond the Cultural Turn: New Directions in the Study of Society and Culture*, Berkeley, CA: University of California Press, pp. 251–52.
Christian, W. (1998), 'Spain in Latino Religiosity', in P. Casarella and R. Gómez (eds), *El Cuerpo de Cristo: The Hispanic Presence in the US Catholic Church*, New York: Crossroad Books, pp. 326–27.

Dupré, L. (1993), *Passage to Modernity: An Essay in the Hermeneutics of Nature and Culture*, New Haven, CT: Yale University Press.

Espín, O. (1997), *Faith of the People: Theological Reflections on Popular Catholicism*, Maryknoll, NY: Orbis Books.

Espín, O. (1995), 'Pentecostalism and Popular Catholicism: The Poor and Traditio', *Journal of Hispanic/Latino Theology*, **3** (2), 14–43.

Francis, M. (1995), 'Popular Piety and Liturgical Reform in a Hispanic Context', in A. M. Pineda and R. Schreiter (eds), *Dialogue Rejoined: Theology and Ministry in the United States Hispanic Reality*, Collegeville, MN: The Liturgical Press, pp. 165–66.

González, J. (1990), *Mañana: Christian Theology from a Hispanic Perspective*, Nashville, TN: Abingdon Press.

John Paul II (1999), *Ecclesia in America*.

Macy, G. (1995), 'Demythologizing "the Church" in the Middle Ages', *Journal of Hispanic/Latino Theology*, **3** (1), 23–41.

Morgan, D. (1998), *Visual Piety: A History and Theory of Popular Religious Images*, Berkeley, CA: University of California Press.

O'Meara, T. F. (1999), *Theology of Ministry*, New York: Paulist Press.

Orsi, R. A. (1996), *Thank You, St. Jude: Women's Devotion to the Patron Saint of Hopeless Causes*, New Haven, CT: Yale University Press.

Rahner, K. (1966), 'The Theology of the Symbol', in *Theological Investigations, Vol. 4*, New York: Crossroad Books.

Sobrino, J. (1988), *Spirituality of Liberation*, Maryknoll, NY: Orbis Books.

West, D. (1995), 'Filming the Chicano Family Saga: Interview with Director Gregory Nava', *Cineaste* **21** (4), Fall, 26–28.

Chapter 4

Notes on Belief and Social Circulation (Science Fiction Narratives)

Juan Carlos Henríquez SJ

The most incisive works linking theology and communication, or more precisely the phenomena of belief with those of their social circulation, concur in that their ideas about religiosity and about communication emerge from broad frameworks and incorporate research findings dealing with mediated society and its forms of symbolic exchange.[1]

By contrast, the least successful attempts at this type of connection usually reduce the phenomenon to concepts about distribution of materials (in this case beliefs, ideas or doctrines), as a result of understanding media of social communications as instruments or vehicles of transportation,[2] without taking into account the media environment (mediasphere) that in fact the media helped to create as of the second half of the twentieth century.

Leaving aside the instrumentalist consideration of communications media and the tendency that all institutions have to control the effect of their symbolic circulations, we should bear in mind that behind any symbol in circulation there is a 'symbolizable' experience that is meant to be recreated when a certain symbolic form that represents it is circulated. It could be said that the construction, consumption, reconstruction and recirculation of a symbolic form is a collective effort to resurrect a now extinct experience.[3]

If we accept the above statement, the phenomenon *theology and communication* or the phenomenon of *belief and its social circulation* surpasses the limited field of the production of messages, channeling them through appropriate media and the eventual reading of those messages. It opens itself up to recognizing and acknowledging 'fields' in which messages or symbolic forms move, are exchanged and, most importantly, in which their meanings are constructed.

Over the past several years, science fiction and fantastic films[4] have been among the texts that most provoke theological or transcendental readings. Many of the films of these genres[5] have even succeeded in introducing into public discourse theological and philosophical discussions that had been relegated to academic or church circles.

In the particular case of the analysis of science fiction narratives read from the perspective of belief, one can identify at least three underlying ideas or premises that are common to this type of interpretation:

1. A theory of *constructive intelligence*[6] which differentiates the moment of experiencing reality from the moment of naming it, and within the latter, the process of constructing the meaning of the lived experience, the elaboration of its symbolic form and its social circulation or communication.
2. A notion of *'field'*[7] or 'cosmos of meaning' as the interpretative framework within which meanings are structured and also as the social space in which meanings are constructed and circulate.
3. A *narrative*[8] *understanding of technology*, in which its manifestations and reaches articulate a metaphoric discourse about other realities, including the human body, Divinity, and so on. This discourse includes the dialectic of opacity and transparency, monstruosity and innocence, all shared by technology, language, body and God.

Constructive Intelligence

The notion that the meaning of the real is not discovered but constructed presupposes the adoption of a theory of intelligence in which, at least analytically, one distinguishes the moment of experiencing a reality from the moment of naming it and placing it in social circulation.

Thinkers such as Xavier Zubiri[9] agree that the naming of a thing is the cosmic moment of intelligence, because in that moment what has been experienced is taken into an order or cosmos dependent on the functional arrangement within a structure of meanings. Thus, sensed reality has meaning not on its own, but to the extent that it is functionally ordered according to a system of meanings. Nevertheless, the meaning conferred is neither arbitrary nor totally dependent on the individual subject. It is intersubjective: the result of a negotiation between subjects who share the same field of interpretation (hermeneutic field). The construction of the meaning of an experienced reality, even though individual, is embedded in the process of intersubjective construction and as a consequence the *name* or constructed symbolic form is incorporated into language.

To experience and to name are operations that harmonize what is experienced with its meaning, most often synchronically. However, there are realities that seem to break the synchronicity of these moments. Such is the case with transcendental realities for which the meaning that is constructed is generally expressed through intentionally open symbolic forms (metaphors). The metaphoric form, because of its openness, is capable of *theological* or *transcendental* readings. In other words, the open symbolic forms can be consumed as theological products quite apart from their initial purpose, since their theological nature lies not only in the production of the message but also in the dynamics generated by their circulation.

A clear example of the provocative potential of open symbolic forms (structures that are not closed) is *2001: A Space Odyssey* (1968).[10] The story was initially based on the short story by Arthur C. Clarke, 'The Sentinel' (1951), and had two versions: the script for the film written jointly by Stanley Kubrick and Clarke, and the novel written by Clarke. Kubrick's film has over time become a cinema classic[11] and a reference point for dealing with introspective philosophical and transcendental themes within the genre of fantastic cinema, but Clarke's novel and its sequels[12] have gone unnoticed. Comparing the movie with the novel, the first thing that one notices is that while Kubrick presents and maintains the mystery of the Monolith, Clarke makes its identity and intention clear from the first chapters.[13] The novel poses an epistemological question with one of the protagonists, the super computer HAL 9000: can there be intelligence without conscience or emotion?[14] The film, however, places all of its weight on the disquieting apparition of the Monolith, a protagonist without any lines of dialog, but whose dramatic action is fundamental from the very first sequence. By doing so, the film makes it possible to pose a question that is no longer epistemological but metaphysical, if not theological: what or who is this protagonist whose mere presence unleashes 'transfigurative leaps'? The first appearance of the Monolith transfigures the ape into a human being. In its second apparition, it transfigures the human being, circumscribed by the limits of earth, into an interplanetary human being. The third apparition transfigures a human creation (HAL 9000) into conscience and emotion, and lastly transfigures the interplanetary human being into a stellar human, atemporal, ubiquitous, old and in gestation, here and there simultaneously.

Let us keep in mind that the theological reading of this work by Kubrick is but one possibility for the viewer and not necessarily the intention of the author, who certainly never considered *2001* to be a story with theological or transcendental propositions. The reading that I propose is only one possibility, but one that is plausible and valid because the film is constructed in terms of symbolic forms that are not closed and thus equivocal.

Narratives that are deliberately constructed with structures and symbolic elements that are not closed assume indirectly the premise that the consumers of symbolic forms have a constructive intelligence and that they become the constructors of meaning, meaning-makers, of those open forms. In science fiction narratives the premise of a constructive intelligence generally appears on two levels. At the level of plot, the stories usually include the problem of an interpreted reality (meaning) versus 'real' reality (experience). The heroes' search consists in resolving the dilemma between experienced reality and its meaning. At the level of reception and circulation, the consumer is assumed to be the meaning-maker and as such exercises his freedom to take the narration and insert it into a field of reference, for example a theological or spiritual one. The premise of a constructive intelligence enables the story in the science fiction film not only to metaphorically evoke texts about revelation, but in a way the film itself becomes a text of revelation.

A Notion of Field

Meaning is constructed not only to be embedded later into an environment. In fact, it is constructed from the environment created by the media (mediasphere) and the language they establish. In a media environment such as the one we are living in, the field of understanding is identified with the medium.[15]

The relationship between constructors of meaning and the media does not begin when the former decide to put their constructions into circulation. Actually, media and constructors of meaning are generated from the same source, inasmuch as the construction of meaning enters a narrative which has been previously established by, but above all within, the media environment. That means that the symbolic forms are impregnated with the technological environment in which they circulate. If a construction of meaning is theological, then that symbolic form is at the same time a theological and a technological narrative. Theology and technology are not two different discourses, but two possible approaches to the same narrative phenomenon: from the theological perspective one glimpses a technological discourse, and from the technological perspective one glimpses a theological discourse.

A symbolic form (constructed meaning) is not merely inserted in a field; the very construction takes place in the field where it will circulate. The *field* is the social space in which a symbolic form is interpreted, constructed and consumed. The field where meanings, including those of belief, are constructed and circulate is always intersubjective and is constructed using as a starting point a reference or language that has already been structured among individuals. Therefore, language is not a regulated code (grammar) but a field of understanding.

One basic characteristic of the field is its *regeneration*. The construction of a particular meaning, expressed in a symbolic form, is not only generated and inserted in its field of origin, but also '*regenerates*' the field. That is, it creates autonomous fields or universes of meaning. In other words, it is neither the product (content) nor the reception, but the circulation that regenerates the field. Something analogous to this happens ecclesiologically: it is not the discourses of belief (orthodoxy) nor the adherence to rituals of worship (ortholatry), but the dynamic circulation of these elements (orthopraxis) by believers that sacramentally recreates the community.[16]

But when all is said and done the creation of an autonomous field of meaning is a constant practice in the socialization of discourses, from children's games to narratives of ultimate meaning. What perturbs the *imaginaire sociale* is that the creation of an 'autonomous field of meaning' will materialize and create not only a field but also a 'real autonomous world'. One of the recurring themes in science fiction narratives is the assumption that at a certain moment we may be able to materialize the fields of meaning and create real worlds, parallel to and autonomous from the world from which the meanings are constructed. The fascination and terror that inspire some science fiction stories lie in the possibility that the worlds we have created might become autonomous and we become trapped in them (total immersion is one of the cores of stories such as *The Matrix*, *eXistenZ* or *Solaris*[17]). Total immersion in an autonomous world different from the one we inhabit is fascinating as a technological accomplishment, but on the other hand its possible monstruosity terrifies.

Imagining autonomous, created worlds and a total immersion in them is often a secular and pragmatic way of responding to the anthropological desire for eternal life. William Gibson, a novelist considered to be the predecessor of cyberpunk and postmodern science fiction, imagines the creation of autonomous technological worlds and the possibility of accessing them without the need of interfaces. The obsession of his characters[18] is to overcome the inconveniences of the biological body (obsolete hardware), by moving memory, emotion and other cerebral operations (software) to interconnected cyberspace. Eternal life achieved in this way certainly overcomes the limitations of time and space imposed by the biological body: there is no more sickness or death, the characters become omnipresent and immortal. Gibson's heaven is the updated technological version of other eternity narratives, all of them stemming from the Greek notion of immortality in which only the spatial–temporal aspects are liberated while the rest of the immanent condition is maintained.[19] Narratives of Olympic, vampiric or cyber-spatial heavens are symbolic circulations that take place coincidentally in predominantly secular fields of understanding. As Gustave Flaubert writes: 'When the gods no longer existed ... there was a unique moment ... in which there was only man.'[20]

A Narrative Consideration of Technology

The word 'technology' is undoubtedly a concept developed in conjunction with the Industrial Revolution in the eighteenth century. As Jean-Claude Beaune (1980) explains so well, the various definitions of the term 'technology' always imply the notion that there are different types of knowledge and procedures regarding the use of raw materials to create final products that will satisfy human needs.

Regardless of which definition is used, technology carries with it multiple discourses, among which is the discourse of implicit belief.[21] There are several works that explore the theological discourses surrounding the different definitions of the word 'technology'. However, it may be helpful, if only for a moment, to explore the concept by de-emphasizing a strict definition and looking at its etymological meaning roots.

The word 'technology' derives from two Greek terms, τέχνη (*techné*) and λόγός (*logos*). In ancient times, as well as in the Middle Ages, *techné* was translated as *ars*, art. Even though in the Middle Ages the so-called *ars mechanica* came to the fore as what was later known as 'technique',[22] the original meaning of *techné* was to make real an idea or purpose.[23] *Techné* implies materialization, the entering of an idea into the sense-perceived world of phenomena. So, for the moment one can consider technology to be the discourse that deals with the phenomenon of materialized ideas and purposes.

In the same way that the phenomena of belief are narratives that circulate in a field of understanding, the technology used for the materialization of those narratives not only plays a role in their material condition (there is no narration without technology) but is itself also a narrative (or sub-narrative).

The link between what is religious and what is technological is not merely instrumental. Technology conditions the circulation of religious matters (construction, consumption and reconstruction) but is also a discursive analogy of that which is religious. As already mentioned, science fiction films such as those by Ridley Scott, David Cronenberg and more recently Larry and Andy Wachowski or literary works by J. R. R. Tolkien, Arthur C. Clarke or Stanislaw Lem (subsequently made into films) are able to trigger thoughtful theological reactions and place into circulation topics that had been ignored or had been limited to fields of specialization.[24]

The theology–technology link and the reflective discourses it raises – even though they are most evident in products such as science fiction narratives – have as their source the first technology (taken as the first materialization of a symbolic form): the word, and they extend through the different steps of orality to writing and then to mass printing, and so on.

The consideration of technology as the performance of a materialized purpose directly impacts the field of theology. The question of materialization, of incarnation, of 'becoming flesh' as a condition for action in the world is the newness of the revealed Christian faith. The intention of the God of Christians, which in Johannine theology is expressed as making 'the Grace and Truth come'[25] in all fullness, can be achieved through the materialization of His purpose.[26] Can we consider the word, including the divine word, as technological? At the very least, the origin of the Greek term *techné* would allow us to make this allegory, and from there consider the metaphor of Jesus as God's *Techné*.

The word as first technology is a controversial notion. Even those who agree with this idea acknowledge a certain strangeness about referring to language as a technological manifestation. This is not surprising. We are so used to our mother tongue that it seems to have always been part of us and yet language is one of our most costly acquisitions in terms of time and effort. Language is one of the least friendly technologies for new users, although it certainly succeeds in becoming fully incorporated by advanced speakers.[27] When that happens, oral technology is not opaque and conscious anymore and becomes so transparent that it is difficult for us to be aware of its presence. This dialectic of opacity and transparency, of perceived and unperceived, of conscious and unconscious is shared by other realities, such as the body or the divinity.[28]

The dynamic of opacity and transparency[29] is common to all technologies, including the ones related to the word. The same dynamic is lived with regard to the body. Perhaps we should say that the dialectic of opacity and transparency occurs in technology as an extension of the body. More often than we think, after technology and the body have achieved levels of transparency, they suddenly go through stages of opacity.

A sign of transparency is unawareness and therefore absence. A sign of opacity is awareness and the discomfort of its presence. Opacity 'shows' what transparency hides. Our closest transparency is in our own body. When healthy, our body is absent, indifferent, hidden from our consciousness. It signals its presence through an alarm, the language of illness. In illness, but also in pleasure, our body's opacity comes to the fore and with it one of its most characteristic signs, the loss of control. Pain as well as pleasure reveal to us the alien side of that which we assumed to be so personal.

Opacity plays the part of revelation in a body. This faculty has an immediate consequence for theological discourse, specifically in ecclesiology. For Christian theology the incarnation event is diffusive and embodying: the church is the body of Christ and as body participates in the dynamic of transparency and opacity. The joy and passion of that body are privileged moments of opacity, sometimes violently so, in which its ultimate identity is forcefully revealed, *casta et meretix*, saint and sinner, intimate in itself and alien to itself.

The same ambiguity of our body (and of the ecclesial body) can be applied to the media (body extensions[30]) we interact with. The media – radio, television, cinema, press – have gone through this see-saw motion and continue to do so when their established languages dare to break commonly agreed-upon rules. Nowadays we can watch tamed cinema and also dark and disturbing cinema.

The media flow dialectically between these two categories. Basically discomfort is associated with becoming stagnant in either of them. Complete opacity is so cryptic as to be meaningless, and total transparency is so innocuous that it becomes trivial. This dialectic is also part of the common premise in science fiction narrative open to theological reading. *Monstruosity* (that shows what was previously hidden) is the main topic in films like those by David Cronenberg,[31] and is also present in the rest of the science fiction narrative productions and in fantastic cinema that has triggered theological readings.

Consideration of the narrative aspect of technology, acknowledgement of a generative field where there is circulation of symbolic forms and the affirmation of a constructive intelligence are three pivotal points related to the analysis of products of mass consumption that are interpreted as *discourses of belief.*

Symbolic forms that are not closed and the insinuations that are provoked by the dynamic of revealing and hiding are in fact an ideal type of language for articulating discourses of belief in postmodernity. Theology in postmodernity, at least that which is done in the public space, is closer to the negative theology of de Cusa[32] than to the positive and speculative theologies[33] developed especially around the eighth century and taken up again in the Renaissance and modernity. Reality, ultimate reality above all, is 'apophatic'[34] for the postmodern because it cannot be named or circumscribed in stable and defined narratives.[35] For the meaning-maker, only figures like the metaphor and the metonym allow a reading that is reflective and transcendental.

The reading of products that can disturb and provoke this kind of transcendental reflection presupposes a previous affirmation by the reader of an absolute, redeeming center that answers the question of ultimate meaning. This previous affirmation could be called transcendental premise, independent of its origin (divinity, nature, idea, etc.); the source of salvation is absolute and extrinsic to the subject. This premise does not necessarily have to be shared by the original constructor of the symbolic form. It is enough that the reader/reconstructor (consumer) of the form accepts it for the discourse of belief to be generated. In that sense the author's conscious or unconscious purpose is irrelevant in validating a theological reading of a product placed into social circulation.

Notes

1   I am thinking principally of the various works by Manuel Castells about the informational society and in the structural model that John B. Thompson sets forth in *Ideology and Modern Culture* (1994).

2   I recommend a review of the analytical and critical work done annually by the Latin American group, Creators of Christian Images, that critiques and offers alternatives to the instrumentalist vision of communication in audiovisual products that have religious ends. See Tavares de Barros *Imagens da América Latina* (1997) and *La Realidad Imaginada* (1994).

3   The idea of re-presentation as an effort to make present anew an absent reality is related by analogy to two Christian notions, incarnation and resurrection, which suppose the body as the possibility of real presence and action in the world. From this anthropological perspective, *image, symbol and logos* are re-presentative realities and, therefore, re-actors, that is to say: capable of taking action in the dynamic of the world.

4   The nomenclature for these films is somewhat variable. I describe science fiction film (*el cine de ciencia ficción*) and fantastic film (*el cine fantastico*) as two separate genres. These are sometimes subsumed under the general category of 'fantasy film', a designation used by the Internet Movie Database. However, the Society of Fantastic Films which convenes the annual International Festival of Fantastic Films in the UK, uses the term 'fantastic films' to describe thee films discussed here.

5   I mention only three films which not only gave rise to this type of discussion among audiences, but produced a considerable number of published articles and essays to sustain a theological reading: *2001: A Space Odyssey* (Stanley Kubrick, 1968), *Star Wars* (George Lucas, 1977) and *Blade Runner* (Ridley Scott, 1982). It is worth noting that at the end of the 1970s a work by anthropologist Joseph Campbell (1949), *The Hero With a Thousand Faces*, became popular after Lucas declared its influence on the writing of *Star Wars*. We have here the acquisition on the part of the public of a first theoretical framework for the development of an analysis and reading of such films that is mythic and religious.

6   Constructivism is a postmodern current represented by Bateson, Gergen, Watzlawick, Maturana and White, among others. It considers intelligence as an entity that reconstructs

experience and knowing, orders them and gives them form. This proposition has Kantian roots, but also has antecedents in the perspectivism of Ortega y Gasset.

7 It is important not to confuse this notion with that of the semantic field, which refers to the relation of significations (grouping of words related by their signification). The field to which I refer does not order minimal features of what is signified (sema), but rather 'feelings' and 'meanings' according to a narrative logic. In any case, the field of the senses precedes, gives grounds to and hosts the field of the significations (semantic field).

8 For Bruner, there are two ways of understanding reality: the Paradigmatic Form whose objective is consensual truth by the scientific community and the Narrative Form which seeks the credibility of that which is known insofar as it becomes coherent (makes sense) with the discourse of a story. See Bruner (1986).

9 Xavier Zubiri (1898–1983). For a better understanding of this subject see the first part of *Inteligencia Sentiente, Inteligencia y Realidad* (*Sentient Intelligence, Intelligence and Reality*) (1993).

10 'A mysterious monolith is found buried beneath the surface of the moon. It sends a signal towards Jupiter. To solve the mystery, astronauts are sent to Jupiter with the help of the super-computer HAL 9000. After series of accidents and HAL's operations, one of the astronauts, David Bowman, is left alone as the ship reaches the planet. After a journey through inner space, a series of spiritual and physical changes, he becomes an embryo, a star child. He embarks on the final step in humankind's next developmental stage.' Synopsis written by Petri Liukkonen. See http://www.biblion.com/litweb/biogs/clarke_arthur_c.html.

11 Even though its release was a failure: *The New York Times* labeled it 'incredibly boring' and Arthur Schlesinger Jr described it in these words: 'morally pretentious, intellectually obscure and inordinately long...'

12 *2010: Odyssey Two* (1982), *2061: Odyssey Three* (1988), and *3001: The Final Odyssey* (1996).

13 Clarke's idea about the Monolith was that it was an alien device that he calls 'The Sentinel', which had visited Earth in the past and now was on its way to some place close to Jupiter. 'They would be interested in our civilization only if we proved our fitness to survive – by crossing space and so escaping the Earth, our cradle. That is the challenge that all intelligent races must meet, sooner or later.' See Clarke (1999).

14 When the austronaut, Dave Bowman, deactivates HAL 9000, it says to him: 'Dave, I'm afraid. My brain is growing empty...'

15 It is in the field of understanding that the *dance of signifiers* is performed, an idea that would be shared by structuralists and post-structuralists such as Derrida and Foucault.

16 James 2:26: 'For as the body without the spirit is dead, so faith without works is dead also.'

17 *The Matrix* (Andy and Larry Wachovsky, 1999) *eXistenZ* (David Cronemberg, 1999), *Solaris* (Stanislav Lem, adapted for the screen in 1972 by Andrei Tarkovsky and later by Steven Soderbergh in 2002).

18 Especially in novels such as *Mona Lisa Overdrive* (1988) but also present in *Neuromancer* (1984) and in *Count Zero* (1986).

19 Other notions, such as Jewish and Christian, conceive of eternal life not only as the liberation of the spatial–temporal aspects but principally as the total entering into another dimension of transcendental fullness and the radical communion with their God.

20 Cited by Margerite Yourcenar in Cahiers de Notes of *Mémoires D'Adrien* (1951).

21   'In each stage of its history, technology has been the consequence of several interdependent factors: raw material available, present accumulation of technical ability ... economic and social conditions, philosophical doctrines, moral and religious principles' Forbes (1965). Quoted by Beaune (1980).

22   See Ferrater Mora (1980).

23   See Brugger (1958).

24   I emphasize the following titles by these authors: *Blade Runner* (1982), *eXistenZ* (1999), *The Matrix* (1999), *The Lord of the Rings* (1966), *The Sentinel* (1951), *Solaris* (1961). All of these works have enjoyed mass distribution and at the same time have generated the type of public discourses and reflections to which I am referring.

25   Jn 1:14b: 'and we beheld his glory, the glory as of the only begotten of the Father, full of grace and truth'; Jn 1:17: 'For the law was given by Moses, but grace and truth came by Jesus Christ.' Some versions translate this as 'love and truth'. It is worth noting that the words *Gratuity* and *Charity* derive from χάρις, *grace*.

26   Jn 1:14a: 'and the word was made flesh and dwelt among us'.

27   Lacan actually denies to language the possibility of being completely adequate to that which it signifies. We reach it through metaphors and metonyms.

28   Paul approaches the theme of darkness and light not as a problem that requires a solution but as a mysterious reality. 'For if the gospel we preach is hidden ...', 2 Cor. 4:3a; 'For it is the God who said, "Let light shine out of darkness", who has shone in our hearts,' 2 Cor 4:6a; 'But we carry this treasure in vessels of clay', 2 Cor. 4:7.

29   Thinkers such as Richard Rorty would be in complete disagreement. Rorty criticizes those who affirm the dialectic of opacity and transparency because they imply the acceptance of essences, while for him the only possibility of accessing reality is through description and re-description. With the motto, 'may conversion continue', Rorty impels hope but not understanding.

30   Expression of Marshall McLuhan. Jean Baudrillard accentuates the phrase, referring to media as 'expulsions from the body' and Paul Virilio goes further and speaks of 'expulsion from the city'.

31   Especially in the films: *The Fly* (1986), *Naked Lunch* (1991), *Crash* (1996) and *eXistenZ* (1999).

32   Nicolás de Cusa (1401–64), See Chap. 26 of Book 1 of *Learned Ignorance*.

33   While for Negative Theology sacred ignorance teaches us that God is ineffable, and that human beings are sensate, it does not seek to affirm what is divine but rather simply name what it is not, for Positive Theology reason and understanding must search for the contents of revelation and faith. Speculative or Scholastic Theology, for its part, proceeds according to the speculative method for the purpose of explaining the faith with clarity. That is to say that the least well-known revealed truths are explained and demonstrated with the help of those that are better known 'and from the articles of faith, this doctrine sustains others' (see S.Th. iq. 1 a 8 – Summae Theologiae Angelici Doctoris Sancti Thomae Quinatis. Prima Pars Quaestio I Articulus 8).

34   ἀπόφασις: 'negation' or 'denial'. 'Apophatic is a term used to refer to a particular style of theology, which stressed that God cannot be known in terms of human categories. Apophatic approaches to theology are especially associated with the monastic tradition of the Eastern Orthodox church.' See. Glossary of Theological Terms, in: Theology and Religion Resources: http://www.blackwellpublishing.com/Religion/Glossary.asp.

35   This idea is shared by Ludwig Wittgenstein, Jacques Derrida and Gianni Vattimo.

References

Beane, J.-C. (1980), *La Technologie Introuvable – Recherche sur la définition et l'unité de la Technologie à partir de quelques modèles du XVII et XIX siècles*, Paris: Librairie Philosophique J. Vrin.

Brugger SJ, W. (1958), *Diccionario de Filosofía*, Bacelona: Editorial Herder.

Bruner, J. (1986), *Actual Minds, Possible Worlds*, Cambridge, MA: Harvard University Press.

Campbell, J. (1949), *The Hero With a Thousand Faces*, New York: Pantheon.

Clarke, A. C. (1999), *Greetings, Carbon-Based Bipeds!* New York: St Martin's Press.

Ferrater Mora, J. (1980), *Diccionario de Filosofía*, Madrid: Alianza Editorial.

Forbes, R. J. (1965), *Studies in Ancient Technology*, Vol. 2, 2nd edn, Leiden: E. J. Brill.

Nicolás de Cusa (1985), *Nicholas of Cusa on Learned Ignorance*, trans. J. Hopkins, 2nd edn, Minneapolis, MN: Banning Press.

Tavares de Barros, J. (1997), *Imagens da América Latina*, São Paulo: Ocic-Brasil Edições Loyola.

Tavares de Barros, J. (1994), *La Realidad Imaginada*, Santafé de Bogotá: Paulinas.

Thompson, J. B. (1994), *Ideology and Modern Culture*, Stanford, CA: Stanford University Press.

Zubiri, X. (1993), *Inteligencia Sentiente, Inteligencia y Realidad*, Madrid: Alianza Editorial.

PART II
MEDIATED CHRISTIANITY

Introduction

This section provides a number of case studies that examine some of the characteristics and complexities of the interaction between media and Christianity within a cultural perspective. In the process they illustrate how research in the area proceeds. The cases reflect a number of characteristics that also illustrate some of the methodological issues in the field.

One is their qualitative nature. In contrast to earlier US studies in media and Christianity which were strongly quantitative, objective and instrumentalist in their approach, these studies are strongly qualitative and interpretative, considering media and religion not as separate entities but as complex cultural phenomena that are intertwined and in many ways inseparable from each other and from other cultural factors such as politics, economics and entertainment.

Kwabena Asamoah-Gyadu's chapter on media and Pentecostal religion in Ghana exemplifies this, locating new religious movements in Ghana as inseparable from the economic and political conditions in which they have arisen, not only using media in their work but also positioning and distinguishing themselves as particular forms of media–religious cultures. Jolyon Mitchell and Germán Rey in this section illustrate another important dimension of research in this area, that is that the study of media and religion in society can no longer be pursued solely in relation to religious institutions and their use of media. Mitchell's chapter explores the growth of commercial religious videos in West Africa and the place they have created for themselves in the wider global market, offering their own distinctive religious narratives to intersect with popular needs and enjoyment. Rey's chapter does similarly with Latin American *telenovelas*, exploring how these soap operas contribute to the development of cultural identity through a meeting of religious icons and popular narrative in the commercial marketplace.

A significant advance in the study of media and religion from a cultural perspective has been a growing awareness of the importance of visual and material culture in religious sensibility and practice. David Morgan, who has done extensive work in religious visual culture (Morgan, 1998, 1999; Morgan and Promey, 2001) explores this dimension with a study of visual media in Ethiopia. Morgan's chapter includes a brief introduction to the study of visual media within Christianity.

One of the most difficult methodological issues in the cultural perspective on Christianity and the media is in managing the complexity of factors that this approach involves. Understanding is complicated by two strong emphases of cultural studies research. One is that meaning is to be understood not just in terms of the intention constructed by the author in producing the text, but also by the meanings taken from, attributed to or constructed into the text by the user of the text at that particular time. A second is the emphasis given by cultural studies to differences between phenomena as well as commonalities as bearers of significance. It is potentially problematic in media and religion research, therefore, to assume that 'religion' means something as a category of analysis or interpretation that the individual being studied would apply themselves to their behavior or perception. These questions mean that actual case studies and ethnographical research are often the best for exploring and handling this complexity. This type of research is illustrated in the chapter by Hoover and Park on the use of the Internet as a source of symbolic resources in the exploration and construction of religious meaning.

References

Morgan, D. (1999), *Protestants and Pictures: Religion, Visual Culture and the Age of American Mass Production*, New York: Oxford University Press.

Morgan, D. (1998), *Visual Piety: A History and Theory of Popular Religious Images*, Berkeley, CA: University of California Press.

Morgan, D. and S. Promey (eds) (2001), *The Visual Culture of American Religions*, Berkeley, CA: University of California Press.

Chapter 5

Pentecostal Media Images and Religious Globalization in Sub-Saharan Africa

J. Kwabena Asamoah-Gyadu

The meetings of the International Study Commission on Media, Religion, and Culture, and the seminal publications emanating from them have helped to generate wide scholarly interest in the ability of the interaction between media and religion to act as a tool for understanding religio-cultural values in several contexts, including sub-Saharan Africa.[1] Modern African new religious movements, including many of non-Christian persuasion, make wide and extensive uses of modern mass media technologies in the dissemination of their messages.

However, academic interest in this area is still in its formative stages. A number of the African new religious movements in question are involved with media production and, when that happens, the content of the programmes tends to 'reflect the media theology of the institution' (Lehikoinen, 2003, p. 34). This could hardly be otherwise because new religions usually see themselves as being in competition with older and more firmly established traditions and therefore make extensive use of the media in order to secure their share of the religious market. In this chapter, we look at the images that Africa's new Pentecostal/charismatic movements and their leaders in particular carve for themselves through their media programmes.[2]

The new Pentecostal/charismatic movements under study here started proliferating in sub-Saharan Africa at the end of the 1970s. These new churches differ from established classical Pentecostal denominations like the Assemblies of God in two significant respects. First, the new Pentecostal/charismatic movements are historically younger. Second, the new movements have remained autochthonous founder-led congregations, and the personal charisma and psychology of the leader is what shapes their orientation. African Pentecostal/charismatic churches boast of large urban-centred 'mega-church' congregations. They tacitly approve a relaxed, modern and fashion-conscious dress code for members. The pastors of these churches are often quite young, well educated (though not necessarily in theology), articulate in English, entrepreneurial and well travelled. Membership here is skewed in favour of youth, which is partly the reason they enjoy such a high profile. The churches are very international, modern, prosperous and flamboyant in outlook. This exotic image is also inspired by the messages of success and prosperity that Africa's new Pentecostal/charismatic churches advocate.

The prosperity gospel teaches that God wills all Christians to prosper in 'health and wealth', especially if they pay their tithes and offerings religiously. This is a message that is inspired by the North American leanings of this nascent movement. On account of their personal charisma, Africa's new Pentecostal/charismatic leaders covet and enjoy great visibility, a phenomenon made possible not only by their message, but also by their presence in the media. On the bestowal of prestige by the media, Hiebert has noted:

> The mass media bestow prestige and enhance authority of individuals and groups by legitimizing their status. Recognition by the press or radio or magazines or news reels testifies that one has arrived, that one is important enough to have been singled out from the large anonymous masses, that one's behaviour and opinions are significant enough to require public notice. (Hiebert et al., 1985, p. 246)

In addition to being constantly featured as news items in the print and electronic media, Pentecostal/charismatic leaders and their churches also covet media attention. For instance, in May 2003, the founder and leader of the Lighthouse Chapel International, Bishop Dr Dag Heward-Mills, a man in his mid-forties, celebrated his birthday. A select number of his church members placed full-page advertisements in at least three top Ghanaian newspapers. The advertisements featured the portrait of Bishop Heward-Mills bearing the signatures of all his colleagues including those serving as Lighthouse pastors in the US and Western Europe. The total cost of the three full-page advertisements amounted to not less than US$5000. Quebedeaux has shown that 'religious figures who utilize the media engender a personal connection with their audience' (Quebedeaux, 1982, pp. 110–11). Today, the birthdays of leading African charismatic pastors are virtually turned into national events as they are announced on radio and TV. Church members and admirers then call in to the stations and pour adulating birthday wishes on 'the anointed men and women of God'. In this discussion, I suggest that the desire to appear in the media attempts to bridge the gap between theology or message and experience. In other words, the images presented in the media are carefully constructed to reflect the message that is preached.

The prominence that Pentecostal/charismatic leaders enjoy also extends to the organizations they lead. Africa's new churches boast of a very forceful presence on the continent. Unlike their mainline church counterparts, the Pentecostal/charismatics invest money in airtime, a phenomenon that popularizes the movements and greatly enhances the charisma of the people behind such religious innovations. The influence of Pentecostal/charismatic Christianity in Africa goes far beyond its impressive numerical strength. This new type of Christianity, as a result of its media presence, continues to have a much more diffused impact on African Christianity in particular and popular culture in general. The presence of the new Pentecostal/charismatic movements has literally transformed the religious culture of Christianity in Africa, leading to what may be referred to as a 'pentecostalization' or 'charismaticization' of African Christianity. Marleen de

Witte captures succinctly the relationship between mass-mediated religion and the transformation of culture, noting that: 'through the mass mediation of religion, a new religious format emerges, which although originating from the Pentecostal–charismatic churches, spreads far beyond and is widely appropriated as a style of worship and of being religious' (de Witte, 2003, p. 1). Against the backdrop of these occurrences within Africa's new forms of Pentecostal/charismatic piety, one is kept imagining the sort of impression an observer would be likely to form of these new religious functionaries and their movements, assuming that the mass media were the observer's primary sources of information.

The chapter therefore attempts to image Africa's new Pentecostal/charismatic churches as portrayed through various mass media programmes and the implications that such images hold for the nature of African church life. The West African country of Ghana constitutes the immediate context for the study. The 'Charismatic Ministries', as the new churches under study are popularly called in Ghana, have deep roots in the conservative evangelical movement. The evangelical movements with their 'biblicist' attitude to life and emphasis on personal holiness were strongest in secondary and tertiary institutions in sub-Saharan Africa in the 1950s through the 1970s. At the end of the 1970s, the new crop of believers who had come through the evangelical movements and whose spiritualities no longer fitted into the historic mission denominations, started founding independent fellowships in order to give expression to their enthusiastic faiths.

One of the first people to lead such fellowships was Nicholas Duncan-Williams, the son of a politician–diplomat whose dramatic conversion experience inspired him to do something new for God. He eventually transformed the fellowship into a church. Duncan-Williams is a protégé of the late Nigerian charismatic pastor Archbishop Benson Idahosa. The 'Voice of Inspiration' hosted by Duncan-Williams on Ghana Television on Sunday mornings is one of the most popular religious programmes one can find in that category in Ghana.[3] These new independent Pentecostals share phenomenological similarities with the American 'electronic church'. These 'new paradigm churches', as Donald Miller designates them, have changed the face of Christianity by discarding traditional attributes associated with established Christianity. The new Pentecostal/charismatic churches appropriate contemporary cultural forms, and are 'doing a better job of responding to the needs of their clientele than are many mainline churches' (Miller, 1997, p. 3).

African Pentecostal/Charismatic Movements and the Media

One of the major strengths of the Pentecostal/charismatic churches is that they are 'successfully mediating the sacred, bringing God to people and conveying the self-transcendence and life-changing core of all true religion' (Miller, 997, p. 3). In this, the mass media have been found to be a most potent tool and they are being used with dramatic effects.

With its extensive use of the media, there is now no aspect of African life that has not been encroached upon by the new 'pentecostalist' culture.

The mass media's ability to give stature, enhance charisma and widen horizons has helped produce religious superstars within modern Ghanaian Christianity whose following extends beyond the registered membership of their congregations. One of such superstars is Pastor Mensa Otabil, 'founder and leader' of the International Central Gospel Church (ICGC).[4] ICGC draws a crowd that is upwards of 6,000 worshippers during the church's two Sunday services. Pastor Otabil's own TV television and radio programmes (dubbed 'Living Word') and the frequent invitations to speak at public functions often covered by the media mean that he is very well known and his influence travels well beyond the Sunday captive audience. His books, video and audiotapes are available for circulation among local and international patrons. During Otabil's TV programmes, viewers are constantly reminded on the screen that copies of tapes could be obtained through the following address: tapes@centralgospel.com.

In keeping with the theology of positives, possibilities, success and prosperity, deliberate correlation is established between the message/theology and the images of the leader conveyed through the mass media. The appearances of the preacher and his church members as shown on TV must be carefully edited to reflect not only the message being preached, but also the demands of television (Horsfield, 1984). In other words, the images 'advertise' the message. This explains why even the poorest churches will spend enormous amounts of money not only to sponsor their media programmes, but also to record major events on video. Such videos circulate among local audiences and Ghanaian migrants abroad, helping to establish a sense of 'globalized' importance as well as specific identities. A number of charismatic pastors may not travel personally, but their video, audio and TV programmes are accessible beyond local contexts, ensuring 'a multi-source diffusion of parallel developments encompassing Europe, Africa, America, and Asia' (Hexham and Poewe, 1994, p. 61).

A filming of the introductions and conclusions to Otabil's weekly TV programme 'Living Word' shows careful editing of the message.[5] The shots feature Pastor Otabil welcoming viewers at the beginning and then at the end, and vicariously mediating God's power to them through prayer so that what listeners have heard would take effect in their lives. 'Living Word', like a number of other programmes hosted by various charismatic churches, is advertised several times before being telecast. The advert shows Otabil with microphone in hand and the appropriate gesticulations completing a sentence that ends with: 'vision, perception, action'. The focus on vision and ambition in charismatic messages meets the aspirations of young people who need to take advantage of what opportunities in education, commerce and industry offer for personal and national development. The image of a successful mega-church pastor as mediated on TV becomes concrete evidence that, true to the Christian gospel, those with the right vision could succeed.

Africa's Pentecostal/charismatic churches have stirred other new religious movements on the continent to emulate their media use.[6] However, the Pentecostal/ charismatic churches dominate the media scene. The implication of imaging success is simply to testify what God can do for those who put their faith in him, which is what Pentecostal/charismatic theology is about: that God is a God of interventions. This is what makes Pentecostal/charismatic Christianity tick in Africa: its theology remains experiential rather than cerebral. Private businesses have thus taken advantage of the popularity of the new churches to sponsor and through that advertise their services during charismatic media programmes. 'Living Word', for example, is sponsored by Kingdom Transport Services (KTS), whose proprietor explains his success in terms of the impact of the gospel preached by Otabil. So the sponsorship by KTS is not without theological implications. In charismatic theology, those who invest financially in the ministry of the church, particularly in the personal ministries of the 'men/women of God', as the pastors are called, are promised huge returns in expanding business opportunities and wealth. In an African context of economic and social deprivation, such motivational theology tends to resonate with popular aspirations. The signs of positive change in a person's circumstances *through* association with charismatic leaders with the right anointing are the images that TV programmes are designed to convey. For in the prosperity worldview, what is for the Lord must be appealing, grandiose, enviable, modern and successful.

'Advertising God'

Pentecostal/charismatic programmes in Ghana are advertised on glossy handbills, posters and overhead banners hung across major streets in the urban areas. The worldview of 'health and wealth' is evident in the choice of rhetoric and themes for such programmes and messages. Banner advertisements available around Accra, the capital of Ghana, include: 'Turning Failure into Success'; 'Enlargements on all Fronts'; 'Moving on to Higher Heights'; 'Possessing your Inheritance'; 'From Glory to Glory'; 'Breaking the Curses of Life'; 'The God of Heaven will make us Prosper'; and so on. Signs of prosperity are expected to follow Christians provided they follow the principles of success, a key component of which is the consistent payment of tithes and offerings. Pentecostal/charismatic pastors are the best real-life examples of these theological values of prosperity and are so imaged through the media as symbolic realities of the messages they advertise and preach. Jesus is supposed to be the ultimate example of prosperity theology, because, as one charismatic pastor argued during a TV interview: 'Jesus wore designer clothes'. 'Jesus' robe was seamless and the donkey on which he rode to Jerusalem was supposed to be the Mercedes Benz of his day.' Therefore to 'advertise God', these are the images that must be articulated in order that he may be presented and properly conceived as the 'creator and source' of all good things.

The theology of 'interventions' is very important for charismatic Christianity and, as with experiential religions generally, divine interventions engender testimonies of new life and new lifestyle. Ultimately, that new lifestyle leads to development that draws African nations closer to the developed ones as important players in world affairs. Testimonies that follow new life experiences are meant for public consumption so the availability of mass media technology affords charismatic Christianity enormous opportunities to present its preferred identities to the public. One of such identities is the desire to appear international.

Internationalism

That the new Pentecostal/charismatic movements are a global phenomenon is evident in the extensive global networks to which a number of them belong. Thus international travel both for the leader and members is highly coveted and cherished. In recent times, requests for visas have come to rank next only to healing during radio phone-in programmes. The international leanings and connections of pastors and their churches are publicized at the least opportunity because in the theology of the new churches, internationalism is considered an important index of a Christian community that is truly blessed by God. In the context of Africa's innumerable woes and economic quagmire, international connections constitute important avenues for receiving 'blessings from God' in the form of either personal acquisitions or remittances from friends and family domiciled abroad. As a recent study points out, once they set foot in Europe and the West, there is enormous pressure on Africans to send money and similar assistance home to relatives whose perception of the West is a very bright one where everything is achievable (Arhinful, 2002, p. 157). That explains why the prayer for visas competes fiercely with healing during charismatic radio phone-in programmes (Van Dijk, 1997, p. 145). In a particularly intriguing instance, a woman who called in to ask for prayer support after her initial application for a US visa was turned down was asked by the pastor to lay her hands on the radio after which he offered a simple prayer: 'In the name of Jesus, receive your visa to travel!' There are real difficulties in obtaining visas to travel from African countries where people do not have the resources to prove that they will return once they travel out. As it happens, even very genuine applications get rejected. Africans believe in religion that serves practical ends, and with that mindset, divine interventions through prayer become the only available means of securing certain desired opportunities.

In charismatic spirituality, giving is theologically reciprocal. The leaders of the new churches are therefore frequent beneficiaries of gifts from members abroad who see their successes as a direct result of God's intervention, with the charismatic leader as the conduit. Giving, as one charismatic preacher has it, 'is a seed you sow not a debt you pay.' Radio and TV presentations of Pentecostal/charismatic churches are constantly illustrated with events that uphold them as having been beneficiaries of international largesse. Preachers are often introduced as having just flown in from another country and congregations are proudly informed of their pastor's impending trips to foreign parts. To have an international image has therefore become for this new type of Christianity one of the hallmarks of a successful church or person.

The global outlook of Africa's new Pentecostal/charismatic movements goes deeper than the mere yearning to participate in the material abundance associated with the West. The spiritual import here is that each of the charismatic pastors lays claim to a global mandate in mission conferred by Christ during their calling into ministry. Bishop Charles Agyin Asare of the Word Miracle Church International, Bishop Duncan-Williams of the Christian Action Faith Ministries, and Pastor Abubakr Bako of the Rhema Ministries International, alongside several others, are keenly sought after as speakers at international crusades. Within the last year, Bishop Duncan-Williams has served as the main speaker at Bishop T. D. Jakes's Potter's House in Texas, and Bishop Agyin Asare held public Healing Crusades in the Ukraine. A number of these programmes have been shown to Ghanaian audiences in lieu of the regular TV programmes hosted by the pastors concerned. In the past, these forays into the arena of mass crusades had been associated with the Oral Roberts, Billy Grahams and Benny Hinns of this world, with Africans serving as the consumers. Things have changed and African healing evangelists and pastors are attracting audiences at international evangelistic campaigns comparable to those of their western compatriots. The Bible verse underneath the pictures on the Bishop Agyin Asare 2002 calendar is very instructive in this direction: 'Ask of me, and I shall give thee the heathen for thy inheritance and the uttermost parts of the earth for thy possession' (Psalms 2:8). In short, your influence will go beyond the local context. These developments underscore the reality of the proverbial shift of the centre of gravity of the Christian faith from the northern to the southern continents.

Pentecostal/charismatic church pastors like Otabil are frequently 'Dr', 'Bishop' or both. Ghanaian bishops of Pentecostal/charismatic movements will almost invariably have an American bishop of that persuasion among those who enthrone them. Several charismatic leaders have also been honoured with doctorates by mostly American seminaries. In addition to these, there is a conscious attempt not only to publish their books abroad, but also to have the foreword to such books authored by charismatic pastors written by international evangelists and pastors. Stan Dekoven, President, Vision International University, US wrote the foreword to Bishop Agyin Asare's book, *Rooted and Built up in Him* (1999). The desire to locate itself firmly within the international charismatic family has also made the globe, often embellished with other symbolic images such as a flying dove, representing the Holy Spirit, a very popular logo among the new churches in Ghana. Pentecostal/charismatic church premises may also be supplied with flagpoles on which the colours of various countries may be mounted. TV viewers thus have the opportunity to appreciate the modern nature and international standing of the churches.

Prosperity Gospel and Media Images of Prestige

The images of Pentecostal/charismatic movements generally, we have noted, are those of self-importance, success in ministry, economic prosperity, and the ability to spiritually empower others. A number of these images were played out at ICGC during the visit of members of the Commission. The events *consciously* portrayed a prestigious image of the 'man of God' and his church. First Pastor Otabil walked into the service after the notices, but just in time for him to preach, literally making his 'entrance' into the 'drama'. In popular African imagination, important people, particularly traditional chiefs, politicians and chief executives, *must* attend functions later than everybody to affirm their importance. So the Pentecostal/charismatic pastor is imaged as the 'chief executive' of a religious enterprise. Second, Otabil was the sole centre of attraction throughout the period he was on stage. The podium was bare except for a few potted plants and the lectern. This had to be so as it is his charisma that pulls everything together. Third, his outfit, the traditional three-piece *agbada*, was made of lace, one of the most expensive fabrics that could be used for clothing in that category. These elements, carefully imaged through the media, especially on TV, signify a redemptive uplift for charismatics that is achieved through God's intervention in lives that were otherwise heading nowhere. Pentecostal/charismatic church testimonies are purposely designed to publicize what God has done for people, and the media provide the means to take these messages of divine intervention beyond local religious collectivities. This process of imaging through the media is motivated by a vision and desire to participate in and contribute to religious globalization from the African context of deprivation and socio-economic and political marginalization.

Much of what is happening in Ghanaian Pentecostal/charismatic movements are local innovations, but they are also very much inspired by developments in other contexts particularly the US. Ghanaian charismatic pastors openly allude to their connections to leading charismatic figures and Pentecostals such as T. D. Jakes and Benny Hinn. On Easter day, 31 March 2002, for example, Bishop Duncan-Williams granted an hour-long interview on Ghana national television. This focused on his high-profile divorce and reunion with his wife Francisca, herself an ordained pastor of their church, the Christian Action Faith Ministries. The story of the reunion and the international influences that made it possible were first passed on to *The Mirror*, Ghana's most popular and widely read weekend paper. A bold picture of Duncan-Williams (posing a victory sign) and his smiling wife accompanied the story, which referred to Duncan-Williams's friendship with the American evangelist T. D. Jakes, who helped bring the couple back together.

During an interview on the popular 'Kwaku-One-On-One' programme, Bishop Duncan-Williams constantly confirmed that Bishop Jakes was instrumental in bringing the marriage back together. Barely three weeks after Bishop Duncan-Williams's television interview, his wife was also featured on the TV3 programme, 'Women of Distinction'. More than three-quarters of the allotted thirty minutes was on the divorce and reunion, the couple's worldwide peregrinations, and the award of a doctorate to Francisca by an American seminary. Obviously a couple must be very important to merit such media attention, travel that much, and have a pastor of Bishop Jakes's standing as their counsellor. This was the impression that the interviews were designed to create. Following these developments, a bold silhouetted picture of Bishop Duncan-Williams and some of his members, in an emotional atmosphere of worship, decorated bus stops along selected principal streets in Accra. The visual representation of Duncan-Williams and his CAFM is accompanied by words that present Action Faith Chapel as 'a place where over-comers never quit'.

The divorce of the 'first charismatic couple' had itself been put in public space through the media, and Bishop Duncan-Williams's reputation as the pioneering founder of a Pentecostal/charismatic church in Ghana had suffered a great deal. The interviews on national television thus gave the couple an opportunity to stage a comeback and they did not allow the opportunity to slip. During the last Valentine's Day, for example, he claims to have given his wife and two hundred other couples from their church a poolside dinner at the plush Nogahill hotel in Accra as evidence of his turnaround. Holidays in foreign countries had also been placed on the agenda. Even in the attempt to win back public confidence, the image of the charismatic pastor and his wife as being more spiritually powerful than most and as symbolizing material prosperity, success, and being at home with modern values were evident.

Ghana's charismatic churches reflect modern African ingenuity in the appro-priation of neo-Pentecostal Christianity enamoured by a repertoire of global, mostly American neo-Pentecostal techniques, style and strategy in organization and expression. The glossy images of pastors and their wives on magazines, posters, book covers and almanacs are Ghanaian imitations of a largely North American phenomenon. In Ghanaian eyes, North America, with its technological superiority and material abundance, epitomizes modernity. For a religion that seeks to be modern and preaches material abundance as signs of right standing with God as the new Pentecostal/charismatic Christians do, things that come from America are a great source of enchantment and inspiration and an ultimate symbol of God's blessing. Video and audiotape recordings of American televangelists abound in Ghana. Programmes like those of the healer televangelist Ernest Angley are part of the regular weekend religious menu on Ghanaian television stations. In an age of unprecedented technological advancement, the role of the mass media in the diffusion of religious and other innovations must be obvious. In the words of Rogers: 'mass media channels are often the most rapid and efficient means to inform an audience of potential adopters about the existence of an innovation, that is, to create awareness-knowledge' (Rogers, 1995, p. 18). The mass media thus play a crucial role in this diffusion of religious innovation by revealing models and styles from other contexts which may easily become the norm for similar movements elsewhere.

The Media and Images of Special Anointing

The emphasis on personal experiences of the Holy Spirit and the manifestations of his gifts and graces in Pentecostal/charismatic churches is relatively more democratized. The principle of the priesthood of all believers is thus emphasized among the new Pentecostal/charismatic churches, yet 'the prestige an extraordinary gifted charismatic person may obtain makes for differentiation' (Droogers, 1994, p. 47). On the back cover of his *Walking in the Power of God* (2000), Bishop Addae-Mensah's credential as a man of sacred power is emphasized by a reference to his having been interviewed on CNN in 1993. For what was a fringe religious movement at the beginning of the 1980s, an appearance on CNN definitely confers a very high status on its leader and the movement as a whole. This personal prestige as a symbol of God's favour is very much coveted in Ghana's new Christianity.

The media are used with dramatic effect in order to make a charismatic person's prestige a public showpiece of what God can do. The constant appearances of charismatic pastors on Ghana television have given them a very high profile as people of worth who need to be taken seriously. Radio and television have acquired ritual status in Ghana. And so preachers frequently encourage listeners to place their hands on the radio or put their open arms on the television screen in order that healing or anointing for particular breakthroughs in life may be mediated to them through these gadgets. Clients who have successfully received mediated spiritual power through television and radio ministries are encouraged to phone in to testify what the Lord has done for them through the ministry of particular preachers. Thus an important image conveyed by Pentecostal/charismatic churches through the media is one that presents the leadership as truly anointed and full of spiritual power. Television advertisements of impending charismatic programmes frequently display images of people falling down or 'being slain in the Spirit', as the phenomenon is called, under the touch of the pastor. This is a movement that has within three decades moved from the periphery to the centre of African Christianity and the media have been used effectively to achieve this end.

The tremendous patronage that the radio ministries of Ghanaian charismatic pastors enjoy transcends local audiences. Local television programmes of Bishop Agyin-Asare of the Word Miracle Church International are also available in London and Amsterdam through the private channels of Inspiration and Salto respectively. Ghanaians in the diaspora and interested foreigners are able to listen to live radio programmes through the Internet, and those looking for prayerful intervention in times of crises constantly phone in so that prayers may be said for them through that medium. In the midst of the harsh realities of life, African traditional worldviews that encourage the search for answers in the religious or theological realm have been reinforced through charismatic theology and globalized through the mass media.[7]

Globalization as a Prophetic Mandate for Leadership

Africa's new charismatics, by their own self-definition, suggest that their participation in the globalization process is not merely an attempt to adapt to modern trends in keeping with change and progress. The leadership believes this to be a divine destiny purposely bestowed on them by God. The following is part of a prophecy that is supposed to have been delivered following a message preached by the founder and leader of ICGC Pastor Otabil in the Bahamas. The prophecy reveals the mind of God about Africa and her future in Christian globalization, but the important point is that it affirms Otabil as God's 'apostle to the nations':

> For says the Lord, 'your voice has not been heard in the nations, your voice has not been heard on the continents'. He that has an eye let him see what the Spirit is doing for I am causing a new wind and that new wind is blowing from a place you never see a wind blow from. That new wind is blowing from a place that was despised. For I will cause my sons and daughters with my anointing and with my power to move forth in the nations of the world and the world will be blessed because of them for the time has come for the nations to be helped. (Otabil, 1992, pp. 64–65)

A 'place you never see a wind blow from' and the 'place that was despised' in this prophecy refer to Africa. The message of the possession of a divine calling to establish Africa as a leading player in world affairs through charismatic Christianity thus informs the images that are brought to the world through the media.

In the pursuit of their globalizing aspirations, preaching tours have become very important to charismatic church leaders. The ability to travel abroad and in the process 'export spiritual power' or 'import' foreign preachers has become in Ghana an index of a leader's charismatic credentials and success as a man or woman of God. It is also a source of great pride for church members. The driving force behind the international image they so keenly covet lies in the global mission to which the leaders claim God has called them. In the thinking of African charismatics, God has raised their leaders to provide the vision and aspirations needed for the continent to take its place in world affairs. Ghanaian theologian Kwame Bediako surmises that the self-definition of the new Pentecostal churches as 'international' organizations points 'to some specifically Christian dimensions of the African participation in globalisation that may escape secular-minded observers' (Bediako, 2000, p. 311).

The renewal of Christianity in Africa through Pentecostalism suggests that in the midst of the political turbulence and other socio-economic problems bedevilling the continent, religion and culture may just turn out to be the areas in which Africa might make some of its greatest contributions to the 'global village' in the new millennium. This explains the emphasis on capacity building, empowerment and the realization of potential that now inform much charismatic preaching and programmes.

Conclusion

There are a number of significant conclusions that may be arrived at against the backdrop of the Pentecostal/charismatic media images that have been discussed. We noted, quoting Quebedeaux, that utilization of the media by religious personalities engenders personal connections with audiences. Benjamin Wagner, building on Quebedeaux's observation, notes that in modern American culture 'leaders who have this personal connection, especially those who are made "visible" by the media, can achieve mass influence simply by virtue of the form of communication' (Wagner, 2003, p. 120). The influences of charismatic pastors in Ghana, particularly on the young, are deep and extensive. In responding to the presence of charismatic renewal movements, historic mainline churches must consider this fact and realize that the theological orientations of their members are, thanks to the media, being shaped by forces beyond their control. Rather than resist the current 'pentecostalization' of Christianity evident in the mainline churches as some are tempted to do, a healthier approach may be to isolate its positive elements and allow their own Christian education programmes to be informed by happenings on the religious front. In the wider public sphere, monitoring is important because what is received through the media also shapes public culture, morality and the future aspirations of young people in particular. Public organizations can therefore not afford to be uninterested in what Pentecostal/charismatic leaders convey to the public through their media programmes.

We have also seen that those who are shown forth as examples to the world in Pentecostal/charismatic media usages are those who have achieved something in life. The idea is that the Pentecostal/charismatic Christian, beginning with the leader, must be visible as a symbol of God's blessing, and the media provides ample space and opportunity for this image of success to be advertised. In the minds of their leaders, God has called them to make a global impact, so the idea of globality is an integral part of the self-definition of Africa's charismatic churches. The movement's activities are therefore consciously planned, designed and executed to emphasize and maintain this global image. This image and others discussed in the essay are coveted and once obtained are very seriously cherished because charismatic theology is one that affirms the worth of the individual. As one of such churches advertises on a giant billboard in Accra, 'this is a place where God makes everybody somebody'. Extensive and innovative use of the mass media facilitates the acquisition of these images.

The image that Ghana's charismatic churches mediate to the public is a reflection of the gospel of prosperity that they preach. Theologically, there may be much in such a message that inspires people to put their God-given potentials to constructive uses. The success of Pentecostal/charismatic Christianity in Africa has lain largely in its ability to propagate itself in a 'powerful and efficacious manner' by enabling people to be set free from the dangers and troubles of life. In that sense, Pentecostal/charismatic churches serve as more credible sources of intervention for

African Christians than the traditional shrines from where stories of diabolical rituals often emanate. Pentecostal/charismatic churches in Africa have developed, for the African context, a crisp, clear and powerful message that speaks directly to people's concerns.

The unfortunate development here, though, is that realities centred on the inevitable difficulties associated with life tend to be played down by the sort of triumphalistic images portrayed through the media by Pentecostal/charismatic leaders. Additionally, as Horsfield argues from the North American context, the insistence that people must give or sow a seed in order to be blessed may very easily lead to a 'return to the purchasing of indulgences, with the only proviso being one's willingness to pay the required amount in order to set the mechanisms of miracle-working in motion' (Horsfield, 1984, p. 34). In the end, the poor, outcasts, marginalized and the helpless, who were actually the centre of the ministry of the Lord Jesus Christ, tend to be ignored because they are not seen as good images or symbols of the gospel of prosperity. The challenge that this raises for African pastoral theologians is enough. Pentecostal/charismatic attempts to globalize their initiatives through the media call for decisive steps for constructive engagements with the religious media in order that they may serve very useful and altruistic purposes in the hands of the Christian church. In that respect, the introduction of courses in 'media, religion and culture' may now have to be considered as non-negotiable as far as the curricula of seminaries and Bible schools are concerned.

Notes

1 Two of the publications are: Hoover and Lundby (1997) and Mitchell and Marriage (2003).

2 The expression 'Pentecostal' refers to Christian movements and churches in which the experiential presence of the Holy Spirit is valued and actively promoted as part of normal Christian life. Newer forms of Pentecostal movements operating within non-Pentecostal churches are normally referred to as 'charismatic'. In this study the combined expressions 'Pentecostal/charismatic' will used to refer to the new independent churches of that persuasion operating in sub-Saharan Africa because the two expressions are used interchangeably for them.

3 Since the pioneering initiative of Bishop Nicholas Duncan-Williams, who formed the Christian Action Faith Ministries International (CAFMI) in 1979, the list of new independent Pentecostal/charismatic churches in Ghana has become endless: Liberation Bible Church International, Global Revival Ministries, Living Streams Ministries International, International Bible Worship Centre, Word Miracle Church International, Victory Bible Church International, Continental Charismatic Evangelistic Ministries, International Central Gospel Church, and so on.

4 Pastor Otabil took part in panel discussions at the Accra meeting. In their various essays, Commission members refer to the privilege we had to experience at first hand the innovative, fervent and vibrant nature of African Charismatic Christianity during a visit to ICGC.

5   On Sunday 21 May 2000, members of the International Study Commission on Media,
    Religion, and Culture worshipped at Pastor Otabil's ICGC. Following the service, the
    team visited Pastor Otabil's private office located in the multi-million cedi Christ Temple
    that also houses the main church.
6   Ghana has four TV stations, GTV, TV3, TV Africa and Metro. Religious programmes
    featured on these channels include: for GTV, 'God's Miracle Power'; 'Winning Ways';
    'Voice of Inspiration'; 'Restoration Hour'; 'Church Bells'; 'Encounter with the Truth';
    'Gospel Trail'; 'Power in His Presence'. For TV3, 'Your Miracle Encounter'; 'Treasures
    of Wisdom'; 'Words of Exhortation'. For Metro, 'Solid Rock'; 'Christ Apostolic
    Church'; 'Mystery Body Church'; 'Gospel Music'; 'Miracle Touch'; 'Great Light
    Worship'; 'Turning Point'; 'Calvary Crusaders'; 'Light House Chapel'.
7   The image of a powerful charismatic pastor also abounds in local video films produced in
    Ghana, a subject treated at greater length in the chapter in this volume by Jolyon Mitchell
    (Chapter 8).

References

Addae-Mensah, M. (2000), *Walking in the Power of God: Thrilling Testimonies about
    Supernatural Encounters with God*, Ontario, Canada: Guardian Books.
Agyin Asare, C. (1999), *Rooted and Built Up in Him: Things which make Sound Doctrine*,
    Accra: Miracle Publications.
Arhinful, D.K. (2002), '"We think of them": Money Transfers from the Netherlands to
    Ghana', in I. Van Kessel (ed.), *Merchants, Missionaries and Migrants: 300 Years of
    Dutch–Ghanaian Relations*, Accra: Sub-Saharan Publishers.
Bediako, K. (2000), 'Africa and Christianity on the Threshold of the Third Millennium: The
    Religious Dimension', *African Affairs*, **99**, 303–23.
De Witte, M. (2003), 'Altar Media's *Living Word:* Televised Charismatic Christianity in
    Ghana', *Journal of Religion in Africa*, **33** (2), 172–202.
Droogers, A. (1994), 'The Normalisation of Religious Experience: Healing, Prophecy,
    Dreams, and Visions', in Karla Poewe (ed.), *Charismatic Christianity as a Global
    Culture*, Columbia, SC: University of South Carolina Press.
Hexham I. and K. Poewe (1994), 'Charismatic Churches in South Africa: A Critique of
    Criticisms and Problems of Bias', in K. Poewe (ed.), *Charismatic Christianity as a
    Global Culture*, Columbia, SC: University of South Carolina Press.
Hiebert, R. E., D. F. Ungurait and T. W. Bohn (1985), *Mass Media IV: An Introduction to
    Modern Communication*, New York and London: Longman.
Hoover, S. M. and K. Lundby (eds) (1997), *Rethinking Media, Religion, and Culture*,
    California, London and New Delhi: Sage.
Horsfield, P. G. (1984), *Religious Television: The American Experience*, New York and
    London: Longman.
Lehikoinen, T. (2003), *Religious Media Theory: Understanding Mediated Faith and
    Christian Applications of Modern Media*, Jyvaskyla, Finland: University of Jyvaskyla.
Maxwell, D. (1998), 'Editorial', *Journal of Religion in Africa*, **28** (3), 255–57.
Miller, D. E. (1997), *Reinventing American Protestantism: Christianity in the New
    Millennium*, Berkeley, Los Angeles and London: University of California Press.
Mitchell, J. and S. Marriage (eds) (2003) *Mediating Religion: Conversations in Media,
    Religion and Culture*, London and New York: T&T Clark.

Obatil, M. (1992), *Beyond the Rivers of Ethiopia: A Biblical Revelation on God's Purpose for the Black Race*, Accra, Ghana: Altar International.
Quebedeaux, R. (1982), *By What Authority: The Rise of Personality Cults in American Christianity*, San Francisco, CA: Harper & Row.
Rogers, E. M. (1995), *Diffusion of Innovations*, 4th edn, New York: Free Press.
Van Dijk, R. A. (1997), 'From Camp to Encompassment: Discourses of Transsubjectivity in the Ghanaian Pentecostal Diaspora', *Journal of Religion in Africa*, **28** (1), 135–59.
Wagner, B. A. (2003), '"Full Gospel" Radio: Revivaltime and the Pentecostal Uses of Mass Media, 1950–1979', *Fides et Historia*, **25** (1), 107–22.

Additional Resources

Duncan-Williams, N. (1990), *You are Destined to Succeed*, Accra: Action Faith Publications.
Gifford, P. (1998), *African Christianity, Its Public Role*, London: Hurst and Co.
Hackett, R. I. J. (1998), 'Charismatic/Pentecostal Appropriation of Media Technologies in Nigeria and Ghana', *Journal of Religion in Africa*, **28**, 258–77.
Heward-Mills, D. (2000), *Catch the Anointing*, Accra: Dag's Tapes and Publications.

Chapter 6

Identities, Religion and Melodrama: A View from the Cultural Dimension of the Latin American *Telenovela*

Germán Rey

Latin America studies of the relationship between communication and culture have shown great creativity over the last several decades. There are various reasons for this dynamism. Communications have been very important in the processes that have modernized our countries, in the connections that exist between new technologies and daily life, in the entry of local societies into a global economy and in the spread of a world culture.

As noted by a number of authors, such as Jesús Martín-Barbero (1992), Renato Ortiz (1997, 1985), Néstor García Canclini (1989) and Carlos Monsivais (2000), the media have played a decisive role in establishing the identity of Latin American societies and of very specific sectors of the population. 'In the first half of this century', wrote Néstor García Canclini, 'Radio and cinema helped organize the narrative of identity and civic sense in these nations' societies. To the epic tales of heroes and grand collective events they added a chronicle of daily concerns' (García Canclini, 1995, p. 107). García Canclini confirms the role played by cinema in the construction of Latin American national identities, and insists that the opening up of national markets to global ones has tended to reduce the role of national cultures and to diminish the importance of traditional reference points of identity.

Visual imagery has always been decisive in the development of Latin American social and cultural identities. This visual imagery expresses itself in indigenous, rural or Afro community imagery or in the colorful and baroque iconographic universe that dominates popular festivities, religious celebrations or the way people decorate their most intimate spaces. Visual displays are cultural manifestations that overlap and lay down a pattern for everyday rituals in the life of most Latin Americans: in an ornamental use for religious expressions (of pilgrimages, saints days, or shrines), in the organization of space in houses and meeting places, in dress and fabric patterns, in the preparation of meals, and in the connection between images and popular literature. But they can also be found in the most contemporary behavior, as for example in the development of modern architecture, the audiovisual industry's means of expression (from movies to *telenovelas*) or in the layout of urban environments.[1] There is a long tradition of combining images, culture and religiosity that runs through the whole of Latin American history, through its aesthetics and its sensibilities, as well as through its ways of life, belief systems and expectations for the future.

It is not difficult to observe temporal manifestations of religious *mestizaje* or racial–cultural mixture. They can be seen in the ludic sense of death in Mexico, expressed in the popular celebration of The Day of the Dead, with its altars full of food and music; or in the iconography of *La Parca* (Death) in sweetmeats and breads; or in the influences of African religious traditions found in Cuban, Haitian or Brazilian religious rituals – from *candomblé* and voodoo to the *orishas*. They can also be seen in their most contemporary art – the paintings of the Cuban Wilfredo Lam come naturally to mind – and in the forms of popular religion, which appear every day in Colombian or Venezuelan *telenovelas*.

These strong relationships, which start in the past and continue into the present, have been described with studied precision by Serge Gruzinski, who dedicated several years to the study of Mexican history and the evolution of its imagery:

> The war of images is perhaps one of the major events of the end of the twentieth century. Difficult to define, entangled in journalistic commonplaces or the meanderings of a hermetic technological sophistication, this war covers – beyond the struggles for power – the social and cultural stakes whose present and future importance we are yet unable to measure. 'Would it not be a great paradox for us to be living in a world of inflation of images, while still believing we are under the sway of text?'[2] From Orwell's omnipresent screens to the gigantic billboards piercing Ridley Scott's humid and illuminated night skies, the image has already invaded our future. (Gruzinski, 2001, p. 2)

Gruzinski demonstrates that the battle of the image, which occurs when indigenous and Christian perspectives meet in the coming together of Catholic beliefs and the native worldview, continues in the technological present of electronic images.

'If certain aspects of muralism were reminiscent of the evangelizing ambitions of sixteenth-century fresco painters, the fantastic rise of Mexican commercial television, under the aegis of the Televisa company, certainly conjured up the miraculous and invasive image of baroque times' (ibid., p. 221). He also states that:

> The spiriting away of transcendence and religion in favor of consumerism – thus making what was only one of the results of the baroque *imaginaire* an end unto itself – is the abyss that separates Televisa from the colonial machinery. A systematic exploitation of the attraction, the ubiquity, and the magic of the image; making *imaginaires* uniform; and the reuse of popular stories – the rhythm and efficiency of soap operas were already present in the Guadalupe legend – brings them closer. (Ibid., pp. 222–23)

It could therefore be said that in the process of creation of identity there is a meeting of Our Lady of Guadalupe and *telenovela*, of religious icons and popular narrative.

The Spanish invasion, set in an Old Testament context, gave rise to an explosion of western imagery, ambiguity in the substitution of images, unequal exchanges, the regarding of idols as evil and abominable plus the concealment of the gods themselves from the invader's control and prohibition (a retreat into hiding). This guiding thread, which differentiates one's perceptions of the images of others from one's relationship with one's own images, is present in the ways that Christian images are produced in video today. That is what I have been able to confirm when analyzing videotapes made by Latin American Catholic producers. While some of them emphasize literal, didactic images that try explicitly to spread the gospel, others steer clear of mere transcriptions, allow variations and generate interchanges between different aesthetics and interpretations. While some Catholic producers work with the image mainly for educational purposes or to motivate and support pastoral work, some of the more daring ones – such as Juan Carlos Henríquez in his video production, *Apocalipsis* – connect the biblical text with daily experience, recovering its symbolic strength to produce an audiovisual narrative that proposes language innovations and enables a much richer and more evocative interpretation on the part of the audience.

It could be said, then, that one trend in Latin American Catholic video images is an attempt to make the text clear to the audience, resorting to traditional symbolic references and to predictable codes of interpretation (some of which are schematically rational while, by contrast, others are excessively emotional). A second tendency acknowledges the transmutation of languages in contemporary audiovisual culture and tries to find, in a dialog with it, other narrative forms (Rey, 1997, pp. 39–52). In addition to the relationships of communication, culture and identity, there is now a much closer relationship between communication and cultural policies, whether this is the relationship between communication and social democratization, the configuration of public space, the expressive dimensions of social movements or the increasing efforts to consolidate modern citizenship.

These relationships reveal a variety of tensions. One is the confluence of social and economic inequality and new exclusions – among them being, undoubtedly, the exclusion of wide sectors of the population from access to information and knowledge opportunities. Another is the difficulty in connecting the local with the global. In fact Latin American cultural (including audiovisual) production has very little circulation, not only at a global level, but also – and this is even more disturbing – within the region. The hegemonic dominance of American audiovisual production (Hollywood) is clearly evident, overwhelming as it does the film distribution circuits and greatly affecting the circulation of television products.

Communications studies, which began by focusing on the media, have moved towards a much richer understanding of the communicative phenomena. The title of the classic 1987 text by Jesús Martín Barbero, *De los medios a las mediaciones: Comunicación, cultura y hegemonía* (*Communication, Culture and Hegemony: From Media to Mediations*), defines this movement very well. Culture – or rather, cultures – have increased their presence, both socially and conceptually, in Latin

America. Socially, this has come about through phenomena such as multiculturality, the processes of hybridization and *mestizaje*, the sociocultural movements that daily increase their social and political prominence or through the convergence of widely diverse cultures that make up dense and complex intercultural realities in the continent.

While vast migrations from the countryside to the cities have taken place, contrasts coexist in the same physical space: pre-modernity and modernity, traditional societies and groups operating with global logics, large social groups that live immersed in their oral cultures and are challenged by audiovisual culture and groups that are actively connected to the new technologies and consumer practices. A number of important conceptual shifts have occurred. Some of these are: anthropologists' study of indigenous communities or ethnic groups, the current broadening of the concept of culture to include the careful observation of phenomena such as the affirmation of youth culture, the symbolic texture of the urban landscape, the interactions between cultural industries and audiences and the cultural importance of the *telenovela* (undoubtedly the most important mass, popular, cultural product).

Latin American research has made clear the intersections between culture and communication, but it has also taken up important inquiries into religion in our countries. Without a doubt liberation theology has had a great impact, joining theological reflection with the social and political problems of a continent that has deep social inequality, serious problems of exclusion (economic and political but also cultural exclusion) and widespread problems of poverty. Theological interpretations have not been separate from the vital contexts of religious experience. On the contrary, liberation theology quickly encountered the church base communities, groups of Christians committed to projects of social change. This has also ignited heated controversy in some sectors of the institutional church.

But there are other advances, besides liberation theology, that have also had an important impact on the study of religion and its connection with communication and culture. Among them are studies on popular religion, analyses of the influence of secularization and urbanization on traditional systems of belief, the role of religious models in the processes of socialization, the constitution of identities and social cohesion, the connections between non-Catholic religious movements and communications media and the symbolic importance – in religious terms – of a very wide range of cultural forms of expression. These range from carnivals, secular festivities, pilgrimages and religious celebrations to youth aesthetics, iconographic blendings, fashion and audiovisual grammars.

Powerful trends in this Latin American thought could serve as useful guides for an enriching discussion of topics that are centrally important. One illustrative example is research into the importance of communications media in the construction of cultural identity, including the relationships between melodrama and Latin American cultural dynamics, the tensions in the encounter between local imaginative frameworks and global media productions (particularly US television and film), and the connection between religious practices, symbol structures and social life.

Religion, Melodrama and Identity in Latin America

The Latin American *telenovela* is a television production that may consist of over 200 episodes, broadcast daily in one-hour segments. The narrative structure privileges a linear story line, highly contrasted characters, and the development of dramatic nuclei that are repeated, such as the son/daughter who does not know who his/her mother is; the poor woman who undergoes great hardships to finally marry a rich and handsome man; the reuniting of members of a family after years of separation, etc. In general, *telenovelas* are centered in love; they are, therefore, a portrait of our emotions (hate, solidarity, revenge, generosity) and a map of basic human relationships.

There are different models of Latin American melodrama. The Mexican and the Venezuelan models have a long tradition and have achieved a solid production infrastructure, in both economic and technical terms. They have also developed strong commercial marketing internationally. But the most outstanding feature of this model is its narrative form, which relies on stories and characters whose outlines are known, and on plots that evolve through exaggeration of emotions and simplicity of description.

The Brazilian model, on the other hand, takes greater care of production quality. It uses stories that are less predictable and plots that are more complex. While the first model leans towards being anachronistic, the second one is more modern; while in the former social issues are expressed in a descriptive and very literal way, in the latter they become part of the story in a more analytical and historical way.

In his book, *Communication, Culture and Hegemony,* Jesús Martín-Barbero established the connections between fairground shows, horror stories, popular *cordel* literature,[3] wandering circuses, tobacconist store tales, *folletines* (nineteenth-century serialized booklets) and radio plays with melodrama.

Melodrama's complicity with the new popular public and with the cultural space which this public marked out for itself provide the keys which help us situate this form of popular spectacle at the turning point of the process which moved from the popular to the mass. Melodrama provided a point of arrival for the narrative memory and gestural forms of popular culture and the point of emergence of the dramatization of mass culture. That is, melodrama is where the popular begins to be the object of a process that erases local cultural frontiers, a process that takes off with the constitution of a homogeneous discourse and with the unification of the images of the popular, a unification that is the first form of mass culture. (Martín-Barbero, 1993, p. 113)

The *telenovela* not only takes up the greatest production efforts of Latin American television companies, but it is also the expressive form with the greatest potential for achieving high audience reception and consumption. Series like *Simplemente María* (*Just Mary*), *La Fiera* (*The Shrew*), *Los ricos también lloran* (*The Rich Also Cry*), *Topacio* (*Topaz*), *Leonela*, *La Intrusa* (*The Intruder*), *Dancing Days*, *Roque Santeiro*, *Café* or *Betty, la fea* (*Ugly Betty*), to mention but a few examples from different periods and countries, have had a truly remarkable reception by large audiences in countries as dissimilar as Russia, Singapore, Spain and China. Further, *telenovelas* are embraced by the Hispanic population in the United States. Countries like India have also made memorable *telenovelas* that have led to relationships between Mexico, for instance, and India.

The structure of the melodramatic text is as important as the conditions of production and reception. *The Practice of Seeing: Audiovisual Hegemony and Television Fiction* (Martín-Barbero and Rey, 1999) was an attempt to explore the evolution of Latin American and Colombian television melodrama, from the *teleteatro* (television theatre of the middle of the twentieth century) to its links with literature, its stylistic renewal and its more recent insertion into the dynamics of international television markets. *Telenovela* is, then, the most important genre of Latin American television production and probably its most outstanding mass, popular, cultural object.

Powerful audiovisual industries, with fairly standardized production and marketing processes, have been structured around the *telenovela*, which makes up a substantial portion of the programming offered by the largest Latin American television conglomerates: Televisa in Mexico, Venevisión in Venezuela and O Globo in Brazil. These companies are among the world's largest media groups.

But beyond its economic importance, the *telenovela* – with its mixture of ingenuity and anachronism – has become a narrative that speaks about social forces, about changes in sensibilities and the reconfiguration of roles and identities. Many factors have forcefully come together in the development of *telenovelas*, as they have been so much in tune with audience tastes and preferences and have taken advantage of new developments in audiovisual technologies in recent years.

What we see represented in the Latin American *telenovela* are the profound changes our societies have undergone in these turbulent decades: the upheavals in social perceptions caused by the complex processes of migration that have altered the rural world and shaped urban centers. *Telenovelas* represent the entry into a modernity that has impacted the way of life, the reference points for our value systems, our religious beliefs and the very nature of human relationships.

In the dramatic core of *telenovelas* (upward social mobility, differences between rich and poor, family relationships, incest, emotional ties, changes in gender roles, and the transition from the country to the city, and so on) one can see powerful social processes, such as the shift from markedly Catholic societies to more secular social organizations. In other words, the transitions that religiosity has undergone leave a clear imprint in the narrative of the melodrama. As Gruzinski writes, Our Lady of Guadalupe (a central moment in Mexican identity) has the rhythm and efficacy of a melodramatic serial. Exploring these connections not only sheds light on the relationship between media, religion and culture, but helps us better understand the processes of identity construction.

The reception of *telenovelas* cannot be explained simply as a phenomenon that adjusts television texts to fit audiences. The *telenovela* is above all a place where people's desires and expectations take shape as recognizable narratives that speak in a readily understandable language about everyday, real-life concerns and the human quest, or seeking. For years, the *telenovela* has enabled social sectors to recognize themselves, to explore the uncertainties caused by situations that are complex and in flux, and to decipher a social context that is mobile and syncretic.

Although it is not a religious object, the *telenovela* usually has explicit religious references and some, such as *Roque Santeiro* in Brazil, have interwoven remarkably well popular religion with social issues, thus showing their deepest connections. Nevertheless, there are dimensions that are central to the *telenovela* and are at the same time familiar to religion, or at least to the popular understandings of Catholic Christianity. First of all, the *telenovela* usually presents good and evil in stark contrast. Traditionally, the characters are placed on one or the other pole of the dichotomy, although there is a recent change in television melodrama that introduces nuances into what was Manichean. Good and evil are highlighted and generate a dramatic tension that maintains the suspense within the melodrama. However, good and evil are depicted in very different ways. Good is usually found in weak but kind-hearted characters who patiently endure suffering, while evil is identified with strong, truculent characters, capable of the most immoral and insensitive actions. Sometimes the evil character is converted, but the good character seldom becomes evil. What happens morally is that good simply triumphs over evil, without any major considerations, even though the triumph is delayed excessively, which of course is an emotive factor in the plot.

Second, the *telenovela* is clearly a moral narrative that underscores virtues and vices and usually tells a story that promotes the former and punishes the latter. The exaggeration of malevolence contrasts with the exaltation of goodness. It could be said that the *telenovela* serves as a moral lesson, recovering the values of traditional societies threatened by changes like secularization. To a certain extent, the *telenovela* is an affirmation – although an anachronistic one – of values that are being reconsidered in people's everyday life. That is the reason for the emphasis on the family, on solidarity, on basic social relationships (what Jorge González has called 'that which is elementally human'. In this sense there are some similarities – which have not been studied in depth – between the *telenovela* and the talk show. While the former is fiction about daily life, the latter is an apparently real depiction of daily conflicts. While *telenovelas* create moral types to explain human relationships, talk shows present stories, usually exaggerated, that try to strike a responsive chord in the viewers.

Third, suffering and guilt – central in Catholic theology – are also central in the *telenovela*. Characters undergo a purifying process of suffering, from which they emerge into a paradise that may be earthly. Suffering is linked to poverty, amorous deceit, estrangement from one's children, or denial of the past. Suffering not only guarantees heaven but saves on earth. This union of suffering and guilt surely has roots in the religious mentality inherited from Christianity. While suffering is a crucible, guilt is weightier because of the importance that family relationships have in melodramatic stories. Common are possessive mothers and weak fathers, mothers who daily face the hardships of poverty and who form relationships based on guilt. Here is a strange mixture of *machismo* and matriarchal families, of the sense of sin and the religious power of resignation.

Fourth, the woman – the mother – is usually in charge of preserving beliefs and guaranteeing the vitality of the religious sense. The mother embodies what is virtuous and pure and regularly overcomes all obstacles, even in the most dire circumstances. It would be interesting to study the relationships between patriarchal societies, *machismo* and the maternal conservation of religiosity in Latin American culture. A novel like *La Virgen del Sicario* (*Our Lady of the Assassins*) by the Colombian writer Fernando Vallejo, recently made into a film, explores the relationship between death, religious sense, superstition and crime. Studies such as those of Alonso Salazar about drug traffic cultures reveal the connections between popular religion, relationship with the mother and the figure of the disapproving and distant father. In Vallejo's novel, the assassin, one of many poor young men used by drug cartels, finds in the Virgin a sense of maternal protection that can even guarantee early salvation (not getting killed during one of his criminal acts). Other figures such as the Divine Child (Ferro, 2001), Our Lady of Carmen, José Gregorio Hernández or the Sacred Heart of Jesus, mix national identity with personal protection, acts of healing with cultural and class identification.

It is interesting to observe all these figures in the formation of the national imagination, as Carlos Monsivais points out in the case of Our Lady of Guadalupe in Mexico:

> Historically 'Guadalupanism', a shared experience of rootedness and continuity, is the most incarnated form of nationalism. But what happens in a post-traditional world? What is the relationship between nationalism and 'guadalupanism'? In my opinion, it cannot be understood as just a bellicose emotion but rather as a bonding that equalizes achievements and limitations: misery, understanding of the world through ritual acts, being at risk, habits, the strong love of symbols, syncretism as a way of adapting (first to the conquest, then to the nation emerging through battles, later to modernization), fanaticism which is also a form of bodily testimony to the rootedness in one's first learning, blind faith: power within the powerlessness of believers who are Mexicans, of Mexicans who are believers. (Monsivais, 1995, p. 40)

Fifth, the depiction of Catholic priests is very important. The priest is an adviser, a mediator in conflicts, someone able to help interpret the difficulties endured by the characters in a melodrama. The priest is usually an interpretative reference point, in addition to being clearly an element of social cohesion (certainly a very important topic in Latin America). The priest acts as a contrast to life, and his figure, associated with the sacred, is also the profane figure of the therapist.

On the surface a simple and predictable text, the Latin American *telenovela* recreates the landscape of our changing societies, of our differences and tensions. Deciphering it is an opportunity to explore the nexus that unites communication with religious representation and social and cultural dimensions.

Notes

1 *Telenovelas* are serialized melodramas and are somewhat similar to soap operas on US television, although they tend to have a limited number of episodes and are broadcast in prime time to large, diverse audiences.
2 Gruzinski quotes Henri Hudrisier, *L'iconothèque: Documentation audiovisuelle et banques d'images* (Paris: La Documentation Française–INA, 1982), p. 78.
3 The literature of the *cordel*, or 'string' refers to printed pages hung on string in the marketplace in Spain (Martín-Barbero, 1993, p. 99).

References

Ferro, G. (2001), 'El Divino Niño: ícono para una nación', in *Belleza, fútbol y religiosidad popular*, Bogotá: Cuadernos de Nación, Ministerio de Cultura.

García Canclini, N. (1995), *Consumidores y ciudadanos*, México: Grijalbo.

García Canclini, N. (1989), *Culturas Híbridas*, México: Grijalbo.

Gruzinski, S. (2001), *Images at War: Mexico from Columbus to* Blade Runner *(1492–2019)*, trans. H. MacLean, Durham, NC and London: Duke University Press.

Gruzinski, S. (1995), *La guerra de las imágene:De Cristóbal Colón a* Blade Runner, México: Fondo de Cultura Económica.

Martín-Barbero, J. (1993), *Communication, Culture and Hegemony: From the Media to Mediations*, trans. E. Fox and R. A. White, London, Newbury Park, CA and New Delhi: Sage.

Martín-Barbero, J. (1992), *Televisión y melodrama*, Bogotá: Tercer Mundo Editores.

Martín-Barbero, J. (1987), *De los medios a las mediaciones: Comunicación, cultura y hegemonía*, Barcelona: Editorial Gili.

Martín-Barbero, J. and G. Rey, (1999), *Los ejercicios del ver. Hegemonía audiovisual y ficción televisiva* (*The Practice of Seeing: Audiovisual Hegemony and Television Fiction*), Barcelona: Gedisa.

Monsivais, C. (2000), *Aires de familia. Cultura y sociedad en América Latina*, Barcelona: Anagrama.

Monsivais, C. (1995), *Los rituales del caos*, México: Era.

Ortiz, R. (1997), *Mundialización y cultura*, Buenos Aires: Alianza.

Ortiz, R. (1985), *Telenovela: historia e producao*, São Paulo: Brasiliense.

Rey, G. (1997), 'Os poros do rostro da vida', in José Tavares de Barros (ed.), *Imagens da America Latina*, São Paulo: Ediciones Loyola.

Additional Resources

Bartra, R. (1987), *La jaula de la melancolía*, México: Grijalbo.

González, J. (1990), *Las vetas del encanto. Por los veneros de la producción mexicana de telenovelas*, Universidad de Colima, México.

Hackett, R. (1998), 'Charismatic/Pentecostal Appropriation of Media Technologies in Nigeria and Ghana', *Journal of Religion in Africa*, **28** (3), 1–19.

Mazziotti, N. (1996), *La industria de la telenovela*, Buenos Aires: Paidós.

Muniz, S. (1998), *Reinventado la cultura*, Barcelona: Gedisa.

Rey, G. (unpublished), 'Polifemo entre pucheros. La telenovela latinoamericana en el fin de siglo'.

Rey, G. (2002), 'La historia de la televisión colombiana', in Guillermo Orozco (ed.), *Historia de la televisión en América Latina*, Barcelona; Gedisa.

Rey, G. (2000), 'La telenovela en el fin de siglo. Cultura y melodrama en América Latina', in *Cultura y medios de comunicación*, Salamanca: Pontificia Universidad de Salamanca.

Rey, G. (1994), 'Los matices de la imaginación', in *La realidad imaginada. El video en América Latina*, Bogotá: Ediciones Paulinas.

Sunkel, G. (ed.) (1999), *El consumo cultural en América Latina*, Bogotá: Convenio Andrés Bello.

Veron, E. and L. Escudero (eds) (1997), *Telenovela. Ficción popular y mutaciones culturales*, Barcelona: Gedisa.

Chapter 7

Visual Media and Ethiopian Protestantism

David Morgan

Religion and Visual Media

Since its origin in the early sixteenth century, Protestantism has relied on several media to shape thought and experience as receptacles of the divine message. Print, architecture, music and imagery have each provided the material means for the 'word of God' to structure Protestant life. Understanding the Bible as the unparalleled self-revelation of the deity, Protestants have tended to apply communications media to the delivery and ritualization of God's message. Architecture is the auditorium for hearing the word; music is the tonal embellishment and interpretation of the word; imagery the visual adornment and elaboration of the word. And each medium immerses the message in a ritualized form of communication, lending it a sensuous, corporeal presence in worship, devotion, instruction and ritual practice. It is not surprising, therefore, that Protestantism is often characterized as a 'culture of the book'. Language, reading, speaking, dogmatic proposition and theological formulation certainly occupy Protestants whatever their sectarian peculiarities. But it is a mistake to overlook the importance of other media (not only among Protestants, but also Muslims and Jews as other religious groups often reckoned to cultivate word-centered media sensibilities). The deft fit between imagery and print in such artifacts as tracts, bibles, devotional books, instructional literature and handbills have secured for imagery a vital role in Protestant practice (Morgan, 1999, 2001). Among Protestants, images more often serve a *rhetorical* rather than an *iconic* purpose. Their primary function, in other words, is to persuade viewers, to deliver a claim, to embellish and illustrate a content that precedes its visual expression. Certainly this subordinates form to content, but we should not miss the fact that without its visual packaging a religious message may suffer a loss of appeal and effect. The iconic tradition, by contrast, stresses the revelatory and sacramental power of imagery as a channel of grace, according images a central place in liturgy and formal worship services.[1] Protestantism rarely allows imagery to function iconically in and of itself. Because they insist on the affirmation of the creedal or dogmatic contents of faith, Protestants generally assign images a rhetorical role. Images have a way of acting like texts.

In fact, Protestants have a way of overlooking the role of visual media. Sometimes they are made anxious by imagery as a form of representation that too easily can become 'idolatrous'. Yet images do assert themselves on occasion, springing forth from the fire under their own power, as Aaron exclaimed of the golden calf to an angry Moses (Exodus 32:24). But the more important reason for underplaying the presence of images is that the imagery Protestants use often works best when it is transparent. In the largely rhetorical purpose to which Protestants put them, images operate as powerful forms of communication when they slip below the threshold of consciousness in delivering their freight of meaning. When an image like Figure 7.1 visualizes how a believer imagines Jesus to appear, issues of race, ethnicity, masculinity, gender, historicity and so forth often pass unnoticed. The image, in other words, may deliver far more than its mere appearance may consciously designate to any viewer. Of course, the same is true with any medium. The deconstruction of words, music, architecture, food or dress may easily show the multiplicity of meanings to be construed in or by means of them. But the power of images consists in their capacity to naturalize the sign. People, it seems, are inclined to believe images. No less, they are strongly inclined to see in an image what they are predisposed to see. This means that not only can images be used to transmit intended meanings, viewers will also apply images to purposes that matter most to them. The power of images, in other words, resides not only in what the creator or sender of the visual message intends, but also in the construction of meaning undertaken by those who view an image in such contexts as commemoration, gifting, instruction, meditation or prophylaxis.

It is important not to overlook Protestant images because of their meager appearance or mundane uses. The low expense and rudimentary technological requirements of print culture and the relative ease with which large amounts of print matter can be placed into circulation make the use of printed imagery quite attractive among religious groups faced with severe limitations in financial resources. Protestant visual culture in everyday life is often modest in artistic skill, lacking in patronage, and prosaic in nature. Yet the reliance on the imagery and the hopes in its efficacy and practicality commend mass-produced Protestant imagery and visual practice to the scholar who seeks to understand what insights visual culture can render concerning Protestant belief and devotional life.

Protestant Visual Piety in Ethiopia: Images and their Uses

Protestant evangelists in Ethiopia today face a familiar set of challenges. Literacy rates are extremely low, infrastructure from schools and churches to seminaries and church facilities are minimal, funding is not abundant for virtually any enterprise, and, in addition to being a religious minority on a national level, Protestants in Ethiopia are plagued by intense and potentially highly fractious clan and tribal rivalries. In spite of these challenges, however, the growth and

Figure 7.1   Warner Sallman, *Head of Christ,* **1940, oil on canvas.**

Courtesy: Anderson University

enthusiasm of many different Protestant groups in Ethiopia was unchecked through the 1990s.

While Ethiopian Christian art is immediately associated with Orthodox icons and architecture, the visual culture of a Protestant group in Ethiopia offers an opportunity to study the place of images in a fast-growing Protestant community in Africa, the Ethiopian Evangelical Church Mekane Yesus ('House of Jesus').[2] A colleague and I conducted interviews with many members of the church in the national capital, Addis Ababa, where Mekane Yesus is headquartered. Further interviews took us to locations in and around four provincial cities: Hossana and Awasa in south central Ethiopia and Nekemte and Aira in the western portion of the country. In each location we interviewed church leadership, faculty, clergy, publishers and laity.[3]

Consistent with the Protestant tradition, which was brought to Ethiopia in the nineteenth century by European missionaries, images were widely understood among those people we interviewed to be effective means of teaching. The principal rubric under which the image was classified was 'communication'. No one understood the image in the sacramental sense of an Orthodox icon that serves as a visual channel of grace, though some made the point of proscribing such a use of images. Comments fall into seven more or less related categories of purpose. Images were signifiers of Christian and sectarian identity; signifiers of educational status; devices for information delivery; instruments of control in teaching; ostensive devices for visualizing historical referents and corroborating biblical accounts and personal testimony; the visual means of evoking empathy in the viewer; and icons, which for many Ethiopian Protestants are images that are tantamount to idols.

The president of a synod of the Mekane Yesus in Western Ethiopia noted in an interview that people hang portraits of Jesus in their homes in order 'to show they are Christians'. Orthodox Christians, he continued, use pictures of Mary and the angels while Protestants prefer pictures of Jesus.[4] A missionary of Christian education who worked for an evangelical organization based in Addis indicated that evangelical churches in Ethiopia won't place images of Jesus in their worship spaces due to the association with icons in Ethiopian Orthodoxy.[5] As we will see shortly, the association of images with the Orthodox Church in Ethiopia is of special significance to many Protestants in or trained in Addis, but not elsewhere. We were also told by a clergyman who is the director of evangelism in a southern synod that 'the learned' hang religious pictures on the walls of their homes because they understand the images and because they are signs of their education.[6]

The greatest purpose ascribed to images consisted of the capacity of illustrations to deliver information in teaching. An evangelical missionary stated that an image is a 'device for understanding the biblical text better without extensive learning'.[7] According to a director of evangelism in a southern Mekane Yesus synod, images 'help organize information and visualize mentally the teaching and the scriptures'.[8] He stressed the application of images to education, stating that they were particularly useful 'on the first level ... at the beginning we use these pictures, illustrations, images in the books and tracts'. Images, he noted, were useful for confirmation classes and with adults coming from traditional religions. In both cases, illustrations facilitated learning where extensive reliance on text would not work due to low levels of reading ability or complete illiteracy.

An instrumentalist notion of communication undergirds the Protestant view of the image as a rhetorical device rather than as a sacramental vessel. One of the textbooks used in the Mekane Yesus Seminary in Addis, and cited explicitly by one church worker in the mission field, stresses the classical instrumental theory of communication. Written by James F. Engel, a professor at Wheaton College, an evangelical institution in the United States that is very active in training missionaries, *How to Communicate the Gospel Effectively* defines communication as 'the process whereby audience understanding is created when a message is sent by a communicator through appropriate media [channels]'.[9] Engel teaches that the effective communication of the Christian message relies on what he calls 'a strategy of audience orientation'. In order to achieve and maintain the listener's attention and successfully deliver the message, the evangelist must understand the audience and adapt the form of the message to the receiver's particular circumstances. This procedure is crucial because of the potentially disruptive nature of human autonomy: 'Because people see and hear what they want to see and hear, the communication process starts with the analysis of the audience' (Engel, 1988, p. 22). One frequently cited reason for using images in American religious pedagogy as well as among Ethiopian Protestants is the power of images to attract and hold the attention of viewers. Teachers are well aware of this purpose and make use of it frequently.

Securing the attention of the audience is always desirable, but the object of the viewer's attention concerned some teachers, evangelists and preachers. Images that threatened to become the focus of attention rather than the message they were to bear were objectionable. A seminary instructor in Hossana maintained that it was 'very helpful to teach with images in hand – pointing to elements of the picture helps a great deal in understanding the gospel message'. But he saw important limits to reinforce on the use of images: 'Beyond illustration we don't expect another understanding' (from an image) because 'worship of images is dangerous'.[10] Images that do more than clearly deliver their intellectual content are in danger of becoming an object of worship. Their usefulness consists in the power to point directly to their factual, empirical referents. For conservative Protestants for whom the Bible represents a reliably accurate historical record, this ostensive function of the image enriches the capacity of the image to deliver information without distortion or confusion. As the seminary instructor put it, a picture provides a view that is comprehensible inasmuch as its purpose is 'to show fact'. Yet he also expressed concern about using images among the uneducated. When he preaches about Christ's crucifixion to literate audiences, such as seminary students, pictures of the crucifixion are helpful because his audience is 'touched by the image'. But when he teaches neophytes to pray, he does not distribute pictures nor does he show them an image to take home to pray under. Instead, he attempts 'to place the image in their mind of praying to the Christ crucified for them'.

Others were much less anxious about images being misused or misunderstood among the laity. A layman in Hossana, though he regarded images as more useful for teaching Sunday school than in adult worship services, affirmed the presence of images in churches. He noted that teachers in Sunday schools teach with pictures, showing children how to praise God and how to recognize creation as God's work.[11] Several people indicated that images were used in the celebration of major days in the liturgical and secular calendar such as Christmas, Easter, New Year's Day and other holidays.[12] The children's Christmas drama in several congregations involved the temporary placement of a mural of Mary and the infant Christ or a scene of the nativity in the narthex or sanctuary, as in the large mural shown in Figure 7.2 from the original mission church in Nekemte. Images of the nativity certainly recall the visual piety of Northern European Lutheranism, which has always been fond of Christmas imagery of the infant Christ and the tender attention of Mary for the newborn. It is also possible that the strictly temporary use of such Marian imagery may be due to the prominence of Marian imagery in Ethiopian Orthodoxy. One evangelist observed that 'evangelists and preachers like images because of the [Orthodox] background of the people', and that illustrations were especially popular 'on Christmas, Easter, and holidays'.[13] If this is true, it may be that clergy and teachers seek to restrict the use of images of Mary out of fear that excessive use may reinstall the iconic function of images among former Orthodox members of Protestant congregations. Yet the Lutherans benefit from the residual appeal of images as powerful ways of celebrating major holidays.

The meanings of images are not easy to control. The very power of the image to fix attention may lead to an unintended response. A seminary staff person trained for audiovisual ministry and currently working in Hossana acknowledged the ability of images to hold the attention of an audience, but considered audiovisual media 'the best way to communicate the gospel with our people'.[14] Why this is so might be inferred from a subsequent interview with him in which he told of taping a presentation made by an emotional German evangelist with a healing ministry in 1995 in Awasa. The staff person taped the presentation, edited it, mixed music with it, and showed it to youth, who cried when they watched it. When the evangelist on tape shouted 'Hallelujah!' the youth raised their hands and cried out as if they were present at the event. 'They feel as if they are there because they are worshipping as if they were there.'[15] A European theology teacher and his wife, a nurse, on staff at a Christian college in Nekemte, related a similar account: 'If we show a video of the life of Jesus, the people think it was recorded while he was alive.'[16]

In these instances, the power of images to refer directly to their referents serves to manifest them, to make the past present. The status of the image as representation vanishes before the luminous presence of the referent, the great religious object of desire. Even among those who are fully cognizant of an image as a cultural

Figure 7.2   Teshale Zerhune, *The Nativity*, 1997, 6½ × 4 feet, Nekemte Congregation, Nekemte, Ethiopia.

Photo: David Morgan

construction, the image retains a moving ostensive power. It operates as a kind of corroboration of the message of the text. A clergyman and evangelist claimed that 'When we show [potential converts and new believers] images and pictures they understand the history of the Bible – they see it is *not* fiction, but history.'[17] The ostensive capacity of images is their ability to corroborate the text, to testify to its historicity, to evoke an empirical referentiality. A seminary instructor and clergyman at Hossana insisted that images of Jesus in the church building were not merely decoration, but allow believers to say: '*This* is Our Savior, Our Lord.' He reported that he had an image of Warner Sallman's *Head of Christ* (see Figure 7.1) displayed in his home and he was proud that his children 'know who he is'.[18] The image furnishes the opportunity to recognize and affirm Jesus publicly and in the home.

The power of images to point demonstratively to historical referents is not only a form of visual testament. Images are able to do more than show the person or event to which they refer; they can imbue it with feeling and establish a felt relationship between the referent and the viewer. A seminary president in Mekane Yesus, when asked why preachers and teachers would show an image of Jesus to those they teach, replied: 'To see and feel how it was. This [image] shows how the love of God was exhibited and [how it] saved us.'[19] According to this view, images add an emotional intensity to the experience of learning about Jesus and the Bible. Indeed, there is some evidence that the emotional resonance of images cultivates among some Ethiopian Lutherans a form of empathy familiar in Pietist traditions of Lutheranism in the United States and Europe. A pastor who worked as an evangelist and counselor in an enthusiastically charismatic Mekane Yesus congregation in a suburb of Addis articulated this view of the purpose of images in his experience. He reported that images of the crucified Jesus were placed in the church during Easter services in order to teach, but also 'to bring to mind, to [make people] think about how hard the crucifixion was – for people to put themselves in the place of Jesus'.[20] Images, he added, help his parishioners to imagine how Christ died. The didactic function of images was, therefore, overlaid with an empathetic, devotional one: imagining the death of Christ meant feeling the event and coming to understand its significance for one's own redemption.

Finally, there is the category of the image as an icon, which is often troublesome for Protestants inasmuch as they regard an icon as an idol or as tantamount to being one. Perhaps because the great majority of images in use among Ethiopian Protestants are mass-produced reproductions and simple illustrations in books, tracts and instructional materials, the anxiety about the icon *qua* idol was rather infrequent. A zealous evangelist in Nekemte objected to the Orthodox practice of bowing before icons and directing petitions to them. A seminary instructor in Hossana expressed concern about the danger of image worship among laity. And an evangelical missionary in Addis indicated that Protestants who come from an Orthodox background 'are often opposed to images because they are worshipped in the Orthodox Church'.[21] In every case that image worship was mentioned, it was associated with the Orthodox Church. No one associated image worship with traditional religion in Ethiopia, presumably because the traditional forms of belief there have not involved the use of images.

Image and Identity

Yet this attitude was exceptional and the negative association of images with Orthodoxy or Catholicism was only the sentiment of some church workers living or trained in Addis, where competition with Orthodoxy is far more keen than in the south or west. In the highlands, Mekane Yesus draws much of its membership from Orthodox converts. There is also a history of association between the Orthodox Church and the government, which, from the late 1970s through the 1980s, had been on poor terms with Mekane Yesus. Most of the imagery we saw in Mekane Yesus churches had been placed there since 1991, when the oppressive Marxist regime known as the Derg ('Committee') fell.[22] Having discouraged the practice of Protestantism for many years, the Derg had extended its attack even to the images used by Protestants. A pastor in Addis recalled that the Marxists confiscated 'images of Jesus and told the people that the foreigners [that is, missionaries] were fooling you with a Jesus who is a foreigner, and not an African'.[23] But near the end of its tenure, the Derg relaxed its policy of prohibiting Protestant worship. Protestant church growth flourished, particularly after the demise of the government in 1991. In celebration of the new religious freedom that came with the regime's defeat, many members of Mekane Yesus throughout the south and west of the country presented gift images to their congregations. The degree of freedom that Ethiopian Protestants felt in the wake of the Derg is also proudly announced in the common southern practice of painting the exterior of one's home. The guesthouse of a Mekane Yesus member near the southern town of Jajura displayed a painting of the Virgin and Child on the exterior (Figure 7.3) and a number of biblical images on the circular wall of the house's interior, including Samson and Delilah and the crucifixion, along with New Testament texts and allegorical imagery taken from the texts.

Several church officials in Addis registered their concern over use of images of angels or Mary, the two subjects of greatest devotion in Orthodox visual piety. A religious publisher in Addis, whose firm caters to many Protestant organizations, recalled that a Mekane Yesus official objected to a book on evangelism produced by the publisher's firm because of the Orthodox cross that appeared on the book's cover.[24] The director of the publishing arm of the Mekane Yesus proudly pointed to the range of images used in church publications, but indicated that carved imagery was associated with the Orthodox Church.[25] A clergyman on staff at church headquarters in Addis suggested that audiovisual media were reliable media for conveying information, but that icons were linked to the veneration of saints, which was not prescribed by the Mekane Yesus constitution, which stresses the Protestant ideal of *sola scriptura*, the view that Holy Scripture is the only source of teaching and doctrine. Meditating on images, he maintained, was opposed to the christological

Figure 7.3   *Virgin and Child*, 1999, painted on exterior of guest house near
                 Jajura, Ethiopia.

Photo: David Morgan

emphasis of Mekane Yesus. The use of icons, he warned, would 'lead to Orthodoxy', would fail to mark the 'big difference' between Mekane Yesus and Orthodoxy.[26]

Since the historical strength of Ethiopian Orthodoxy is in the northern half of the country, we were especially interested to note variations in thought and practice as we moved west and south into the lowlands, where Mekane Yesus enjoys its greatest numerical strength. In provincial churches images were quite common, gifts that were either purchased in the marketplace or hand-produced after models in circulation. The further we traveled from Addis the less concern we encountered about the visual signifiers of Orthodoxy. Indeed, by the time we reached the far west, Mekane Yesus congregations felt entirely free to incorporate Orthodox crosses into worship, as in the altar in a large congregation in Aira (Figure 7.4). In Nekemte, images proliferated in the stone church built after the turn of the century by Scandinavian Lutheran missionaries, where our conversation with the zealous evangelist took place. He was the only person in Ethiopia to mention Catholicism as a negative association with Protestant piety. Among the nine separate images displayed in this church was the Sacred Heart of Jesus placed above and behind the pulpit (Figure 7.5). This was at first surprising to find in a Lutheran church. But Roman Catholicism enjoys little presence throughout major parts of Ethiopia, so it is not at all unusual that Lutheran homes and churches displayed this image. In fact, another version of the Sacred Heart hung in the living room of the president of the Lutheran seminary in Addis Ababa. When asked what it meant, he provided a very articulate reading of the heart as the emblem of Christ's compassion and the theology of grace that is central to Lutheran doctrine. Likewise, when asked to explain the significance of the Sacred Heart above the pulpit in the Nekemte church, the evangelist indicated that it 'shows the love of Jesus'.

Certainly the inexpensive images used among the Protestants of Ethiopia pale as aesthetic artifacts in comparison with the artistic accomplishment, venerable age, and liturgical richness of Orthodox Ethiopian art. Yet, though they may appear at first glance to offer little interest to the scholar, careful scrutiny of the visual practices in which Protestants employ imagery demonstrates that even the most ephemeral images participate in the everyday worlds of belief. The frail paper illustrations and mass-produced portraits of Jesus that circulate in villages and cities across the nation are a prosaic, but revealing part of a dynamic church body whose members are realizing new forms of worship and evangelism every day and finding use for imagery as the church enters a new age.

Notes

1   As Alain Besançon has pointed out, the rhetorical understanding of the image is also a generally western Christian view, evident in the Latin Middle Ages and inherited by the Protestant Reformation (Besançon, 2000, p. 150). It is also a view that has been reinforced in the modern day by the Second Vatican Council (Gamboni, 1997), pp. 250–54.

Mediated Christianity

**Figure 7.4   Orthodox Ethiopian cross on altar of Lutheran church, 1999,
           Aira.**

Photo: David Morgan

Figure 7.5   *Sacred Heart of Jesus*, **pulpit, 1999, Lutheran church, Nekemte.**

Photo: David Morgan

2   From 1988 to 1998, Mekane Yesus experienced a 193 percent growth rate (from 776,673 to 2,274,200) in spite of the manifold harsh conditions mentioned above in one of the most impoverished of developing countries (statistics from the Evangelical Lutheran Church in America, Appendix 3, p. 2). Professor Charles Schaefer and I spent three weeks in May 1999 interviewing several dozen church leaders and staff, teachers, evangelists, clergy, business persons, missionaries and laity in numerous cities and villages in central, southern and western Ethiopia. All of the thirty-two structured interviews (and several additional informal conversations) were conducted in English. On Mekane Yesus, see Bakke (1987) and Arén (1978).

3   While in Addis we also visited SIM, the Society for International Ministries (originally Sudan Interior Mission), an evangelical organization, examining its publications and meeting with some faculty, staff and the organization's president. And we visited congregations of the Mulla Wengel, the growing Pentecostal organization in Addis and elsewhere in Ethiopia. On SIM, see Donham (1999), pp. 82–121. On the charismatic movement, see Fargher (1988), pp. 349–50.

4   Interview 18, Synodical president, Ethiopian Evangelical Church Mekane Yesus (EECMY), 21 May 1999.

5   Interview 17, Educational missionary, Society for International Ministries (SIM), Addis, 20 May 1999.

6   Interview 15, ECCMY director of evangelism, southern synod, 18 May 1999.

7   Interview 17, 20 May 1999.

8   Interview 15, 18 May 1999.

9   Engel (1988), pp. 17–18. Engel's book is used at the Mekane Yesus Seminary in Addis in tandem with (as well as cited in) Jørgensen's *Communication Means People*.

10   Interview 12, clergyman and seminary instructor, EECMY Seminary, Hossana, 15 May 1999.

11   Interview 12, 12 May 1999.

12   Interviews 5, evangelistic pastor, suburban EECMY congregation, Addis, 12 May 1999; 16, ECCMY clergyman, Awasa, 18 May 1999; and 24, teacher and nurse, Christian Education College, Nekemte, 24 May 1999.

13   Interview 23, lay church member, Markofa preaching station, Didessa Valley, 23 May 1999.

14   Interview 12, 15 May 1999.

15   Interview 13, technician and teacher, ECCMY Seminary, Hossana, 17 May 1999.

16   Interview 24, 24 May 1999.

17   Interview 15, 18 May 1999. Emphasis in original.

18   Interview 12, 15 May 1999. Sallman's picture of Jesus was widely recognized and explicitly cited by several of our informants (interviews 2, 12, 16, 17, 19, 29 and 32).

19   Interview 18, 21 May 1999.

20   Interview 5, 12 May 1999. For a discussion of empathy and its role in Protestant visual piety, see Morgan (1998), pp. 59–96.

21   Interviews 19, ECCMY evangelist, Nekemte, 22 May 1999; 12 and 17.

22   On the history of the revolution and the relationship between the Derg and Mekane Yesus, see Eide (1996).

23   Interview 30, ECCMY clergyman, church headquarters, Addis, 26 May 1999.

24   Interview 26, private religious publisher, Addis, 26 May 1999.

25   Interview 1, director, Yemsirach Dimts ('Voice of the Word of God'), 10 May 1999.

26   Interview 2, ECCMY official, church headquarters, Addis, 11 May 1999.

References

Arén, G. (1978), *Evangelical Pioneers in Ethiopia: Origins of the Evangelical Church Mekane Yesus*, Stockholm: EFS and Addis Ababa: Mekane Yesus.

Bakke, J. (1987), *Christian Ministry: Patterns and Functions within the Ethiopian Evangelical Church Mekane Yesus*, Oslo: Solum Forlag A.S.; and Atlantic Highlands, NY: Humanities Press.

Besançon, A. (2000), *The Forbidden Image: An Intellectual History of Iconoclasm*, trans. J. M. Todd, Chicago: University of Chicago Press.

Donham, D. L. (1999), *Marxist Modern: An Ethnographic History of the Ethiopian Revolution*, Berkeley, CA: University of California Press.

Eide, Ø. M. (1996), *Revolution and Religion in Ethiopia: A Study of Church and Politics with Special Reference to the Ethiopian Evangelical Church Mekane Yesus 1974–1985*, Studiea Missionalie Upsaliensia, no. 66, Stavanger: Misjonshøgskolens Forlag and Uppsala Universitet.

Engel, J. F. (1988), *How to Communicate the Gospel Effectively*, Achimota, Ghana: Africa Christian Press.

Evangelical Lutheran Church in America (1998), Board of the Division for Global Mission (March 20–22) Appendix 3, page 2, 'Membership Statistics of Companion Churches'.

Fargher, B. L. (1988), 'The Charismatic Movement in Ethiopia, 1960–1980', *Evangelical Review of Theology* (12), 344–58.

Gamboni, D. (1997), *The Destruction of Art: Iconoclasm and Vandalism since the French Revolution*, New Haven, CT: Yale University Press.

Jørgensen, K. (1995), *Communication Means People: Manual on Communication in Society and Church*, Addis Ababa: Mekane Yesus Seminary.

Morgan, D. (2001), 'For Christ and the Republic: Protestant Illustration and the History of Literacy in Nineteenth-Century America', in D. Morgan and S. M. Promey (eds), *The Visual Culture of American Religions*, Berkeley, CA: University of California Press, pp. 49–67.

Morgan, D. (1999), *Protestants and Pictures: Religion, Visual Culture, and the Age of American Mass Production*, New York: Oxford University Press.

Morgan, D. (1998), *Visual Piety: A History and Theory of Popular Religious Images*, Berkeley, CA: University of California Press.

Scribner, R. W. (1994), *For the Sake of Simple Folk: Popular Propaganda for the German Reformation*, Oxford: Clarendon Press.

Additional Resources

Banks, M. (2001), *Visual Methods in Social Research*, London: Sage. Written by a leading British figure in visual anthropology, this book is a fine introduction to research methodology.

Barnard, M. (2001), *Approaches to Understanding Visual Culture*, New York: Palgrave. A readable introduction to the subject of visual culture, which includes different interpretative models, but no mention of religion.

Drury, J. (1999), *Painting the Word: Christian Pictures and Their Meanings,* New Haven, CT: Yale University Press. An accessibly written study of Christian painting from the fourteenth to the seventeenth century that incorporates theological reflection with careful visual analysis.

Freedberg, D. (1989), *The Power of Images: Studies in the History and Theory of Response*, Chicago: University of Chicago Press. A sophisticated, pioneering book that argues for the importance of studying the fear and devotion to images that traditional art history has often ignored.

Morgan, D. (2005), *The Sacred Gaze: Religious Visual Culture in Theory and Practice*, Berkeley, CA: University of California Press. A study of images and visual practices in many world religions that seeks to show how visual evidence can assist scholars and students in their non-art historical study of religion.

Chapter 8

From Morality Tales to Horror Movies: Towards an Understanding of the Popularity of West African Video Film

Jolyon Mitchell

It is an unforgettable experience to sit in a packed cinema or video house in Accra and watch a locally produced Ghanaian or Nigerian video film. The audience is rarely entirely silent, and often actively cheers, boos or prays out loud for the characters.[1] This experience stands in sharp contrast with sitting in a western multiplex watching a Hollywood film, where the audience is usually almost entirely silent. The peace is occasionally disturbed by a cough, or the rustle of sweet wrappers or the crunch of popcorn. Any talking is normally 'shushed' and exclamations are rare, the exception being laughter during comic moments or screams at sudden surprises in horror movies or thrillers. The silencing of the Western audience is a fascinating story well told elsewhere.[2] Appearances, however, can be deceptive. As other chapters in this book demonstrate, this comparative silence does not mean that audiences are necessarily entirely passive.[3] Research by Hoover and Clark (2002), for example, illustrates how the opposite is in fact the case. Audiences actively weave complex patterns of meaning on the basis of the media that they consume. Nevertheless, precisely which films are viewed and the cultural context in which they are watched remains a significant element for understanding the complex triadic relationship between the spectator, the producer and the media text.

In this chapter I focus on these three components of West African video film: the audience, the film producer and films themselves. This is in order to investigate why these video films have displaced Hollywood productions that dominate in so many other parts of the world. Why have these locally produced video films become so popular? I will suggest that these films dominate the market in Ghana partly because they articulate local concerns and customs in highly realistic cinematic forms. More precisely, the popularity of these video films is derived from the fact that they often make concrete and visible the hidden forces of evil that are perceived as lurking behind the modern urban life of cities such as Accra. These feature-length films are eclectic, drawing upon a range of cinematic and theatrical traditions: from local street drama to Hollywood action movies. They have evolved considerably over the last decade. In the 1990s the majority of these films focused primarily either on the family (exploring themes such as faithfulness between marriage partners, loyalty between parents, children, siblings or the extended family), or the quest for money and power in relation to the occult.[4] These are morality tales that are invariably played out against the backdrop of spiritual warfare. Sometimes films show how the family can be shattered by involvement in the occult. Initially, the vast majority of Ghanaian video films lacked the suspense or explicit violence embodied in western horror movies, but with the increased popularity of more violent Nigerian and jointly produced Ghanaian–Nigerian films, the local film industry in Ghana in the late 1990s has evolved into producing and marketing movies that have closer parallels with the horror genre (Figure 8.1).

Elsewhere I have identified a range of conversations currently taking place in the emerging field of religion and media.[5] By focusing upon these highly popular and religious video films in Ghana and Nigeria, and in particular the emerging horror element, this chapter contributes to a number of these ongoing discussions. This unique phenomenon in West Africa merits close attention, and is also pertinent to research into the relationship between religion and film.

Ignoring and Interpreting Horror

Recently there has been a rapid increase in the amount of writing produced on religion, theology and film (for example Mitchell and Marriage, 2003; Johnston, 2000; Jewett, 1999; Marsh and Ortiz, 1997; May, 1997; Baugh, 1997; Miles, 1996; Martin and Ostwalt, 1995).[6] The conversation to date has primarily focused on western films, ignoring both Bollywood and the burgeoning video film industry in Ghana and Nigeria. Given the frequent appearance of religious symbols and imagery in horror films, it is also surprising to discover that in nearly all the recent books on religion and film there is remarkably little mention of horror. A few exceptions stand out, notably Zwick's discussion of 'The Problem of Evil in Contemporary Film' (Zwick, 1997, pp. 72–91). Zwick suggests that the divide between good and evil has become more ambiguous in recent Hollywood films. As we shall see later this is definitely not the case in the vast majority of Ghanaian and Nigerian video films. More recently Kreitzer's analysis of *Dracula* in *Pauline Images in Fiction and Film* (1999) represents a more text-based approach. He focuses first on the Lord's Supper in Paul's thought, and then analyzes communion imagery in both Bram Stoker's novel *Dracula* (1897) and some film adaptations of *Dracula*. Imaginative as this approach is, it does not encompass an in-depth analysis of why horror films exert such a strong hold over many viewers' imaginations.

'Why would anyone ever be interested in horror, since being horrified is so unpleasant?' This is the question that Noël Carroll considers from a range of perspectives in *The Philosophy of Horror* (1990). He suggests that audiences find watching horror in the safety of the cinema or the comfort of their own homes both

Figure 8.1   Video shop in Ghana.

Photo: Stewart M. Hoover

pleasurable and fascinating. Seeing what happens to characters can satisfy curiosity, while also appealing to sympathetic inclinations towards the victim. Like many other recent writers working on understanding horror (for example Wells, 2000), Carroll does not seek to tackle in depth the appeal of the religious dimension found at the heart of many horror narratives. Instead, he asks: 'How can anyone be frightened by what they know does not exist?' One answer is that the effects overwhelm audiences; another is that viewers suspend their disbelief for the duration of the performance. While these and other sets of answers provide valuable insights into understanding horror, I will demonstrate how the questions themselves are open to criticism in the light of Anglophone West African video film.

Understanding the New Wave of West African Popular Video Films

The year 2001 saw over 600 video films produced in Nigeria and nearly 100 in Ghana. The number has increased every year for the last ten years. In 2002, however, most productions in Nigeria ceased for several months. This 'recess' was an attempt to bring order to a market that was becoming saturated with new productions.[7] This was only a brief pause in the production of local films. Given that 'Anglophone Africa remains far behind francophone in the production of feature films' (Magombe, 1996, p. 670), these video films represent a vital new development in film production in Anglophone Africa. With a lack of investment and scant resources for creating indigenous African films, American films have dominated the cinemas of Ghana and Nigeria until the last few years. 'With the advent of video', Nigerian film historian Frank Ukadike suggests, 'Ghana has been able to cultivate an indigenous film and video culture' (Ukadike, 1998, p. 570).

William K. Akuffo has produced over thirty films in Ghana, and is one of the leaders of the new video movement there. He was originally a cinema projectionist who approached various film-makers with the suggestion that they should use video rather than celluloid for film production. In spite of being a vastly cheaper alternative, this idea was rejected, so he decided to work on his own. In the early 1990s, he purchased a VHS camera and made his first film *Zinabu* independently, editing on two video machines. No one would purchase this video film so he rented a cinema house, Globe Cinema in Accra, and advertised the video as a Ghanaian film. He assumed that most people had a bias against video at that time. So for the première he camouflaged the bulky video machine and put it right in front of the film projector so that nobody would actually know where the pictures were coming from. When they started showing the film Akuffo admits: 'I was quite scared because I didn't know how people were going to receive it because of how the professionals were going about it, and to my surprise they [the audience] clapped, they laughed and everything' (Interview, William K. Akuffo, Accra, Ghana, 21–27 May 2000).

The popularity of locally produced video films is clear even after a brief walk through the streets of Accra. These videos are sold not only in video shops and general stores, but also off the back of carts and from stands in the city's markets. Locally produced videos, not the Hollywood films, tend to dominate the shelves. Franklin Kennedy-Ukah has spent several years researching these video films in Nigeria. He points out that there are also video cafés, which become the location for vigorous discussions provoked by the films.

> Often we come together and watch some of these tapes. People, especially young people, discuss these videotapes in groups. Even on [Nigerian] university campuses we have little video cafés, we have group video viewing sessions on campus and each week about four, five sessions are held in the university where young people come together; friends come together to watch these videos. It goes to show how tremendously popular, how tremendously important the people think this aspect, this sphere of popular culture is (Interview, Franklin Kennedy-Ukah, Accra, Ghana, 21–27 May 2000).

It is interesting to note how audiences use these films. The sheer ubiquity of video houses and video outlets in Accra and Lagos illustrate that it is by no means only in universities that they provoke discussion. Local people now watch many of these films on television, and sometimes even in churches. Increasingly, films are watched and discussed at home, in front of the VCR. But what aspect of these films generates the liveliest discussions?

Demonizing, Marginalizing and Exemplifying Religious Figures

One of the most common areas of debate is the portrayal of religious figures in many of these video films. Traditional African religious leaders are frequently caricatured, stereotyped or even demonized. They can be the cause of sickness, violence or death. In short, they are the catalysts or agents of horror. They are sometimes portrayed as having direct links with actual spirits, who in turn are depicted as having real power. In the Ghanaian film *Namisha* (Akwetey-Kanyi Productions, 1999), the protagonist Slobo exerts terrible revenge on those who have stolen his wife and were responsible for the death of his two daughters. He uses Namisha, one of the spirits beholden to the earth spirit Abadzen, to seduce his enemies and then brutally murder them. Ministers from the historic mission churches (such as the Methodists, the Presbyterians or the Anglicans), on the other hand, are often represented as well intentioned but ultimately ineffectual and marginal to the outcome of the story. They neither contribute to nor counter the horror. Pastors from the independent Pentecostal or charismatic churches, by contrast, are typically portrayed as dynamic and spiritually powerful. They often use the accoutrements of power, such as mobile phones or computers, alongside a large black leather-covered Bible. Frequently, it is they who overcome or at least help to overcome the evil forces which let loose the agents of horror. At times, the three-way dynamic is simplified to a sharply defined two-way conflict. Africanus Aveh teaches film and video at the University of Ghana in Accra and believes that:

In most of the videos we see the Christian pastor is always neatly dressed in a suit or in a white cassock. He is always a peace-broker who is welcome in every home, who mends broken marriages, who will be consulted and bring life through counselling, etc, etc. But on the other hand you see the African traditional priest being portrayed as a killer, being portrayed as a fraud, being portrayed as a liar who kills for a fee, who helps people achieve all their evil and demonic intentions. For example, if you are a young lady and you see a man that you like and the man is already married, it is portrayed that these young ladies consult the African traditional priest and then he is able to help them snatch legitimate husbands from other women. (Interview, Africans Aveh, Accra, Ghana, 21–27 May 2000).

At other moments the battles between the faiths are more explicitly represented. In the final scene of the Nigerian film *Magic Money*, for example, the Christian pastor and African traditional priest call, even shout, for the help of their respective Gods. They both dance on the spot and gesticulate aggressively, but the traditional priest is literally laid low, overwhelmed by the more powerful force called upon by the Christian pastor.

This literalistic battle scene is taken a step further in *Namisha* where one character commits his life to the elemental spirit Obadzen. He has a secret room to which he adjourns to pray to this spirit. She declines to assist him. So he tries to use his own power. In a scene reminiscent of a science fiction movie, he hurls curses out from his room; with them go superimposed circles of light thrown towards his opponents in the sitting room. They are accompanied by echoing sound effects. The pastor, who has been praying with three women associates, is knocked down and lands back on the sofa. The praying in tongues does not abate; if anything it continues more vigorously. The pastor recovers and this time rays of light burst from him and the three women, and knock out their opponent. This scene is more comic than horrific, with some audiences in Ghana laughing out loud at the weakness of the traditional religionist enacted in this sequence. Intentional and unintentional comic episodes balance moments of suspense, surprise and horror. Only later when Namisha murders her unfortunate victims or turns into a black raven to escape her pursuers is there anything redolent of the more traditional forms of the horror film. Nevertheless, it is clear from the scene described above that the forces are portrayed semi-realistically and that the stronger force is to be found with the prayerful Christians.

These and other similar portrayals provoke fierce criticism from a number of local commentators. Elom Dovlo is head of the religion department at the University of Ghana in Accra:

I think the films should be more authentic in reflecting traditional culture and should be geared more towards how there could be interaction between Christianity and traditional culture, rather than be geared towards condemnation of that culture and the people who follow it. [At present it] simply causes tension within the society (Interview, Elom Dovlo, Accra, Ghana, 21–27 May 2000).

This tension has its roots in Ghana and Nigeria's colonial past, where traditional religion was perceived in particularly negative, even horrific terms.

Historical awareness leads some commentators to be deeply suspicious of these video film portrayals. Elizabeth Amoah teaches at the University of Ghana in Accra:

> For me, it's the content and the images and the impact of these on the audience that I am more concerned about, because there are some of these home-made videos that are very violent, that are very negative to some religious traditions, that are very controversial. This has a long history and it's part of our colonial and missionary history, because if you read how Islam and Christianity came to Africa – these two major religions, because of where they are coming from and their ideology behind their coming, portrayed the indigenous beliefs very negatively. (Interview, Elizabeth Amoah, Accra, Ghana, 21–27 May 2000)

Up to this stage in the discussion a number of points have emerged. First, horror is largely ignored in many studies on religion and film. This is unfortunate, as it is a rich seam ripe for exploration. Second, Ghanaian and Nigerian video films have provided an alternative source of entertainment to Hollywood films. In many shops and most video cafés, particularly in Ghana, they have actually displaced Hollywood films as the most popular item for viewing. They offer a rare example of a local industry that, whilst lacking extensive production and post-production facilities and budgets, nevertheless resists the domination that Hollywood exerts in many parts of the world. Third, one regular criticism of these films is the negative stereotyping of traditional African religious figures and the positive stereotyping of Christian leaders. Given these observations and criticisms, and given the lack of technical sophistication, why is it that many of these films are so popular in Ghana and Nigeria?

Explaining the Popularity of Ghanaian and Nigerian Video Films

'Prior to being sold as a video cassette for home viewing, a popular movie can easily be seen by tens of thousands of people in Accra's cinemas in the center and suburbs and become the talk of the town. Often its story is "broadcast" through mobile people such as taxi drivers, street vendors, and traders in Makola market' (Meyer, 2001). The popularity of these video films can be explained from several different perspectives. One of the most persuasive explanations concentrates upon the belief systems that they embody. Many of these films reflect dominant popular beliefs, in particular a belief in the reality of evil powers. From studying particular films and listening to audience responses it is clear that many of these videos are popular because they enact, in highly realistic forms, the horror that evil forces can bring and their ultimate demise in the face of the Christian God.

This understanding challenges the basis of Carroll's question cited earlier, 'How can anyone be frightened by what they know does not exist?' On the basis of several local interviews, it is clear that many Nigerian and Ghanaian viewers believe that evil spirits, evil characters and evil powers really do exist, and are indeed responsible for bringing about horror and tragedy in people's lives. Given this belief system, cinematic portrayals may be seen as fictionalized accounts of reality. These portrayals thus reflect common beliefs, common concerns and common anxieties. In the video-film houses of Accra it is common to find audiences applauding and cheering as the Christian character vanquishes the apparently evil witchdoctor or traditional religionist. Another research project would be required to analyze the extent to which the audiences recognize these scenes as genuinely reflecting everyday concerns, practices and experiences of faith, and how this might vary in different parts of Ghana and Nigeria.

Nonetheless, it is valuable to highlight the 'realistic' way in which themes are enacted in these films. For example, consider one scene from *Time* (Miracle Films, D'Joh Mediacraft and Igo Films, 2000) one of the first jointly produced Ghanaian and Nigerian films. In it one of the key characters has kept the corpse of his wife in his wardrobe in their bedroom (Figure 8.2). He is following the advice of the traditional healer who had told him that if he does this, she will provide him with all the money that he needs. In the scene under consideration, his son nervously enters the room, crosses himself and then opens the cupboard door. He is shocked by the sight of the body of his dead mother and falls back on the bed in horror. The following shots include an image of the corpse essentially vomiting money. There are actual bank notes coming out of its mouth. When I saw this in central Accra, there were gasps of shock from the audience. These became louder as the father bludgeons the boy to death with a baseball bat for uncovering the corpse.

Recent Hollywood horror movies have tended towards more graphic, realistic and gruesome scenes (see the *Nightmare on Elm Street* and *Friday the 13th* films in the 1980s or the *Scream* films in the 1990s). It is interesting to note how a film such as the *Blair Witch Project* (1999) represents a return to a more allusive style that suggests horror to the imagination of the viewer rather than explicitly showing it. *Time*, like several other recent Ghanaian and Nigerian films, belongs to the more explicit category of horror films. It is hard, for example, to forget the scene of a pregnant woman being murdered and then having her baby cut from her womb to be used in a sacrifice to the ancestral gods. To borrow Kristeva's concept, the 'abjection' of the baby and surrounding fluid, and the 'abject' nature of the corpse and the money in the scene described above, places *Time* firmly with some of the most explicit horror films made in Hollywood, (Kristeva, 1982).

Seeing Video Films as Moral Parables

My argument up to this point is that many of these locally produced video films are popular not because they borrow elements of the horror genre from Hollywood, but

Figure 8.2 *Time* video cover.

Photo: Jolyon Mitchell

partly because they 'give expression to local issues' and 'local perspectives' in highly realistic forms. As anthropologist Birgit Meyer suggests, some films, such as the extremely popular Nigerian produced film *Blood Money* (OJ Production, 1997), articulate popular anxiety in Ghana about the trade of body parts for ritual sacrifice in Nigeria and Ghana (Meyer, 2002). The popularity of many of these videos is clearly a complex phenomenon. It is worth noticing the resonance in some of the films, especially those produced in Nigeria, with traditional Hausa and Yoruba theatrical melodramatic genres, as well as their cultural appropriateness in terms of geographic and social space. In other words, viewers will recognize settings, customs and dramatic genres as their own, rather than as located in a foreign sphere seen only through Hollywood's lens.

This ensures that these films can, in the words of Seth Ashong-Katai, one of Ghana's most experienced producers, continue to act as 'moral parables'. Embedded in many of their narratives are warnings about the dangers of money, ambition or unfaithfulness. According to Birgit Meyer, 'many women in fact want their husbands or boyfriends to come along and watch the latest Ghanaian movie in order to see that bad or morally unacceptable behavior really will lead into all sorts of disasters. So these men should learn that it is better not to take a girlfriend out and drink, squander money and so on. So for women they are really moralizing and educating devices' (Interview, Birgit Meyer, Accra, Ghana, 21–27 May). As morality tales these films therefore play a vital social role, and are used by many women as a way of showing their partners the right way of living. There is a sense in which some films are Ghanaian or Nigerian versions of *Faust* where the protagonist sells his, and it normally is 'his', soul for immediate benefits. The wages of such a contract are often a horrific end or, if he's more fortunate, a painful conversion. Thus horror, though not in the traditional horror genre sense, bolsters the current moral order and shows how people should live. Invariably there is a moral conclusion where good, normally inextricably connected with Christianity, is victorious.

In interviews a number of the producers and directors made it clear that many are not creating film for proselytizing or pastoral purposes. Another one of Ghana's most prolific directors and producers, William Akuffo, confided that his thirty films:

> don't reflect my beliefs at all. They've got nothing to do with my beliefs because to start with I don't believe in all the Christianity crap that is going around me, although I don't believe in this Africanian thing so ... I am not an atheist; but I believe there should be a supreme being somewhere but since I haven't seen him, I don't bother myself very much about him. I don't think my films reflect what I think at all. (Interview, William K. Akuffo, Accra, Ghana, 21–27 May 2000)

For Akuffo the bottom line of making films is to appeal to large numbers of Ghanaians and make himself rich. This is his stated objective. He recognizes that the majority of his potential audiences are Christian and he makes his films accordingly. Horror represents a small, but significant element of his expanding repertoire. In Nigeria targeting films appropriately is more complex as film-makers face an audience composed of Christians and Moslems. Many make video films with one particular faith group, or even sub-group, in mind. Moreover, as the anthropologist Brian Larkin points out, 'there's a tension in Northern Nigeria between local, Hausa-produced videos and Lagos-based videos. For Hausa film-makers, they couldn't possibly, nor would they necessarily want to, get away with certain sorts of licentious activity that goes on in Lagos videos' (Interview, Brian Larkin, Accra, Ghana, 21–27 May 2000). Thus audiences exert a significant influence over the practice of film-makers, often encouraging a moralistic and Christian approach to cinematic story-telling.

Horror in the West African context is far from 'unpleasant' (see Carroll, 1990). In fact as a component of these recent celluloid moral parables, it offers viewers a counterpoint to resist, celebrate with and even laugh at. Few Ghanaian or Nigerian video films conclude like David Fincher's *Se7en* (1995), with no sense of 'redemption from its apocalyptic tale of fundamentalist obsession' (Wells, 2000, p. 108). As post-colonial productions the majority of these films are both hopeful and problematic: hopeful in that they provide an example of a burgeoning local film industry, and one that is resisting the dominance of Hollywood; problematic in the ways they represent diverse religious traditions, and problematic in another sense, in that even the more recent films do not fit easily into the western horror genre. Some claim to be horror films on the back of the video boxes, but employ a whole range of tropes and styles to develop their narratives. Music and action reminiscent of 'Keystone cop' chase scenes can be juxtaposed in the same film with piercing electronic screeches and moments of suspense. This is not horror in the usual sense, nor is it satirizing horror, rather it often draws upon horror as one among a whole palette of colors used to create pictures that are memorable and popular with the audience.

Conclusion

I have suggested that there are many explanations for the popularity of these video films in Ghana and Nigeria. Their ability to adapt to the market and to develop new themes and approaches partly accounts for their continued popularity. There is a sense in which these film-makers are creating a new genre, which breaks open traditional understandings of the horror genre or action genre. It is a genre which has its roots firmly fixed in West African cultural soil, but still bears fruit in a surprisingly diverse fashion. Several movie-makers have moved beyond producing the simple family drama or occult spectacle to more eclectic and violent representations. The horror element in various recent films is but one aspect of these movies. Unlike many Hollywood horror films, the horror is not an end in itself.

The elements of horror in these films can be seen as cultural artifacts that provide valuable insight into the moral landscape, the anxieties and the questions commonly found in Ghana and Nigeria. For example, how do the beliefs of the village-dweller change when they come into contact with the city? Does or should such a shift inevitably lead to a violent abandonment of traditional beliefs and practices? Why does Pentecostal–charismatic Christianity have such a tremendous appeal? How do charismatic Christians relate to other Christian, Islamic and African traditional groups? How can these religious groups coexist when they all have competing claims to the soul of both countries? Alongside these issues the local video film phenomenon is itself evolving. New sets of questions are raised, such as: why is there now in Ghana a strong preference for Nigerian films, and why are Ghanaian producers struggling to meet their own production costs? How far is the reception of these films influenced by the social spaces in which they are watched? Given the extent of the video film phenomenon in Ghana and Nigeria, these and other related questions deserve further investigation.

Notes

1   I am indebted to Birgit Meyer, Rosalind Hackett and the International Study Commission on Media, Religion and Culture for providing the opportunity to experience this first hand in Accra, Ghana. I am particularly grateful to Birgit Meyer, who has shared many of her insights from extensive research into this phenomenon. She suggests in her article on 'Popular Ghanaian Cinema in the Fourth Republic' that watching a film in such a corporate and active way 'triggers moral engagement, and one of the satisfactions audiences get from this is the temporal feeling of moral superiority, of being on the good side, while at the same time being able to peep voyeuristically at the powers of darkness'. Birgit Meyer is senior lecturer at the Research Centre Religion and Society, Department of Anthropology, University of Amsterdam. (Website: http://www.pscw.uva.nl/media-religion). I am also indebted to Brian Larkin for generously sharing his insights about Nigerian video culture.

2   See Levine (1988).

3   Audience studies has a long, complex history. For a brief summary see McQuail (1997).

4   See Birgit Meyer's insightful article (2002) for a more extensive discussion of these themes, including a helpful discussion of the move beyond family and occult dramas in Ghana.

5   See Mitchell and Marriage (2003). In the final chapter of the book, 'Emerging Conversations in Media, Religion and Culture', I set out seven areas of developing concern: the participative turn, the narration of identity, the multi-religious perspective, the quest for communicative justice, the historical perspective, the transformation of religious and theological reflection and the ethics of the audience. I argue on this basis that developing a single coherent methodology is premature if not impossible.

6   See Steve Nolan's extensive annotated bibliography on religion and film in Mitchell and Marriage (2003).

7   See Steinglass (2002).

References

Baugh, L. (1997), *Imaging the Divine: Jesus and Christ-Figures in Film*, Kansas City: Sheed & Ward.

Carroll, N. (1990), *The Philosophy of Horror, or, Paradoxes of the Heart*, London and New York: Routledge.

Hoover, S. M. and L. S. Clark (eds) (2002), *Practicing Religion in an Age of Media*, New York: Columbia University Press.

Jewett, R. (1999), *Saint Paul Returns to the Movies: Triumph over Shame*, Grand Rapids, MI: William B. Eerdmans.

Johnston, R. (2000), *Reel Spirituality: Theology and Film in Dialogue*, Grand Rapids, MI: Baker Academic.

Kreitzer, L. J. (1999), *Pauline Images in Fiction and Film: On Reversing the Hermeneutical Flow*, Sheffield: Sheffield Academic Press.

Kristeva, J. (1982), *Powers of Horror: An Essay on Abjection*, New York: Columbia University Press.

Levine, L. W. (1988), *Highbrow/Lowbrow: The Emergence of Cultural Hierarchy in America*, London and Cambridge, MA: Harvard University Press.

Magombe, P. V. (1996), 'The Cinemas of Sub-Saharan Africa', in Geoffrey Nowell-Smith (ed.), *The Oxford History of World Cinema*, Oxford: Oxford University Press.

Marsh, C. and G. Ortiz (eds) (1997), *Explorations in Theology and Film*. Oxford: Blackwell Publishers.

Martin, J. W. and C. E. Ostwalt (eds) (1995), *Screening the Sacred: Religion, Myth, and Ideology in Popular American Film*, Boulder, CO: Westview Press.

May, J. (ed.) (1997), *New Image of Religious Film*, Kansas City: Sheed & Ward.

McQuail, D. (1997), *Audience Analysis*, Thousand Oaks, CA: and London: Sage.

Meyer, B. (2002), 'Prayers, Guns and Ritual Murder: Popular Cinema and Its New Figures of Power and Success', English translation of the French published text from *Politique Africaine*, **82**, 45–62. See: http://www2.fmg.uva.nl/media-religion/publications/prayers.htm.

Meyer, B. (2001), 'Money, Power and Morality: Popular Ghanaian Cinema in the Fourth Republic', *Ghana Studies*, **4**, 65–84.

Meyer, B. and P. Pels (eds) (2003), *Magic and Modernity:Dialectics of Revelation and Concealment*, Stanford, CA: Stanford University Press.

Miles, M. (1990), *Seeing and Believing: Religion and Values in the Movies*, Boston, MA: Beacon Press.

Mitchell, J. (2002), 'Western African Popular Video Film', *Omnibus*, radio documentary, BBC World Service, 28 May.

Mitchell, J. and S. Marriage (2003), *Mediating Religion: Conversations in Media, Religion and Culture*, London and New York: T&T Clark / Continuum.

Steinglass, M. (2002), 'When There's Too Much of a Not-Very-Good Thing', *The New York Times*, 26 May, Sunday, Late Edition, Final Section: Section 2, Page 16; Column 1.

Ukadike, N. F. (1998), 'Critical Approaches to World Cinema: African Cinema', in John Hill and Pamela Church Gibson (eds), *The Oxford Guide to Film Studies*, Oxford: Oxford University Press.

Wells, P. (2000), *The Horror Genre: From Beelzebub to Blair Witch*, London: Wallflower.

Zwick, R. (1997), 'The Problem of Evil in Contemporary Film' in John May (ed.), *New Image of Religious Film*, Kansas City: Sheed & Ward.

Additional resources

BBC World Service, 'Western African Popular Video Film', *Omnibus,* radio documentary
(producer and presenter, Jolyon Mitchell, 28 May 2002). This documentary provides a
lively account of the West African popular video film phenomenon. It includes comments
by Kwabena Asamoah-Gyadu, Stewart Hoover, Peter Horsfield, Patrick Larkin, Birgit
Meyer and many of the local film producers quoted in this article.

Gelder, K. (ed.)(2000), *The Horror Reader,* London and New York.

Ginsburg, F.D., L. Abu-Lughod and B. Larkin (eds) (2002), *Media Worlds: Anthropology on
New Terrain,* Berkeley, CA: University of California Press. This volume includes work
from the ethnography of media, a burgeoning new area in anthropology. Particularly
relevant to this article on West African film is Brian Larkin's 'The Materiality of Cinema
Theaters in Northern Nigeria'.

Larkin, B. (2002), 'The Materiality of Cinema Spaces in Northern Nigeria', in Faye
Ginsburg, Lila Abu-Lughod and Brian Larkin (eds), *Media Worlds: Anthropology on a
New Terrain,* Berkeley, CA: University of California Press.

Larkin, B. (2000), 'Hausa Dramas and the Rise of Video Culture in Nigeria', in Jonathan
Haynes (ed.), *Nigerian Video Film,* Athens, OH: Ohio University Press.

Meyer, B. (2002), 'Pentecostalism, Prosperity and Popular Cinema in Ghana', *Culture and
Religion,* **3** (1), 67–86; Meyer, B. and P. Pels (eds) (2003), *Magic and Modernity,
Dialectics of Revelation and Concealment,* Stanford, CA: Stanford University Press.
Birgit Meyer has produced ground-breaking research in the field of film and religion in
West Africa. These are two examples from her extensive published work in this area.
Details of her up-to-date research are to be found at http://www.pscw.uva.nl/media-
religion.

Mitchell, J. and S. Marriage (eds) (2003), *Mediating Religion: Conversations in Media,
Religion and Culture,* London: T&T Clark Continuum. This is a comprehensive range of
twenty-nine essays on media and religion, with four extensive annotated bibliographies.
The chapters and bibliography on film and religion are particularly useful background to
this article on the West African video film industry.

Mitchell, J. 'Film and Theology' (forthcoming), in David Ford (ed.), *The Modern
Theologians,* 3rd edn, Oxford: Blackwell. This essay explores the relationship between
film and Christian theology. It begins with a survey of the range of approaches to
theological criticism, then goes on to investigate examples of directorial theology. The
final section briefly situates West African video film in a wider discussion of audience
uses of the cinema.

Chapter 9

Religion and Meaning in the Digital Age: Field Research on Internet/Web Religion[1]

Stewart M. Hoover and Jin Kyu Park

Among the many speculations that have circulated about the nature and implications of the digital era has been a robust discourse about *religion* in the digital/online age. What seems to reside beneath this discourse is a deceptively simple question: 'How is the emergence of digital and online communication changing religion?' It goes almost without saying that to answer this question it is necessary to understand both *online* and *religion* better than most scholarship in either area has previously seemed to. It is our purpose here to explore this question through reference to both emerging scholarship on the net/web/online/digital world, and to ongoing fieldwork on religion and meaning-making in the media age.

A scholarship on media and religion is emerging around the notion that the natures of both 'religion' and 'the media' are undergoing change and are, in fact, converging in important ways (Hoover, 2001). Religion in the industrialized West is becoming increasingly an individual matter. Based on late-modern trends identified by Giddens (1991), modern consciousness now finds itself in a more or less constant quest to construct an ideal 'self', with much social and cultural practice oriented toward that project. Religion – including practices that share a family resemblance to religion but that may no longer be thought of as 'purely' religious – can be seen as a dimension of that project of the self. In fact, an important strain of contemporary scholarship on religion identifies a self-oriented, autonomous spiritual seeking as one of the primary modes of contemporary religion and quasi-religion (Roof, 1999). At the same time, the media sphere seems to offer more and more material of a religious, quasi-religious, or implicitly religious nature. Further, there is reason to suspect that the online world is particularly prone to be a site of certain kinds of religious and quasi-religious seeking and formation (Brasher, 2001).

As an emerging social and cultural reality, the net/web/online/digital world has been approached by scholars in a range of ways. Recent work has included descriptive and anecdotal studies, case histories, case studies, observations, interpretations, and (as the Pew Internet in American Life project has demonstrated) even large-sample representative studies. The thinking and work we present here are intended to represent only one of many possible approaches to these questions. Reflexively speaking, our project is intended to (1) bring a more sustained focus on questions of religion and those ideas, symbols and practices that bear a family resemblance to religion, and (2) explore what can be learned from a specific kind of fieldwork: ongoing qualitative interview studies in media households. Here, we will briefly review some of our initial work, focusing on two areas: (1) the emerging textual landscape of religion on the web, and (2) the results of initial interviews relative to these questions in our sample households.[2]

Religion Online versus Online Religion

Christopher Helland (2000) has introduced an elegant way of looking at this turf, the distinction between *religion online* and *online religion*. Simply put, *religion online* is the self-conscious use of the online context by religious organizations or movements for purposes of publicity, education, outreach, proselytization and so on. *Online religion*, by contrast, is the far more interesting issue of the online context becoming or being used as a locus of religious, spiritual (or other similar) practice. In a way, *religion online* is the easier side to study. Its sources, intentions and resources are easier to see and account for. *Online religion*, by contrast, is more difficult and elusive.

Helland's concern is to categorize the different forms of religious participation on the Internet. He distinguishes the two forms, *online religion* and *religion online*, based on whether or not traditional religious hierarchical structures are involved in the online participation. Accordingly, he defines *religion online* as 'an organized attempt to utilize traditional forms of communication to present religion based upon a vertical conception of control, status and authority', while *online religion* is 'a new development in religious praxis, reflecting the configuration of the Internet medium itself' which has the idea of 'unstructured, open and non-hierarchical interaction' (p. 207). Indeed, Helland's categorization is designed to explain the phenomenon around virtual religious communities on the Internet. Employing Victor Turner's concept of *communitas*, Helland points to the liminal conditions that *online religion* is able to provide, upon which virtual *communitas* are developed and operated.

Although our use of these two concepts does not follow his original conceptualizations, we found Helland's distinction insightful and very helpful for our purposes. Here, we reconceptualize *religion online* and *online religion* from a different perspective. Whereas Helland pays attention to the creators or organizers of web sites, we focus on the audience or users and the meanings they make of those online resources. While both *religion online* and *online religion* provide the audience with resources for meaning-making, they are differentiated by the audience's intentions, motivations and products involved in the meaning-construction process. From this perspective, *religion online* is conceptualized as the online resource to which an audience member turns to embrace his/her beliefs in traditional, established, institutional, religious systems. On the other hand, *online religion* is defined as the online resource an audience member uses to seek his/her more subjective, reflexive, autonomous, religious beliefs.

Both of these 'sides', of course, evolve from a set of concerns that should be entirely familiar to us. Throughout modern history, each succeeding evolution or revolution in communication, from the printing press to television, has evoked hand-wringing about its potential impact on religion. In the case of television, the controversy really took hold in the 1970s and 1980s with the emergence of televangelism. Some contemporary concerns are the same. For example, with both televangelism and the potential for *online religion* some religionists are concerned with how this new medium might be *harming* 'traditional religion'.

As was found with televangelism (see, for example, Hoover, 1988), it is likely that such concerns are too simplistic and facile. The situation is surely more complex. It is likely, though, that one of the major implications of televangelism also applies to the net/web/online context. In both cases, one important 'effect' will have been in the area of social legitimation. Just as televangelism served to legitimize certain aspects of religion, in all probability, so will the Internet. But this remains to be seen.

Returning to Helland's taxonomy, how do we go about understanding the intriguing area of *online religion*? Much of the most interesting work, such as that of Brasher (2001), Zaleski (1997) and Lawrence (2002), has emphasized description and explanation. The basic outlines are that in the online world, a vibrant religious, spiritual and transcendent set of discourses and practices has emerged – a significant point. To the extent that *online religion* has developed in the ways they detail, there are potentially very important consequences for religion and culture as we have known them.

Our purpose is to look in a different direction. As media audience researchers, we are interested in what we can learn by standing with the audience, 'looking back' with them, as it were, toward the mediated cultural world they inhabit, and in understanding the symbols and practices that emerge as meaningful – even religiously or spiritually meaningful – to them in that context. This theoretical and methodological approach has been described in detail elsewhere (Hoover, forthcoming, 2002, and Hoover and Russo, 2002). It is rooted in interactionist social theory and posits that the media sphere constitutes a 'symbolic inventory' out of which audiences select symbols, values, associations, discourses and ideas they use to infuse their lives with meaningful identities. Looked at in this way, both *religion online* and *online religion* potentially provide resources for meaning-making, though with radically different associations, saliencies and potentials.

Contemporary Religion Theory and Research

Valuable emergent scholarship in the area of religion, or what Stephen Warner (1993) calls 'new paradigm' religion research, offers a way to understand these things. As opposed to traditional ways of looking at religion, where history, symbol and doctrine were seen as determinants of belief and action, Warner argues that we now must begin to look at religion *as achieved* rather than only *as ascribed*. The focus of this work is thus on the meaningful actions of communities and individuals in achieving meaning and insight, rather than investigating the ways that adherents do or do not 'get' the orthodoxies of various religious *traditions*.

This dovetails, of course, with the most persuasive directions of contemporary cultural studies as they have been applied to the media. Qualitative methodologies and interpretative sensibilities dominate in this new religion research, along with narrative studies and a focus on popular practice.

A basic assumption of this new religion research is the powerful idea, itself derived from the work of social theorists such as Giddens, that the contemporary religious project is – like the contemporary social project – a project of the construction of the *self* and *identity*. In the context of religion research, this has evolved into a range of studies and approaches stressing the autonomous actions of individuals in making these kinds of sense. Most prominent among these ideas – as we noted above – has been the idea of religious or spiritual 'seeking.' Most extensively understood through the work of Wade Clark Roof (1999), seeking underlies religious practice across a range of traditions and contexts. At its most basic, it replaces other structures of motivation and action with a process whereby the individual is self-consciously and reflexively engaged in a process of cultural-, identity- and meaning-construction. The terms of reference revolve around the individual and his or her needs and motivations.

This religious seeking pervades most traditions and contexts today, from the more traditional movements to those that are on the religious and spiritual fringes. The most obvious examples of seeking come from the package of sensibilities and practices generally referred to as 'new age' spirituality. The new age defies a normative definition, but generally includes those groups and practices that combine seeking with active processes of cultural and symbolic appropriation, creating hybrid traditions combining Christianity with eastern and Native American traditions, for example.

While the new age is in some ways the proto-example of seeking, it is in fact the sensibility of seeking itself that is most important here. As an emergent religious practice, seeking expresses itself across a wide range of traditions and sensibilities. More important for our arguments here, though, is the relationship of seeking to the online context. As a religious/spiritual practice, seeking fits well with this context. The marketplace of symbols and contexts on the web is open to the seeker. There is no priesthood, no dominant tradition or doctrine. There are no barriers to entry or participation. Further, the web is a place of tremendous creativity, variety and volubility. It is typified by playfulness, invention and novelty.

In fact, many of the web sites representative of *religion online* assume that seeking takes place. They provide resources, handles, information, links, and so on, designed to attract the seeker and bring him/her in. More interesting, though, is the relationship between seeking and *online religion*. The elasticity and subjectivity of the 'selves' that presumably 'seek' online enable them to integrate their quests into the kinds of settings and locations present on the web (see, for example, Brasher, 2001 for a more complete discussion). A further issue is rooted in the inherent subjectivity of these practices. As autonomous seekers move into the online environment, their practices need not bear any necessary relationship to established or ascribed categories of religious-, spiritual- or meaning-practice. Put another way, there is no necessary contingency between the constructions and intentions of the creators of Internet sites and the meanings or practices they invoke or relate to in online 'seekers.'

The Focus of this Study

The balance of this chapter will chart in a rudimentary way a theoretical and methodological route through the terrain of online/web/digital religion/spirituality. The basic argument is as follows. The most interesting and challenging aspect of these matters is the *online religion* side of Helland's typology. It is interesting because it would be the most portentious in terms of its implications for what we used to think of as 'religion'. It is challenging because it is the most difficult to study. It is possible, as previous studies have demonstrated, to locate an online community of interest and carry out interviews, observations and other sorts of research interventions. Online activity by audiences that is most relevant should be that which is rooted in the mode of religious practice called 'seeking', and the net/web/digital context should be particularly amenable to this mode. The nature of practice, as well as the outlines of the *online religion* achieved should be of certain kinds – more individualistic, more subjective, less 'traditional', more open to construction and reconstruction, less 'fixed', more 'fluid', yet grounded (Roof, 1999) in certain kinds of histories, meanings and symbols.

In reality, it is far more difficult to study these matters in a way that addresses questions such as: (1) the varieties and levels of meanings, motivations and practices that underlie or lead to online spiritual or religious activity; and (2) the relationship between interest, motivation, the mode of 'seeking' and actual online involvement or behavior.

These questions require a kind of sampling of Internet options, audiences and practices in order to learn more about what might be going on. The field research below approaches this type of method. We engage members of households in in-depth discussions of their narratives of self, family and community, with special attention to the place of their media use in these constructions. Households have been included in our study by means of what Lindlof (1995) calls 'maximum variability sampling', where households are chosen for their variability along a range of demographic categories. Thus, our conversations look for both particularities and commonalities in their expressions, and seek to probe the capacities of various media practices to support various kinds of social and cultural action.

Examples from Field Data

The following excerpts from our field data give a flavor of the kind of material we work with. The interviews were conducted with the idea of getting at the question of how the Internet could be part of religious practice. *Online religion* in some of these excerpts seems to interact with other religious sensibilities and seems especially linked to the practice of seeking. In other excerpts, informants who are not seekers seem to regard religion on the Internet as *religion online* and do not connect it with their own spirituality.

Chris Chandler[3] is a 35-year-old single father. He was interviewed by Anna Maria Russo.

I: Would you describe yourself in terms of religion or spirituality?

C: Confused [*laughs*]. You know I have my core Christian Catholic belief but then there is also I love Zen, I love the beliefs of the American Indians, Tao. It all fascinates me but ultimately all comes down to God and I try to ...

I: The Catholic God?

C: Yeah, for the most part. And I try to pray, I try to count my blessings. I try to say thanks God everyday, I try to thanks for giving Alicia, thanks you know for keeping me healthy you know it's not like I get down and kneel. Usually when I get in the car, you know because I spend all day driving for work and so usually when I get in the car.

I: So do you ever seek out anything related to religion or spirituality on TV or on the Internet or on other media, movies?

C: Definitely Internet.

I: Yeah, where, what about it?

C: Uhm, I can't really give sites' names but definitely I you know when I am in those moods where I just search you know and I think to myself well OK I am going ... I will have a search like ... I always had a thing for the American Indians, you know so. But I can't say definitely that is all religion but you know ... but I can't say about TV at all. Do you mean as far as like religious?

I: Or spirituality, spiritual things or themes.

C: Let's say if it's on and I see something but I can't say that I search for it. Maybe we are just different in semantics ... I don't watch *Touched by an Angel*.

I: You can find meaningful things related to your spiritual beliefs in movies or TV shows or anywhere else that relates to your value ...

C: I would say probably more music for me in that way. I would say definitely more music. When I am searching for some kind of spirituality I would say definitely more in music.

I: Do you have a favorite music, band, group ...?

C: I've got a couple of hundreds CDs out there and you know I worked in a record store for a long time so I like everything. I mean I got punk rock, country, Sinatra, I like almost all.

For Chris Chandler, a 35-year-old field credit representative, the Internet is the most useful medium for providing cultural resources to construct his own spirituality. He employs the Internet to incorporate spiritual traditions such as Zen, American Indians, and Tao into his 'core Christian Catholic beliefs'. His use of the media for religious purposes seems to be very important in positioning his religious identity. In addition, while Chris clearly recognizes his use of the Internet for religious purposes, he refuses to relate his television viewing to his spirituality since he does not want to be identified with the kind of people who search for religious meanings by watching such TV shows such as *Touched by an Angel*. In that sense, the Internet provides him an acceptable and efficient way to seek resources for his own spirituality. It fits with his 'seeker' sensibility (in his view) in that it is not as determinative as television.[4] Chandler is an example of a new age seeker, motivated by his own internal logic. He is engaged in *online religion* in that he finds resources for meaning-making online but not necessarily on sites that self-consciously use the Internet for *religion online*. His extensive use of other media (particularly his seeking spirituality in music CDs and his refusal of television spirituality) is an important aspect of his spirituality, as he clearly uses all these media in his open-ended approach.

Laura Allen is a 16-year-old high school student who lives with her sister and her single mother. She was interviewed by Scott Webber.

I: ... do you seek out information or inspiration online or through other media? You mentioned in the previous interview *It's a Miracle* and *Seventh Heaven*. Have you done anything beyond that or have you continued to do that?

L: Yeah I've continued to do that and I do a lot of research on the Internet.

I: About?

L: Everything and anything. Like the last research I did on the Internet I was doing extra credit and I was looking up minerals and rocks and diamonds and precious gems and things like that.

I: Have you done anything online in relation to your church or your involvement there or inspiration or things in that area?

L: Um ... I did go online during, when I was on the Daniels program. We went online and we answered a bunch of questions and they brought up colleges in Colorado that would be good for me.

I: Last time most of the things you mentioned, *It's a Miracle*, *Seventh Heaven* and *Touched by an Angel*, were on the TV. Anything online like that?

L: Not that I know of since I haven't looked at it.

I: Well ... I'm wondering if you use the Internet in that way?

L: No.

Laura Allen's case illustrates audiences' active integration of media practice – in this case, television, not the Internet – in their religious meaning-making processes.

She is actively involved with her Lutheran church, and the entire interview shows her strong religious identification as a Christian. Even though she does not have a computer in her home, Laura fairly frequently uses a computer and the Internet at school and at her grandparents' house. For her, the computer is so familiar a medium that she claims in another interview to use it 'all the time'. Nevertheless, she does not find a connection between her religiosity and Internet use. It is much easier for her to document her experiences of TV viewing in relation to her spirituality. It may be that she does not see the need for any other cultural sources for her spirituality or that she has not found any benefits in the medium for her already-established religious beliefs and values. Her use of the Internet for information suggests that she may regard the possibility of religion on the Internet as *religion online*, something she does not need because she has her church. This case shows that we should not assume that technological conditions are sufficient to guarantee the use of the Internet for religious purposes by 'religious' people. The religious use of the Internet should be seen with reference to the larger context in which people dynamically integrate the whole media practice including other popular media into their daily 'religious' lives.

David Mueller is a Mormon and 30-year-old father of three. He, his wife, and his children were interviewed by Joseph Champ.

I: Getting back to beliefs. We touched on it a little bit. Do you ever seek out inspirational, transcendent, religious information in media at all? Or do you mostly get that when you go to church?

D: The church has an extensive amount of web sites. And you can go there and you can get spiritual thoughts, there's resources as far as scriptural resources, like, you know, a lot of talk preparation type of materials, teaching materials, like to teach young children, to teach other people. It's really, if you want to learn anything about the church, their web site is ... I mean, you can do anything from family history, genealogy, you can find your ancestors, as far as a religious point of view, they've utilized the available media to get that out. It's more for a distribution kind of thing.

The Muellers are a distinctive case among our respondent families because of their relatively high income as well as their elaborate knowledge of computers. Computers are so ingrained in this family that even Reese, a four-year-old boy, sometimes emails his friends. For this 'committed' Mormon family, the Internet is a medium in which they can easily find much information and many resources to reinforce their commitment to Mormon religious beliefs. David also believes that the Internet has a great potential for the church (not as a local church, but as the whole organization of Mormonism) in order to 'distribute' the religion and that these efforts have been successful. In other words, to this family, the virtual space of the Internet is very much concentrated in, or confined to, their religion. Compared with Chris Chandler, the Mueller family is decidedly 'non-seeking'. As to the question of the utility of the Internet, David Mueller is clearly unable to think outside of an 'informational' mode, and clearly regards the web as a resource for Mormons such as himself. His definition of religion on the Internet as information from an institutional source is, if anything, a view of *religion online*.

Rayna Hancock is a 37-year-old single mother of a young son. She was interviewed by Joseph Champ.

[Interviewer's note: When asked about bookmarked web sites, Rayna mentioned the singles' site maintained by the Mormon Church. It is a site with information and photos of single people who choose to subscribe.]

R: I don't really have time to date, but, you can still have a relationship over the Internet.

I: So you can actually meet people and that's the service that church has kind of . . .

R: I don't know that they would that's *their* thing, but . . . it's a group of. . .well, somebody that's in the church came up with that. You know, it's a service, you pay 35 bucks and you become a member and they have thousands of people on there . . .

I: And so you can e-mail . . .

R: Uh-huh.

I: . . . and communicate?

R: Uh-huh.

I: How do you get involved? Did you know someone, some friends who are Mormons?

R: Yes. You know, I lived in Provo, with all the Mormons there, but . . . but I did make a friend, this girl, and she was just wonderful, and . . . I was pretty much a hellion . . . [and a] partier person for most of my life, but I always stayed in touch with her because I just liked her so much. And um, I started going to church over here at the Vineyard, because you know it's casual . . . it's a nice church. I really liked it. But um, my friend, I was talking to her one day and I said, 'I'm in church, you'd be so happy for me, I'm in church,' and she goes, 'Well, you know, you need to go to the *right* church. You need to go to church that, um . . .' You know, when you're a Mormon, you're *very* . . .

I: Dedicated.

R: Yeah . . . to the beliefs and everything of the church. And I told her that I'd have the missionaries come over and, the more I heard about the church and the more people I met there . . . it is a wonderful church, I have a great support system.

I: The sense of community is real strong.

R: They're just the most sincere, caring people I've ever met. So, I made some great changes. Quit drinking, you know, try to quit cussing [*laughs*].

Rayna is a recent convert to Mormonism from the Vineyard Fellowship, an evangelical group identified with an evangelical type of 'seeking'. The story of conversion she articulates implies that the most important aspect in her 'great changes' were the good impressions she had of the 'people' who are 'the most sincere, caring and supportive'. Rayna's use of the Internet appears to reflect this aspect with an association of her situation as a divorced single. The importance of relationships with other people within the religious community is extended to online relationships in her case. This is a complex example of *online religion* because the informant seems to regard as non-institutional a singles site that the interviewer has identified as institutional and Mormon. It is significant that Rayna does not think of the singles site as an institutional site, as she corrects the interviewer by noting that some Mormon individuals, not the church, constructed the site. This is consistent with her own internal process of seeking, as she describes searching for a religion that would help her change her 'hellion' ways. The singles site reinforces her seeking, as it helps her sense of community. It may well also represent *religion online* to the extent that it reinforces her membership in the Mormon church, but she does not see the site this way.

Katy Cabera is a 32-year-old single mother of two who was interviewed by Christof Demont-Heinrich.

K: ... I was pretty much clueless. Um, and I didn't, you know, I wasn't involved in any kind of youth group or anything. We just went [to church]. Usually if my mom felt bad about something we went because we were Catholic. We could feel bad and then we could be, you know, we could repent on Sunday and everything would be okay. Act bad and then go back on Sunday and everything would be okay. And I had a really big problem with that because as a young kid I didn't think that that's exactly how it's supposed to be. I know that's not how it's supposed to be. You try to be just as good as you possibly can all the time. You don't try to buy your way into heaven or you don't try to justify evil or immoral acts, or whatever it is people do during the week before church on Sunday. Um, and I see a lot of that on certain shows, that it's okay to be one way but then you can be a good Christian on Sunday. So, I have big problem with that.

I: Which shows?

K: Ah, usually movies. If you watch gangster movies, the mob movies, they go out and kill people and then they go to church on Sunday. What are they? They're Catholic!

I: Ah-huh ...

K: And I don't like seeing that. I have a big problem with it. A huge problem with that. And, um, it can also be joked about late night, you know. On *Saturday*

Night Live I've seen a couple of skits like that and, so, um, that's one of the reasons why I left the Catholic Church and stopped going to church. And when I started dating this one man four years ago, ah, he's the one who introduced me to the Lutheran faith. And there's a very close connection with Catholicism. I don't know if you knew that Martin Luther was a Catholic priest married to a nun. So, I, you know, started researching it and found that it, ah, was something that I fit into very well. So, I really like it.

I: So you talked a little bit about movies that weren't too favorable in terms of some aspects of Catholicism. Do you think – have you seen any of that in terms of the Lutheran faith do you think?

K: I don't know. Really with the Catholic thing, I've seen several like that. I remember one show in particular – oh yeah, I must have been maybe 12 or 13 – and the show was called *The Wanderers*. It was a movie set in the 1950s about gangs. And, you know, rival gangs, you're in my neighborhood, you're on my turf and we're going to beat you up now. I mean, it was an interesting movie, but I remember this one gang went to the church to pray for forgiveness before going out and killing.

I: And the movie was called *The Wanderers*?

K: *The Wanderers*. Yeah. That was the first glimpse that I had of it and I can't pinpoint every single movie that I've seen but I know there are Catholic churches, you know there's the cross, the priest, the kneeling, and the praying, blah, blah, blah. And I just have big problem with that, just having to see that [*laughing*].

I: Do you ever seek out anything related to religion on TV or on the Internet or on radio?

K: No, uh-uh. I don't do any of that. I think the reason I don't really touch on going to any religious sites or anything is because I've got my mind set on what I believe and that's what I believe.

I: So what about Lutheran sites, does your church have a web site?

K: Our church does have a web site. But I'm there [at the church]. I don't need to go to the web.

I: So even surfing to sites that align with your beliefs is not of interest?

K: I've never tried it. But I probably will now. I've got my sports and news. As soon as you leave I'm going to put the news on. I do that way too much at work too.

The case of Katy Cabera suggests at least three dimensions of relationship between media and religion. First, as she noted in several references to TV programs and movies in her account of her journey from Catholicism to Lutheranism, popular culture provides crucial resources in some people's religious identity process. Second, the Internet seems to have less potential for religious use for someone for whom religious identity is strongly established. Katy maintains her reason for not using the Internet for religious purposes is that she has already set religious beliefs.

Third, online religious community-building is closely related to involvement in the offline religious community and subjective feelings about that involvement. She has no desire to go to the web site of her church because she is already 'there'. This is clearly an instrumentalist view of the Internet. Also it is clear that she sees the Internet's primary significance to be influence over religious choice, reinforcing her 'not-for-me' view. She seems to think of religion on the Internet as *religion online*, and she's clearly not interested.

Wyonna Fallon is a 39-year-old single mother of two, interviewed along with her daughter Jill, 14, by Christof Demont-Heinrich.

J: And there's – what's that site [*to W*] that you have that you can look at bible verses?

W: Heartlight.org.

J: Yeah.

W: And every day you get –

I: Heartlight.org?

W: Yeah. You get different things every day. Like that screen saver is different every day.

J: You have a different wallpaper every day.

I: Oh, really, what is that one [*pointing to the computer*]?

J: 'Blessed is the nation whose God is the Lord'. Psalm 3:12. They're usually Bible verses. They used to be important quotes. But now we got Bible verses. And then there's always a little picture that goes along with it.

I: And that's what heartlight.org focuses on?

W: It's actually done by the Church of Christ in Texas somewhere. And it has daily verses, or like articles and Bible – [*W. and J. talking right through/across one another here as they often do*].

J: Stories and whatnot –

W: – study things that you can look at different verses or something like that. Put in a word and it'll show all the verses with that in it and stuff like that.

I: How did you find out about it?

W: Ahh … somebody told me about it, I believe.

This is an example of a use of the Internet to 'prime' religion in daily life. This family has no television set in their living room. Three years ago, Wyonna decided to get rid of a cable connection because her daughters were spending too much time watching TV. The only television set used for video watching is kept in the daughters' room, and a computer with a religious screen-saver takes the place of a television in the living room. From the site where she got the screen saver, Wyonna also gets wallpaper containing Bible verses and religious pictures delivered automatically through email. The technology of the Internet is thus seen to provide more efficient ways for people to integrate religiosity into their everyday lives.

Wyonna's use of Bible verses online indicates that she defines this particular form of religion on the Internet as *religion online* because she consciously takes part in a religious use of the Internet.

Donna Baylor is a 38-year-old mother of four, interviewed along with her husband by Christof Demont-Heinrich.

I: OK, we're going to switch gears and then come back to computers at the end. There's a section here on media and beliefs. We talked about this a little in the family interview, but not in depth. Do you ever seek out inspiration or information or encouragement in the media? And, if so, where and when have you done this – can you think of any specific examples? I think you talked about going – you have a whole set of bookmarks. You have a religion folder.

D: Yeah. I do.

I: So you're doing some seeking out online?

D: Yeah.

I: What kinds of stuff are you doing more specifically?

D: Well, first, I have a daily email that comes that's just a scripture. I can't tell you what it's called right off hand: *The Daily Manna*. But I like it because it's just a scripture. It's not a commentary on it. It's just what's in the Bible. I like that. I like to read that every day. And then in my folder, I've got – well, my Crossings book club is in there. They're a religious book club. I think it's called Power and Glory. It's like Columbia House. It's a division of Columbia House, their Christian side of it. So that's in there.

I: And that's music?

D: Ah-huh. And then I've got a thing in there – I don't know if it works anymore – but Hobby Lobby is a Christian organization and they used to every Christmas put in a full page ad that had nothing to do with their stores, just the Christmas message. They also had it online. So I had saved some of those. Because they're really cool.

I: Are you going online often to search for things and bookmark them? Or is this is something – you have a folder that's already been created and you don't add to it very often? You keep going back to the same places?

D: Well, it depends. If I find something new, I'll stick it in there – I've cleaned it out a couple of times because some of the things that I had found previously were gone, were not good anymore. I'd review it and go through it every now and then and put in new things and take out the old. You know, what's relevant and what's not. I have some web sites in there on different religions that I've looked at – if I've gotten into a discussion with someone over. Well, I guess my big thing would be Mormonism. Since I have in-laws and relatives that are Mormon and Bill used to be Mormon. I try and research that a lot so that I have a lot of information to work with that way.

I: So you don't have anything bookmarked on Islam or Buddhism ...

D: I haven't found any. I look around for ones that I like and that I can understand, are clear enough for me to get.

Like Wyonna Fallon, Donna uses the Internet to get daily scripture. An interesting point she makes is that she likes the daily email system because it sends passages of the Bible and not commentaries on it. She emphasizes her own ability to make meanings out of the scripture by refusing to take religious authorities' intervention in the process. This suggests that she is a bit of a contradiction – at least according to a conventional view of the relationship between scripture and authority. She also uses the Internet to seek information about various religious traditions. This is not so much an act of 'religious/spiritual seeking' as in Chris Chandler's case. This excerpt shows two distinctly different uses of the Internet in regard to religion and illustrates the difference between *online religion* and *religion online* from the point of view of an informant. Donna approaches the web sites containing scripture as *online religion* in her own religious seeking. The creators of the sites might have established them as *religion online*, but that is clearly not how Donna regards them. In contrast, she goes to *religion online* in the form of Mormon sites in order to get information on beliefs her relatives hold, although she does not. She is not 'seeking' in the second approach, as what she finds is not connected with her own internal sense of religiosity.

Discussion

There is much of interest here. Informants typically have difficulty in connecting their media and Internet use to questions of religion. Even Chris Chandler, who so definitively states that he uses the Internet for religious purposes, does not describe his practice with specific genres or programs. He clearly exhibits the characteristics of new-age seeking, but does not articulate Internet-specific practices of the kind we might assume he would engage in. While we wish to explore this issue in more detail, perhaps in further conversations and interviews, other evidence from our interviews suggest that it might be a problem of language. That is, the way we would expect people like Chris to describe their spiritually inflected Internet use is simply not the way they describe it themselves. On some level, we are talking about the same thing, but may be using different ways of describing it. Or Internet use may be articulated into spiritual practice in a different way or at a different level than we conventionally expect.

Others, such as Katy Cabera, eschew any notion that the Internet might have a place in religious or spiritual activities for her. She is a 'seeker' in terms of the means by which she came to her current religious position, and seems to have come there in part through other media, such as movies and television shows that depicted Catholics negatively in a way that resonated with her. Now that she has settled in her current religious position, she sees no need to go online. Katy shares something in common with many of the informants here, a sense that the primary purpose of the Internet/Web is a kind of 'informational' function more closely associated with Helland's *religion online* category.

There is some evidence here, then, that the category of 'seeking' does seem to go with an *online religion* morphology of Internet use. And, if it does, we can see how that might be so, and how contrasting categories of use might also function. For informants whose religion/spirituality is more or less 'fixed', a contrasting source of symbolic or meaning resources naturally is seen as less important. For informants for whom 'seeking' has become dominant, sources such as the Internet/web seem somehow logical contexts for working out religious/spiritual identity. In neither case could it be said that the digital context is somehow determinative of practice, rather that it must somehow fit into existing lines of motivation and behavior.

Our method here differs markedly from that of previous studies that have looked at religion and the Internet. We did not select these households because of their religious, quasi-religious, or 'seeking' status. What we have, then, are interviews that begin with a different premise, and get to the question of the Internet as part of an overall discussion of religious practice. In that way, the conversation is 'about' conventional religious practice more than it is about Internet religion. These interviews have provided insights into ways people might regard *religion online* and *online religion* in the context of their own religious identities. The complexity with which some informants regarded religion in the online world suggests fertile ground for further research.

Notes

1   An earlier version was presented at the Association of Internet Researchers 3.0, Maastricht, the Netherlands, October, 2002.
2   The field material and analysis presented here comes from an ongoing, multi-year qualitative study of meaning-making in the media age under the direction of the first author and Lynn Schofield Clark. The research team includes the second author, as well as the interviewers responsible for the specific interviews excerpted here, Joseph G. Champ, Scott Webber, Christof Demont-Heinrich, Anna Maria Russo and Michelle Miles. The authors wish to acknowledge and thank these colleagues for their efforts, advice and input into this article. More information about the overall project, including notes on method, is available at: http://www.colorado.edu/Journalism/mcm/mrc/mrc.htm.
3   In keeping with our protocols, we have changed the names of all informants. All live in the Front Range area of Colorado, within a 100-mile radius of our base at the University of Colorado at Boulder. Under our protocols, none of our informants comes from the city of Boulder itself.
4   Chris's articulation of a 'received cultural script' about the differences between television and the Internet is significant of a much larger and more interesting set of issues. For a complete discussion, see Hoover, et al. (2004).

References

Brasher, B. (2001), *Give Me That Online Religion*, San Francisco, CA: Jossey-Bass.

Giddens, A. (1991), *Modernity and Self-Identity: Self and Society in the Late Modern Age*, Stanford, CA: Stanford University Press.

Helland, C. (2000), 'Online-Religion/ Religion-Online and Virtual Communitas', in J. K. Hadden and D. E. Cowan (eds), *Religion on the Internet: Research Prospects and Promises*, New York: Elsevier Science Press, pp. 205–23.

Hoover, S. M. (forthcoming), *Religion in the Media Age*, London: Routledge.

Hoover, S. M. (2002), 'Religion, Media and Identity: Theory and Method in Audience Research on Religion and Media', paper presented to the Annual Meeting of the International Communication Association, Seoul, Korea, July.

Hoover, S. M. (2001), 'Religion, media, and the cultural center of gravity', in D. Stout and J. Buddenbaum (eds), *Religion and Popular Culture: Studies on the Interactions of Worldviews*, Ames, IA: Iowa State University Press.

Hoover, S. M. (1988), *Mass Media Religion: The Social Sources of the Electronic Church*, London: Sage.

Hoover, S. M. and A. M. Russo (2002), 'Understanding Modes of Engagement in Research on Media and Meaning-Making', paper presented to the Conference of the International Association for Mass Communication Research, Barcelona, July.

Hoover, S. H., L. S. Clark, D. F. Alters, with J. G. Champ and L. Hood (2004), *Media, Home and Family*, New York and London: Routledge.

Lawrence, B. B. (2002), 'Allah on-line: the practice of global Islam in the information age', in S. Hoover and L. S. Clark (eds), *Practicing Religion in the Age of the Media:Explorations in Media, Religion, and Culture*, New York: Columbia University Press.

Lindlof, T. R. (1995), *Qualitative Communication Research Methods*, Thousand Oaks, CA: Sage.

Park, J. K. (2002), 'Constructing a Religion: Issues of the study of religion on the Internet,' paper presented to the International Communication Association, Seoul, July.

Roof, W. C. (1999), *Spiritual Marketplace: Baby Boomers and the Re-Making of American Religion*, Princeton, NJ: Princeton University Press.

Warner, R. S. (1993), 'Work in Progress Toward a New Paradigm for the Sociological Study of Religion in the United States', *American Journal of Sociology*, **98** (March). 1044–93.

Zaleski, J. (1997), *The Soul of Cyberspace: How New Technology is Changing our Spiritual Lives*, New York: HarperCollins.

Additional Resources

Clark, L. S. (2002), 'Young People's Internet Practices and Spirituality: Preliminary Findings from the Teens and the New Media@Home Project', presented to the first meeting of the Pew Internet and American Life Advisory Board, Chicago, April.

Jones, S. (1999), 'Studying the Net: Intricacies and Issues', in S. Jones (ed.), *Doing Internet Research: Critical Issues and Methods for Examining the Net*, Thousand Oaks, CA: Sage.

PART III
MEDIA CULTURE AND CHRISTIAN INSTITUTIONS

Introduction

In many ways the traditional Christian institutions of western societies have taken shape through their engagement with and negotiation of the social, intellectual and media frameworks of western culture. The theoretical and methodological developments being explored in this book have profound implications for those religious institutions because they name developments in the fundamental communication structures of societies on which those religious institutions have been built and which supported the meaning of their activities.

This section explores some of the implications of shifts in media culture on Christian institutions. Mary Hess in her chapter reflects on the implications for the nurture of faith of the growing importance of popular mediated culture as the culture in which people are now living. She explores possibilities for Christian education in making the cultural shift from being focused on religious institutions to the lived context of popular media culture.

Adán Medrano, an independent film producer with extensive experience in church media, reflects on the tensions experienced by a religious artist in a life lived and work produced between those two contexts.

From a different cultural context, Siriwan Santisakultarm considers similar changes, from a Catholicism nurtured in village life through strong oral media and cultural practices to different media and cultural practices when that religious tradition is translated to the quite different contexts of urban life.

Frances Forde Plude in her chapter links the recent exposure of sexual abuse within the Roman Catholic Church to changing patterns of communication and media structures. Plude argues that old authoritarian and propagandistic communication patterns that once worked in a media culture dominated by the power of institutions does not work in a media culture that is diverse, has decentralized patterns of production, where information spreads rapidly and cannot be controlled, and where institutions have a changed social position. Her argument is that this new media culture requires different institutional forms and communication styles, in which listening becomes as important as speaking and communicating faith through dialogue becomes of greater importance.

In the final section, Bob White, one of the pioneers of research in the field of media, religion and culture, surveys the field, integrating the various practical, theoretical and methodological issues facing the field by looking at ten major issues to be explored further or yet to be considered. His chapter in many ways sets an agenda for the next twenty years of research.

Chapter 10

Making Religious Media:
Notes from the Field

Adán M. Medrano

Introduction

Producers of religious media often face two different models or understandings of what media are and how they function. One model sees media as vehicles that transmit messages while the other understands media as constructions that enable the creation of meaning. This essay reflects on how these two different understandings have interacted with each other in the making of Catholic Spanish-language TV programming in the US, and what their implications are for faith communities.

A Spanish-language Catholic TV Series

Festival '73 was the first national TV series that I directed. It was a thirteen-week series of religious half-hour programs broadcast on the Spanish International Network, SIN. A Catholic foundation grant given to a religious congregation, the Missionary Oblates of Mary Immaculate, in San Antonio, Texas, paid for the production costs. Broadcasting the series on SIN was the result of an agreement between the network and the producers such that the producers did not have to buy the airtime and the network could obtain a US-produced program without having to pay for production costs. (Except for this series, virtually every broadcast hour of each SIN affiliate was imported from Mexico). (Rodriguez) The broadcast of this US-produced series was a mutually beneficial arrangement.

I worked with a producer, who was a priest, to create the series concept. As we brainstormed about what the series might be, the guiding question was: what is the religious message that we should deliver to the Spanish-speaking audience? Although this seemed a logical way to proceed, I felt a disconnection between our process of conceiving messages and the life of the Latino community that we were trying to serve.

As a Mexican American, I was part of the 9 million Spanish surnamed residents counted by the US 1970 Census (Arredondo, 2000). The average annual income of a Latino household was low, $10,500, because higher-paying jobs were beyond the reach of our low level of education. It seemed to me that with high poverty rates and too few educational opportunities, the Mexican American community was looking for affirmation, celebration of identity, and an imaginative space to envision the future. More than a religious message, we needed to see ourselves as US Latinos and to feel the uniqueness of our strength and faith.

Sending Messages or Evoking Symbols?

The producer and I struggled back and forth between the responsibility we felt to deliver important content and the persistent feeling that we should affirm a reality that was already out there in the community. How do we serve when we make media? If we are intent on delivering a message that in our judgment is relevant and important, how helpful are we really being, if the audience is already dealing with many messages while in a process of working out its identity and coherence? Is it not that instead of packaging and delivering a message we are designing an imaginative framework within which viewers can use their memories, individual stories, thoughts and symbols to celebrate and affirm who they are? At the same time, they project their own future, a future steeped in faith. This latter seemed right.

We therefore decided that the TV series would celebrate identity and present open-ended reflections about the Catholic faith. The result was a series of entertainment programs that would feature traditional and popular music of the US Mexican American community. We called the series *Festival '73*. Each half-hour program consisted of three elements. Amateur and professional performers sang and danced in outdoor natural settings, introduced by a ventriloquist host who traded barbs with his puppet. Depending on the theme of the music or song, nature sequences with biblical quotations appeared from time to time during the program. Finally, a series of animated reflections about sacraments and community wove themselves throughout the series.

The series was seen in every major city with a Latino population: Los Angeles, Fresno, San Francisco, San Antonio, Chicago, New York and Miami, among others. Since this was before the days of satellite, SIN distributed programs to the various TV outlets by shipping tapes as luggage on passenger buses. During the thirteen weeks that the series aired, we were busy driving to the San Antonio Greyhound bus station to receive and ship tapes, since we had to help the local station executives with this distribution task.

The successful distribution of this series was due to the personal and professional relationship between the SIN network and the producers of this religious program. Each needed something from the other. SIN, as the US subsidiary of the Mexican entertainment conglomerate, was struggling to network TV stations that were all on UHF frequencies, making it necessary for the viewer to purchase and install an additional antenna on the TV set. Moreover, at that time the US Spanish-speaking population was so small and so poor a community that it was not considered a viable advertising market (Rodriguez, n.d.).

Also important was the Federal Communications Commission (FCC) regulation called 'sustaining time' that required every local station to air programming for which it did not receive advertising income. *Festival '73* helped the TV stations fulfill their 'sustaining time' programming requirement.

El Visitante

Six years later, I again teamed with the Missionary Oblates of Mary Immaculate and SIN to produce a religious TV series. At that time I was publisher of the national weekly Catholic Spanish-language newspaper, *El Visitante Dominical*. The plan was to produce a weekly program with the same name and feature current affairs and entertainment. I knew many of the executives at SIN and could rely on professional courtesies, but the TV landscape had changed substantially since 1973 and it would be necessary to invent a new collaborative arrangement between the producer of religious programming and the TV network.

The FCC 'sustaining time' regulation had been removed from the broadcasting requirements. Whereas in 1973 religious producers could rely on mandated free airtime, now the only way to get on TV was to buy the time. Only the evangelical Christians were doing so.

The SIN network had grown spectacularly through a combination of five technologies: the UHF band, cable television, microwave, satellite interconnections and repeater stations. By the early 1980s SIN could claim it was reaching 90 percent of the Spanish-speaking households in the United States, with 16 owned and operated UHF stations, 100 repeater stations and 200 cable outlets (Rodriguez, n.d.). The US Latino population had grown to 15 million, according to the 1980 census, and this did not include an unofficial estimate of 5 million immigrants. Annual household income had grown to $17,000 (Arredondo, 2000).

The advertising revenue of Spanish-language TV stations was also growing fast, from $6 million in 1977 to $32 million by 1982 (Arredondo, 2000). Clearly, Spanish-language television, relying on the growing buying power of US Latinos,[1] was amassing capital rapidly. The logical question that had no clear answer was: What possible benefit could such a successful TV network obtain from a religious producer? Nevertheless, since most of the programming was still being imported from Televisa in Mexico, it seemed to me that the Latino community could be enriched by US-produced Catholic Latino programming.

Production costs for commercial television are high. Fortuitously, the Catholic bishops of the United States had decided in 1978 to take up a collection in every parish church and to use those funds for communications projects. This was called the Catholic Communication Campaign. We requested support and received $175,000 from this national parish collection. The Oblates provided the administrative infrastructure and expenses while additional production funds were obtained from generous Catholic foundations.

As producer, I worked with a creative team to design a 'magazine' concept for the series and a pilot program to demonstrate what the series would look like. Interestingly, no one on the creative team asked the question that had surfaced seven years earlier, namely, what is the message that we wish to deliver? Instead, we discussed what was happening in the Latino community, what trends and symbols were popular, what was happening currently that hurt or helped the development of our community. We asked ourselves, as Latinos and Latinas, what were the traditional, indigenous stories and figures that were guiding us and our families? This would give us the connections between faith and life that might capture the viewer's imagination.

During the process I realized that the production team was working with the symbolic elements that enable us to understand ourselves, our world and our ultimate meaning. They were constructors – of an imaginative, emotional space in which to encounter God in familiar and meaningful ways. The opening line that the host delivered on the pilot program was: '*Quiénes somos, y porqué seguimos adelante*' ('Who we are, and why we continue onward').

The pilot featured a humorous interview with singing star, Freddy Fender, since it was clear to us that star entertainment value was a requisite for the network. With the pilot in hand, I visited the SIN Vice President for Programming in New York City. He found the pilot provocative and the interview with Freddy Fender made him laugh. SIN agreed to air our show on the network on Sunday mornings. My personal connections had opened his office door to me, but what closed the deal was the strength of the production combined with our modest but sufficient financial capital from Catholic sources to fund an entire season. The Oblates, the bishops and our production staff were elated. But a stumbling block was to confront us within weeks.

The Institution as Enabler

During the initial broadcast season of thirteen weeks, the Oblates informed me that they would no longer continue being a partner. Other priorities had surfaced for them. Since there was now no longer a bona fide institutional church producer, the religious program had to end. When our series season ended the network filled our Sunday morning slot with another program. It was this event that deepened my understanding of the function of religious media.

If media function as delivery systems for institutions to produce and send gospel messages to audiences whom they serve, then *El Visitante* should in fact end. But it did not end. Three things had come together to create strong momentum: the willingness of the commercial network, the money from Catholic sources and a creative team comprising persons who had chosen to produce religious media because it was deeply meaningful. This momentum had made the production possible and had thus enabled a community to create meaning in their lives about the ultimate mystery, God. Once I realized this, it became clear that it was not necessary for the institution to be a producer. The institution was a powerful enabler and one of the essential collaborators.

As before, we would have to invent a new collaborative arrangement, this time without the religious institution as producer. With the strong financial support of the bishops' Catholic Communication Campaign and from some Catholic foundations, we established an independent not-for-profit corporation with no formal relationship to any church institution. We called it Hispanic Telecommunications Network, HTN. It would be the vehicle whereby the bishops, Catholic foundations, the commercial network and the creative media producers would collaborate on the TV series.

Since we no longer had the equipment and infrastructure of the Oblate religious congregation, my first duty as founding president of this new corporation, HTN, was to sign for a $300,000 personal loan guarantee to purchase equipment. As soon as I signed the loan document, I knew that the financial capital we were receiving from the bishops and from foundations was generous but in the long run would not be sufficient. Although SIN had said, 'Why did you stop? We need more,' I knew that our reliance on their good will was not a sufficiently stable commercial arrangement.

The only religious producers who were financially viable in the US were the evangelical Christians. Some owned broadcast stations, but many functioned as producers and purchased airtime on commercial stations. I attended their annual convention, the National Religious Broadcasters, in Washington, DC. During one of the workshops on marketing, one of the presenters struck me as both knowledgeable and inventive. He was the director of marketing for The Rex Humbard ministries, the pioneer in evangelical television. I explained to him what we were trying to do in the Latino Catholic Church and, to my great surprise, he agreed to provide us with consulting services. I was surprised because revenue-generating strategies and information are closely guarded trade secrets. In fact we developed a very open and productive relationship.

We agreed on his fee and he traveled to San Antonio to meet with our creative team. What happened was both affirming and disquieting. We were in immediate agreement concerning the creative and participative nature of the audience and about the strength of imagination, symbols and narrative structure. Two things gave us pause. First was the technical complexity required to follow up the program with computerized direct mail solicitations, market research and audience development. The second was the narrowness of the religious Sunday morning TV format. That is, the format allowed for only sermon, music, testimonials and direct-response ads. The strictness of the format was surprising even though we already knew that commercial television in general works with formats that deal with topics within a limited range and depth.

We set about transforming *El Visitante* into a Catholic version of evangelical programs. The name changed to one that had broader appeal, *Nuestra Familia*, or *Our Family*. We conducted a casting call and hired a priest-host. Computerized direct mail programming was installed. Cubicles with telephones were built and telephone operators trained.

There was a constant struggle between the constricting format and the broad range of Latino experiences we wished to express. We added reportage of issues we knew were important in the Latino community such as education and immigration. Books were offered as over-the-air incentives to call. The creative team negotiated heatedly with the hired consultant about when and for how long the telephone number should appear on the screen.

A Space for Meaning-making

Keeping to their agreement, SIN cleared *Nuestra Familia* on the entire network, reaching 90 percent of the US Latino population. As the first program was broadcast, the telephone lines began to ring off the wall. When as a courtesy I presented the audited financial statement of our first year to the Archbishop of San Antonio, we could rejoice that our income exceeded our expenses by $100,000. Since callers to our program were also mailing us donations, over the next five years *Nuestra Familia* continued to grow financially. The personal and sometimes deeply moving letters that we received with the donations were always a reminder of the depth of religious relevance and meaning that the program had for each viewer. The half-hour was truly a space for the viewers to encounter God in their lives. The hand-written letters demonstrated that each viewer was constructing a personal and unique meaning which was helping them in their relationship with God and neighbor.

In 1985 I left the program, which was still operating as of 2004. I am confirmed in my view that media are constructions that enable the process of meaning-making. For the viewer of institutional and traditional religious TV, the program series we constructed was appropriate. It evoked a religious world within which one could celebrate and be affirmed. Although the number of viewers in Sunday morning broadcasts and daytime cable is enough to finance a program, it is nevertheless a miniscule number when compared to daytime and primetime television audiences. One of the reasons that Sunday morning TV time is sold to religious groups is that advertisers cannot justify spending advertising dollars on such a small and mature audience. For the religious media producer, serving this group is important because everyone in the church is equally important. But other groups, much larger, could also be enriched by religious media. This will take the form of media that are not so narrowly constructed and that can evoke the religious worlds of people who are not the Sunday morning TV watchers.

Currently I am working with the US Conference of Catholic Bishops, Secretariat for the Church in Latin America, to produce a documentary about the relationships between Catholics in North and South America. It is an exciting opportunity to design a program that relates to young adults and adults who live in popular culture and whose religious reference points are not traditional. We know that we will certainly not include a 13-minute preacher, but we do not know exactly which symbols, metaphors and narrative structures we will use to construct the documentary. This will become clearer as we research, shoot and edit.

As I work on this documentary, I expect that the institution today still wants to deliver a message. However, I am hopeful that we will construct an evocative documentary because church leaders who have some pastoral experience see the importance of media productions that touch the heart and stir the imagination. This is what we are trying to do.

As seen in other chapters of this book, religious meaning circulates in the community through media practices. If this is the case, most often there is no need to produce media to deliver a religious message. Instead the need is to listen to the religious meanings that are circulating in the community through popular media practices and to affirm and deepen them.

Perhaps it is helpful here to describe what I have found to be implicit, operative assumptions about media among institutional church leaders with whom I have worked. Describing these four assumptions may help to understand the appeal of an instrumentalist message-delivery model of media as opposed to the more complex and challenging view of media as constructions that enable meaning-making. I can point to moments in my own career when these were also my operating assumptions.

The Institutional Church's Four Operative Assumptions

The first assumption is that media and church are distinct, bounded, separate realities. Although they are related to each other, they nevertheless exist as two separate worlds. By contrast, in my experience as a religious producer, I find that these two worlds are conflated and share the same space. By this I mean that we are encountering religious experience in everyday media culture, and it is in media culture that our religious symbols and myths are alive. It is in media culture that we create our understandings of who we are, who God is, and how we should live. Whether watching a movie in the theater or eating while watching a TV soap opera, audiences gather to encounter God in parables of good and evil, the here and the hereafter.

The second operative assumption is that media are instruments of transmission and they are necessary to the church so that we can deliver a message. Much like trucks or trains are used to deliver products or merchandise, we are accustomed to say that we must deliver the message of the gospel. This is a transportation model which conceives of media as instruments which move products from point A to point B. It seems to me that we need a new metaphor, a more appropriate model of media, one which conceives of media as an environment, a context, a culture. Media technology has become naturalized in our daily environment and is in fact the material with which we form and inform our habits, relationships, conversation and identities. In terms of our church life, shared media experiences provide the symbolic material for our imagination and the construction of our religious identity.

The third operating assumption is that the voice of the church commands attention because of its traditionally strong moral authority both in the family and in society. As we can see from the chapter in this book by Frances Forde Plude (Chapter 13), this operating assumption no longer works. Yet although we seem to know this fact, given our many experiences, nevertheless we design television programs, purchase TV and radio stations and publish newspapers convinced that if we identify ourselves as church, this is in itself an advantage.

US television marketing studies have revealed, time and again, that people in general do not want to watch religious TV programming. But they do want to watch moral, or ethical, or values programming. Where media are concerned, people are seeking the gospel, but do not care for the institutional wrapping. This is why the audience for 'electronic church' programs like *Nuestra Familia*, the Eternal Word Network of the American nun, Mother Angelica, and many others, have such a minuscule audience. The fact that audiences for religious programs are so small is the reason that those types of programs have never been able to compete with so called 'secular' programs on television, and consequently they must always beg for donations in order to stay alive.

It seems to me that part of the problem is that we have not found a way to do two things which are both necessary. On the one hand, we must exist in the public arena of media as church. This is necessary in order to strengthen our identity and to witness. But on the other hand, we are unable to find a compelling voice among the many others offering 'traditional programming' which to the viewer well satisfies a religious need, satisfies it much more than specifically religious programming. I believe that this quandary is one of the most important issues facing the church today.

More and more the church must recognize that it is one voice among many. It seems to me that as we search deeply and thoroughly to find our appropriate voice, as a church we are operating from strength. That strength is a prophetic voice, a witness of community, and a storehouse of symbolic, narrative and sacramental resources.

Lastly, church leaders assume that the meaning of media messages is determined by the producer, and the practice of media use and consumption is predictable. That is, one can more or less determine the effects of media and their messages upon people. Changes in behavior because of those messages are also predictable.

As a producer, I know that I certainly determine what my program will look like and I hope that it will evoke certain reactions. But I also know that most of what the viewer experiences upon watching my programs will be determined by him or her. The meaning of media messages is constantly being created, negotiated, constructed *between* the producer of the text and the receiver of the text. The locus of meaning is the viewing experience. My videos do not have a meaning until the viewer constructs that meaning. Further, each viewer will construct the meaning differently.

The producer's control over the meaning is further diminished when we consider 'media talk' as the extension and prolongation of the meaning of a media product. The meaning of the TV program, movie, or radio show does not stop when the show ends. The meaning continues in the discourse of the community and its various groups. Fan clubs and gossip about a soap opera continue the meaning and add countless nuances. Teenagers often use topics from their favorite TV show to open discussions with their peers and work out their feelings and values about sex, authority and relationships.

The Media-maker

The person who either chooses or is charged with making media within church communities is a constructor of symbols and imaginative frameworks. A producer feels his way through the production process by constantly making judgments about both the clarity of rationale structures and the power of emotional responses. He relies on instinct and takes risks. Because media-making is always a new creation, the final outcome is not completely known until it unfolds in the process. Its success can be judged by the meanings that circulate among those who watch it.

This description contrasts with the understanding of a media-maker as a designer of media messages. According to this view, he is then an artful technician who can package knowledge with clarity and impact. Seen in this light, the task of the media producer is to transmit knowledge by packaging it in a visual and aural form that is appealing to the senses. The final outcome can be judged successful based on whether or not the media product is faithful to the original knowledge that was to be transmitted.

Along the way, from 1973 to 2003, religious media producers with whom I worked have combined both roles described above, sometimes even in the same production. With hindsight I understand more clearly that how a church understands media and their function determines how it will situate itself prophetically, symbolically and prayerfully in today's media world. For example, if the role of a media producer is to transmit messages that are faithful to the knowledge that constitutes our faith, the producer's participation in worship and liturgy is a narrow one, perhaps limited to discrete media productions or PowerPoint presentations. These will elucidate and illustrate.

Moreover, if the media producer's role is to package content in a manner that is contemporary and attractive, then perhaps she will be useful for those who work in religious education, spiritual retreats or social justice because she can design brochures, posters, newsletters or educational multi-media presentations. She can be strategically instrumental in the achievement of the goals that have been determined by a particular ministry. However, if the media-maker is integrated as an authentic interpreter of faith experience, she will be a full member of ministries like worship, religious education, spiritual retreats and social justice. Her appreciation of the sounds and rhythms of the culture will help redesign liturgical music and sound so that the prayer experience will resonate deeply, bodily, with the natural sounds of daily life. Contemporary stories, heroes and heroines of popular culture will find their way as reference points for discerning good and evil in today's language. The essay by Juan Carlos Henríquez in this book (Chapter 4) explains this more fully. In other words, media-making will be a collaborative work among all who work in the specific ministries, with the media producer contributing a special skill in the design of symbolic elements based on sound and vision. The contribution of the media-maker is at the heart of ministry, for media experiences nurture the experience of the sacred and as such are constitutive of the faith community, not simply illustrative or instructional of concepts and ideas.

The Praying Community

Religious media-making at its best is grounded and finds its echo in a praying community. In this context, media production is a process of meeting God, affirming community and committing to the well-being of the other. Churches in the US have often ignored these faith dimensions of media production. The reason may be that the division of labor among the various church ministries lends itself to relegating media into the category of strategic instrument as described above.

Such a division has not been present in communities where there are natural working relationships of co-responsibility among ministries. For example, when a poor urban community in Montevideo, Uruguay decided to produce a video about their trash recycling cooperative, the members did not make a distinction between their re-cycling program and the making of a video.[2] To them media is both product and process. The act of making media is a process that reinforces the community and clarifies its utopic vision.

Making a video was important to the development of this community because it wanted to become incorporated into the larger city. The video was eventually viewed by the mayor of Montevideo at city hall and this helped the community's efforts to resolve serious issues in health, housing and education. The video also cemented the community and aided in their continued dialog. The process of making it clarified their vision of who they are, what they want to achieve and why. The editing process, deciding what gets cut and what stays, engaged them in a dialog about the larger community that would view the video and how they wished to relate to this larger public sphere. When the finished video was played during small group gatherings, it was celebrated. It became the 'song of praise' during liturgy.

If a liturgical worship service is both the source of inspiration for daily life and the offering of one's life to God, then church media productions have their source and their culmination in worship. Roberto Viola SJ, a novelist and media producer in Uruguay, says that a worshipping community is constantly breaking boundaries as it strives to find God. He says that the task of a religious leader is to find out *'Dónde se escucha el hablar de Dios?'* ('Where can one hear the speaking of God?'). Oftentimes the speaking of God is found outside the normal boundaries of one's community. Therefore, the important question for church media producers is 'What is the Spirit in this community doing and saying?' It is a question of discernment, a people of God trying to be faithful.

The worshipping community is also the final point where media productions are celebrated. Churches integrate music, gestures, dance and material objects into worship but find that media (video, multi-media, recorded pop music) create difficulties beyond the obvious technical ones. Most churches do not have forms of worship that are conducive to the integration of media productions. Could it be that the general form of Sunday worship itself is from an age and culture that is foreign to people today? What are the new forms of praising God that speak in today's language? I suspect that as churches experiment with new forms and sites of worship, they are both discovering and creating the new media productions for today.

The church will produce media in the same way that it prays and witnesses, for media are vital expressions of its faith. Understood in this way, I believe that praying communities will undoubtedly make religious media that enable profound meaning-making in the cultures of our times. The spirit will not be quieted. 'I tell you, if these keep silence the stones will cry out' (Luke 19:40).

Notes

1 Estimates of the US Latino buying power range between $25 and 35 billion annually (Valenzuela, 1986).
2 The video, *Nosotros los Clasificadores*, was produced in Montevideo, Uruguay by the Organización San Vicente of the Obra Padre Cacho in December 1999.

References

Arredondo, P. (2000), 'Televisión Mexicana en Estados Unidos: ¿Extinción o Reconversión?' http://www.felafacs.org/dialogs/pdf21/arredondo.pdf .
Rodriguez, A. (n.d.), 'Spanish International Network', http://www.museum.tv/archives/etv/ S/ htmlS/spanishinter/spanishinter.htm.
Valenzuela, N. (1986), 'Spanish Language TV in the Americas: From SIN to PANAMSAT', in J. Miller (ed.), *Telecommunications and Equity: Policy Research Issues*, New York: Elsevier, pp. 329–38.

Additional Resources

Martín-Barbero, J. and G. Rey (1999), *Los Ejercicios del Ver*, Barcelona, Spain: Gedisa Editorial, 144 pages. This is an analysis of the place of television and specifically the Latin American *telenovela* in a changing, globalized society. It explores the connections among memory, narrative, traditions and changing political climates.

Tavares de Barros, J. (ed.) (1997), *Imagens Da América Latina*, São Paulo: Ocic-Brasil Edições Loyola, 142 pages. Another in the series resulting from the seminars, 'Creators of Christian Images', the collection of essays by Latin American film and video makers. Chapters include: 'Narratives of Theological Videos'; 'And the Word Was Made Digital'; and 'Evaluation of the Use of Religious Videos'.

Tavares de Barros, J. (ed.) (1992), *La Imagen Nuestra de Cada Día: Situación del Video Pastoral en América Latina*, Santa Fé de Bogotá, Colombia: Ediciones Paulinas, 203 pages. This book contains theoretical and practical essays by Latin American film and video makers about the role of a religious media producer; grassroots video, and video as cultural artifact. It is the first in a series of books published as outcomes of an annual Latin American seminar, 'Creators of Christian Images' that convenes media producers.

Chapter 11

Rescripting Religious Education in Media Culture

Mary E. Hess

During my last ten years of research I have grown convinced that religious meaning-making takes place all around us, often in places rarely identified by religious institutions as 'religious'. This conviction has grown as scholars of media, religion and culture have turned their analytical lenses on mass-mediated popular culture.[1] Rather than welcoming this insight, however, religious communities have often seen in it further evidence that religion is declining, that societies are becoming more secularized, and so on. Alternatively, some religious institutions have concluded that their most effective response is to 'encode' their central messages into particular 'frames' – thereby using the tools of mass media as yet another instrument with which to evangelize.[2]

Both of these responses ignore the underlying dynamics of mass-mediated popular culture, which far from being an 'instrument' to passively extend a message's reach is instead a cultural playground in which meaning is 'produced, contended for, and continually renegotiated and the context in which individual and communal identities are mediated and brought into being' (Davaney, 2001, p. 5).[3,4] The disconnect between the rich descriptions scholars are providing of the ways in which people make religious sense of their lives, and the instrumental modes by which religious institutions seek to respond to contemporary culture is clear evidence of an 'adaptive' challenge that religious educators face in mass-mediated cultural contexts.

Adaptive challenges

Ronald Heifetz, long a leader in professional education, has identified two specific kinds of challenges that adults face: *technical* challenges and *adaptive* challenges.[5] The first kind is met by specific concrete skills, often of a technical nature. The second is the kind of challenge that cannot be solved by the application of technical skill. Heifetz's classic example is of the difference between healing a broken arm and healing heart disease. In the first example, the extent to which healing happens depends in large measure on the doctor's ability to align a person's bones properly and get the cast made well. The patient's responsibility is primarily to interfere as little as possible in the process. In the second instance, the healing challenge becomes one of supporting a patient in coming to terms with their illness, and adapting to the necessary changes in their lifestyle. In the case of heart disease the doctor and the patient together face an adaptive challenge: they must work together in ways that have very little to do with technical skill, but much to do with relationality and meaning-making, with habit and behavior. The challenges that religious educators face in media culture are much more akin to this second example. It is no longer – if it ever was – a simple matter of 'putting on a cast', or implementing a specific curriculum well.

As scholars of media and religion are quick to point out, religious meaning-making takes place across all genres of media, and that meaning-making is neither easily controlled nor linear. As theologians struggle with bringing consistency and systematic clarity to our words about God and God's relationship with creation, we are living in institutions that are increasingly marginal to the broader structures of cultures. Clarity and consistency are good things, but clarity and consistency pursued to the point of irrelevance become nonsense. Religious educators and theologians, communications professionals and artists – all those who wish to live and work and create within communities of faith – are discovering that they must 'see anew' what their tasks are. Christian religious educators, for instance, have to re-imagine our role within communities of faith. Rather than being transmitters of doctrine, we need to become interpreters of culture – speaking both to and from the church about the ways in which the Holy Spirit is moving in the world.

Knowing How

Terry Tilley writes:

> It is hard for Christians ... to hope for heaven in a culture wherein immediate gratification is the norm, or to understand what holiness of life could be in a culture idolizing conspicuous consumption and material possessions. To believe in heaven and hope for eternal life require participation in a practice or practices that are *not* immediately gratifying ... To seek holiness requires participating in practices that shape one's desire *not* to consume and to have 'things,' but to love God and one's neighbor as oneself. The means are *knowing how* to engage in those patterns of actions and attitudes that seek the goals and carry the vision; mere *knowing that* cannot suffice. Mere notional belief will not do. (Tilley, 2000, p. 78)

If religious educators in any community – for myself that is the Christian community – are going to be successful in what we do, we need our teaching and learning in communities of faith to be about *knowing how*, not simply *knowing that*. Yet *knowing how* ought not to be confused with the kind of 'technical' skill required of the doctor with the cast, mentioned earlier in this essay. Instead, *knowing how* has to be understood as 'participating in practices that shape one's desire' and as engaging 'in those patterns of actions and attitudes that seek the goals and carry the vision' – in short, it is a form of knowing that is deeply participatory. But how is that kind of knowing supported educationally?

Parker Palmer argues that we have tended to think of education as an instrumental and linear process, indeed a 'technical' one. In such a model of education the teacher is the one who provides the bridge for the 'pure' content of the subject to reach the amateurs. In this very linear process the teacher becomes, in effect, the 'instrument' by which the information is conveyed. It is this model that Palmer's first image, (Figure 11.1a) is meant to illustrate (Palmer, 1998, pp. 107–8). Palmer suggests, however, that there is another model we could retrieve from religious communities. In that model the subject is placed at the epistemological center. That is, the thing or things, the ideas or concepts, the feelings and actions that we want to learn from are at the heart of a dynamic process around which we gather. Each of us becomes a 'knower' who is in relationship with the 'great thing' that we desire to know. Each of us is also in relationship with each other. Palmer's second image describes this communal model, with information flowing in many directions, and with multiple ways in which to learn about something, multiple relationships by which we come to know (Figure 11.1b). Indeed, at the heart of Palmer's model is his assertion that 'we know as we are known' (Palmer, 1993).

This model of teaching and learning suggests that knowledge is a dynamic, relational process, rather than a formulaic, regulated one. It suggests that the 'great thing' in the middle of our knowing *might be a script for our participation in the construction of knowledge,* as compared to the first model, where knowledge is something apart from the learner, and simply transferred to them through the mediation of a teacher.

This second model also highlights an adaptive understanding of *knowing how,* implicit in many of the stories Christians, for example, narrate about the ways in which Jesus taught. Various gospel authors describe Jesus amidst groups of people, working with their questions; using analogies drawn from the contexts around them; often answering one question with another question. 'Who are you?' receives 'Who do you say that I am?' 'Who is my neighbor?' evokes a story and a question in response. The communities of people who gathered around Jesus were hungry for answers, but they received stories and more questions, and were thereby drawn into new patterns of practice. At the heart of this adaptive model is a recognition of the deeply collaborative, relational elements of knowing – a recognition that is bubbling up from within many numerous attempts to revision Trinitarian theology, as well.[6]

This is a model for Christian *learning,* above all else, and it provides a way to engage our differences as crucial insight, crucial knowing. If we are all knowers, all teachers and learners, and if the great thing we put at the heart of our study is a script for our participation in Christian practice, then deepening our learning of this script, of these practices, is not only possible, but life-giving and transformative.

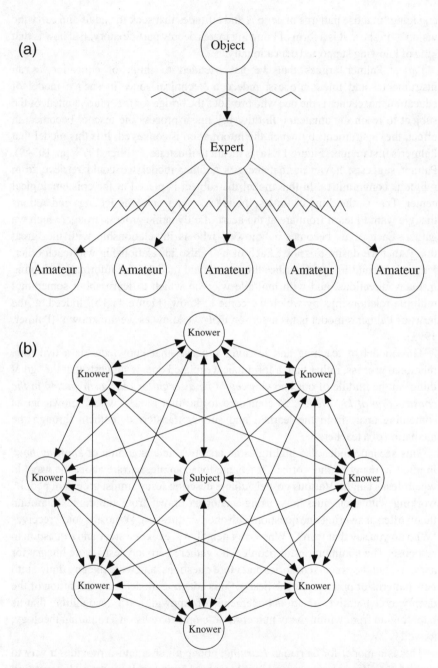

Figure 11.1   Models of teaching and learning Parker Palmer, *The Courage to Teach***, San Francisco, CA: Jossey-Bass, 1998.**

Courtesy of the publishers

What does religious education look like within media culture when it takes seriously this model of teaching and learning? Over and over in our travels, the International Study Commission on Media, Religion and Culture was presented with numerous examples of the ways in which people locally were 'playing' with and 'improvising' with mass-mediated popular cultural materials in their religious meaning-making. They were quite literally 'gathering around' sets of vivid stories (films, television, pop songs and so on), and thinking/feeling/acting their way religiously through and within them.

At our meeting in Bangkok, for example, we learned of the enormous crisis the advent of economic globalization has created for Catholic families seeking to nurture their children's faith in a country in which only 2 percent of the people are Christian (let alone Catholic). Siriwan Santisakultarm writes more about this challenge elsewhere in this book (Chapter 12), but I would highlight here her conviction that meeting that challenge well requires engaging 'human media' responsibly. Palmer's second model, relationally based as it is, provides a better foundation for meeting the adaptive challenge Christians in Bangkok face than any instrumental, 'banking' notion of doctrinal transmittal.[7]

Another example from the Bangkok meeting came in the form of a video produced by the Jesuit Communications Project that told the compelling story of a young Jesuit who had embraced an injured boy carrying a bomb into a Cambodian school – in so doing, dying himself but protecting other children from injury.[8] The video used the biblical phrase – 'there is no greater love than to lay down one's life for a friend' – to explore and describe Christian witness without ever implying that such witness must be triumphal, colonial, imperial, or so on. Indeed, for me one of the strongest insights emerging from the meeting in Thailand had to do with what evangelization might consist of in a globalized world. Much as Roberto Goizueta points out in his essay in this volume (Chapter 3), the people we met with in Bangkok convinced me that the mission of the church is one of being present to those most marginalized, to bring hope, love and mercy in the face of oppression. That contributing to such hope might be pursued through a medium such as video was particularly compelling to me.

Yet another example emerged in our meeting in Quito, Ecuador, where among other 'trinkets' I brought home with me was a computer CD that had been decorated with an image of the Virgin Mary, and hung with a chain to make it into a car accessory. This might appear to be a very ephemeral, trivial example, but I have since been struck by the play of rainbow light that encircles the image as it hangs in my office window, and the extent to which it has been a focus of conversation for visitors. This small piece of 'junk' has actually provoked more thoughtful and interesting reflection upon the role of Mary in Christian spirituality than any number of abstruse theological tomes that also grace my office bookshelves. This object has become a very present example for me of the ways in which people improvise meaning with the materials around them, of the ways in which they 'perform' religious meaning-making in their daily practices. This question of what constitutes 'performance' of religious meaning is one that religious educators must take seriously.

Performative Practice

In my own context, of North America, there is an argument taking place over what it means to inhabit the Christian witness, over the 'performance' of that script. The argument includes disputants as diverse as the President of the United States, various peace movements, televangelists, children's cartoons, pop music artists and so on. Christian religious educators need to enter into this argument, finding ways to participate constructively, and creating a wider space in which others can do so as well. Lately I have found that taking the metaphor of a 'script' seriously can be quite evocative.

Consider, for a moment, what is involved in preparing to perform a play. To begin with, the play's actors 'learn the script'. But learning a script entails far more than memorizing words. Wooden, parroted dialog does not in any way feel real. The actors need to explore the contexts in which the words were written, they need to imagine the motivations and feelings behind them, and they need to explore their way into making the script their own. This is a process that requires a community of people who are so deeply steeped in the 'script' that they can assist others in 'catching' a vision of it. Many people will pick up a script and not be able to imagine how its words hold any meaning for them. 'Learning' a script requires first wanting to learn it, and that requires – particularly in the context of religious education – some sense that the script holds something of value, something that will touch one's meaning-making.

In a mediated sphere, where simply having a religious institution 'proclaim' truth is not enough for people to take the utterance seriously, let alone 'authorize' it as truthful, religious educators are challenged to make immediate and engaging the central narratives of our script. The 'words' we use to tell this narrative will likely vary widely between educators, let alone amidst different communities. Within the Christian context, for instance, some will understand 'word' as 'Word' – meaning the sustained witness of Jesus Christ. Some will understand 'word' as 'biblical narrative' – meaning human interpretations of human renderings of sacred speech. Some will understand 'word' best as music, as dance, as drumming, as festival preparation. But the point here is that this is both a communal and an interpretative process, and one that begins with a community that holds these stories central to its identity.

In some ways, this aspect of 'enacting' our script holds much in common with the ways in which religious education has traditionally been understood, particularly when that process took on the depth elements of socialization into religious community.[9] Immersing people in liturgical celebrations, placing beautiful children's books with explicit religious language into the midst of bedtime reading rituals, adding candles and flowers to family prayer, teaching biblical stories through music – these are all examples of traditional Christian practices that have helped people to 'learn the dialogue' of the Christian scripts they are seeking to construct together. The Study Commission saw numerous examples of this kind of work scattered across the multiple contexts we visited. Some of it was moving into digital formats, and beginning to penetrate other new media. Uruguayan religious educators, for instance, have created a series of materials that incorporate video stories and in Japan and Korea animated filmmakers are at work on biblical stories.[10]

This process of 'learning the words' of the script, however, really only comes alive in rehearsal, as people begin to play with different interpretations. *Practicing* or *rehearsing* is much more about 'knowing how' than 'knowing that' – it is a form of knowing that is deeply adaptive, deeply interpretative, not merely technical. Actors preparing to enact a play practice over and over again in multiple contexts, sometimes on their own but more often with their collaborators; sometimes with minimal sets and costumes, and eventually with a full dress rehearsal as they collaborate in the creation of specifically nuanced meaning.

Right now the 'words' of a religious script – whether that is defined as biblical witness, confessional heritage, sacred symbol and so on – are afloat all over media cultures. Every day people are 'practicing' with snippets of the script, constructing meaning in numerous contexts across multiple cultures. Some are practicing the whole thing in full costume – perhaps enacted liturgically in grand cathedrals – and some are practicing it in *avant garde* dress – perhaps on the airwaves of the local pop radio station, or embedded in a comic book. An alert religious educator will be able to support the actors in picking up the resonances and connecting them with other narrative streams, identifying the allusions being made and highlighting the references.

Our meeting in Hollywood, CA alerted us to the many ways in which creative professionals in that environment are playing with, practicing and rehearsing, religious meaning. Mass mediated popular culture in the US is full of opportunities for religious educators to practice this kind of interpretive accompaniment, whether they are engaging the obvious (films like *The Matrix*, *Bruce Almighty* and *Harry Potter* come to mind), or the more subtle or allusive (music like that of U2, Bruce Springsteen, Dave Matthews band and so on). Still, in some ways these two moments in performance – learning the dialog of a script, and rehearsing it – remain moments that typically occur 'within' the circle of the play's actors, authors, and so on.

Yet no play is truly 'whole' until there is also an audience engaged in participation. The audience brings the context alive, and participates in hearing and making meaning out of the dialog. No matter how well and how hard the actors have practiced, the audience can change the meaning of what is happening. Here is where the metaphor of dramatic performance perhaps begins to break down, because the line between the 'performer' and the 'audience' is not clear, perhaps can never be clear, within a religious community. There will always be, for example, people for whom the script is central to their identities, and people for whom the script belongs to some other community and they are simply visitors. Here, then, the metaphor points to something very important, that Christians (in particular, speaking personally) need to attend to.

Christians are called by sacred scripture to 'go and make disciples', but far too often we have heard that imperative in narrow, technical ways. Rather than hearing it as an invitation to learn more about our own script, we have instead heard it as a demand to simply pass the script along. Understanding knowing in relational, collaborative terms, seeing clearly that the twenty-first century demands adaptive responses, we can begin to see that we are called to *perform* our script in multiple contexts.

This is an imperative for mission, not because Christians seek ways to impose our script on others, but because we know, deep in our bones, deep in our communities, that we can only really *know* this script with as wide a circle of fellow learners as possible. As the Catholics in Bangkok know, these stories have meanings people from other faiths can bring alive to us. As the Catholics in Quito know, these stories mean differently in the many and varied contexts of Ecuador. Media culture has something to add as well. When U2 sings of 'grace' it adds nuance to that term, and when Springsteen devotes an album to 'The Rising' and sings of 'strength, hope and love' we can be reminded of the Pauline exhortation.

Indeed, our sacred narrative invites us to move outward in the deep humility of a pilgrim on a journey of transformation. We are invited to 'perform' our script in multiple contexts not to 'prove' our interpretation, but to *risk* it; not instrumentally or technically to 'apply' our narrative to a larger context, but in fact to enter into the larger context in order to see what God might be telling us there. This is a moment in the construction of meaning that is obviously dynamic and uncontrollable. It is precisely also the moment in which mass-mediated popular culture is at its most persuasive, and thus religious institutions often find themselves backing away from this kind of engagement.

Here the work of Alejandro Garcia-Rivera and Roberto Goizueta ought to be most compelling for religious educators, at least those of us working within the Christian context, for it invites us into this kind of participation and performance, and suggests that there are in fact rubrics we can follow to maintain congruence and authenticity.[11] Tilley, too, has something to say about this when he writes that:

> Human beings engage in practices that constitute traditions; as contexts vary, those practices change, sometimes radically and sometimes deliberately. The grammar of the tradition, we could say, is both made (by the participants' practices) and found (as intellectuals reflectively analyze those practices and write rules for the practices like the present one). The grammar of the practices shapes us in the ways in which we live and move and have our being; but we also reshape and reinvent the grammar of the practices, and perhaps even change the rules as practices are translated into new places. In this sense traditions are both made and found. (Tilley, 2000, pp. 150–51)

Further,

> *tradita* alone do not carry the tradition ... the greater the difference between the context in which the *traditor* learned the tradition and the context in which the tradition is transmitted, the greater the possibility that a shift in *tradita* may be necessary to communicate the tradition. Paradoxically, fidelity to a tradition may sometimes involve extensive reworking of the *tradita*. (Ibid., p. 29)

Indeed, it may be that it is this very reworking that is the most essential task that religious educators engage in, in mediated cultures. People who are involved with improvisational theater note that it is crucial to know the moves and gestures that convey meaning, to know how stories work so deeply in your being that you can perform even when the story is being changed or you are inventing it as you play. The circumstances around us, the contexts in which we live, are changing rapidly; so rapidly that some commentators say we live in a perpetual state of 'blur' (Davis and Meyer, 1999). Others write that we must learn to live while navigating constant whitewater (Vaill, 1996). Whatever metaphor you find powerful, increasingly religious educators working in media cultures have to recognize that we are being called upon to practice improvisation. Business leaders respond to this adaptive challenge by transforming their businesses into learning organizations (Senge, 1994). Religious leaders need to do the same, as Cormode points out when he references Bolman and Deal's work (1997) and suggests that '"visionary leadership is inevitably symbolic", ... during periods of significant social change, society looks to such symbolic leaders to weave troublesome events into a coherent narrative of hope' (Cormode, 2002, p. 94).

Learning our script, practicing it, performing it in multiple contexts and improvising to learn/learning to improvise take on greater urgency when the contexts are always changing around us. Communities of faith have thus far focused on the challenges of media culture in much the same way that we have conceived of learning – instrumentally. We have worried about electronic screens and we have worried about the content of popular culture, and in doing so we have sought to figure out how to have either a better 'technique' for conveying our own content, or how to have a better way of inoculating people against the dangerous content carried by the electronic pipelines. Yet each of these worries assumes that mass media work in instrumental ways, and even more so, assumes an instrumental model of teaching and learning. They assume that religious experts can and must control the performance of our shared script.

Neither of these assumptions is adequately descriptive of the world we inhabit. Religious educators need at once both to let go of our control over our 'scripts', and be even more engaged in enacting them. We will not succeed by asking everyone to participate only in 'religiously approved' content, or by asking everyone to boycott problematic 'secular' content. In doing so we force people into narrow enclaves of religious identity or we force them into vast trivialization of religious truths.[12] We force them to flee the adaptive challenge into the technical 'solution' of authority, or into the ignorance of denial. This cannot be what we mean by religious identity, and it does us no good to conceive of teaching and learning in these narrow ways.

Instead religious educators need to think about the ways in which we can invite religious resonance that is always and everywhere present, into our lives every day and in every way. We need to find a way to respond to the sacred invitation to play. We need to find a way to live into the script of our religious witness, to live in such a way – performatively – that our religious witness rings true, and we need to teach and learn in such a way that we can support people in this kind of improvising. The International Study Commission on Media, Religion and Culture has been, for me, the primary way in which my own imagination has been challenged into adaptation. It is my hope that this volume will now provide an entry point for others, as well.

Notes

1   Here, in particular, I think of the work shared within the international media, religion and culture conferences. Some of that work has been published by Hoover and Lundby, Hoover and Clark, and Mitchell and Marriage.

2   There are numerous sociological studies that document the varied responses of religious communities to this changing landscape. Two that I have found evocative in the US context are Roof (1999), and Cimino and Lattin (1998).

3   I have written about the implications of this paradigm shift in Hess (1999).

4   Lyon has also written about this, noting that 'people construct religious meanings from the raw materials provided by the media, repositioning and patterning the elements according to logics both local and global, both innovative and traditional' (Lyon, 2000, p. 57).

5   See, in particular, Heifetz (1994), pp. 73–84.

6   Classic texts here would be LaCugna (1991), and Johnson (1992).

7   The negative implications of understanding education as 'banking' of concrete information is powerfully articulated by Freire (1970).

8   The video, entitled 'Greater Love', is dedicated to the memory of the young Jesuit, Richie Fernando, and can be acquired by writing to Sonolux Bldg, Ateneo de Manila University, Loyola Heights, Quezon City, Philippines (jcf@pusit.admu.edu.ph).

9   See, in particular, Boys (1989).

10 See, for example, the work of Eloisa Chouy in Uruguay, and Clotilde Lee in Seoul, Korea.

11 See, in particular, Goizueta (1995), pp. 73 ff., and Garciá-Rivera (1999), pp. 87 ff.

12 See, in particular, Heifetz (1994) and Heifetz and Linsky (2002) for their description of ways to meet adaptive challenges, and John Hull (1991).

References

Bolman, L. and T. Deal (1997), *Reframing Organizations: Artistry, Choice and Leadership*, San Francisco, CA: Jossey-Bass.

Boys, M. (1989), *Educating in Faith: Maps and Visions*, San Francisco, CA: Harper & Row.

Brown, D., S. Davaney and K. Tanner (eds) (2001), *Converging on Culture: Theologians in Dialogue with Cultural Analysis and Criticism*, New York: Oxford University Press.

Cimino, R. and D. Lattin (1998), *Shopping for Faith: American Religion in the New Millenium*, San Francisco, CA: Jossey-Bass.

Cormode, S. (2002), 'Multi-layered Leadership: The Christian Leader as Builder, Shepherd, and Gardener', in *Journal of Religious Leadership* (2), 69–104.

Davaney, S. (2001), 'Theology and the Turn to Cultural Analysis', in D. Brown, S. Davaney and K. Tanner (eds), *Converging on Culture: Theologians in Dialogue with Cultural Analysis and Criticism*, New York: Oxford University Press, pp. 3–16.

Davis, S. and C. Meyer (1999), *Blur: The Speed of Change in the Connected Economy*, New York: Little, Brown and Company.

Freire, P. (1970), *Pedagogy of the Oppressed*, New York: Herder and Herder.

García-Rivera, A. (1999), *The Community of the Beautiful: A Theological Aesthetics*, Collegeville, MN: The Liturgical Press.

Goizueta, R. (1995), *Caminemos con Jesús: Toward a Hispanic/Latino Theology of Accompaniment*, Maryknoll, NY: Orbis Press.

Heifetz, R. (1994), *Leadership Without Easy Answers*, Cambridge, MA: Harvard University Press.

Heifetz, R. and M. Linsky (2002), *Leadership on the Line: Staying Alive Through the Dangers of Leading*, Cambridge, MA: Harvard Business School Press.

Hess, M. (1999), 'From Trucks Carrying Messages to Ritualized Identities: Implications of the Postmodern Paradigm Shift in Media Studies for Religious Educators', *Religious Education*, **94** (3), Summer, 273–88.

Hoover, S. M. and L. S. Clark (eds) (2002), *Practicing Religion in an Age of Media*, New York: Columbia University Press.

Hoover, S. M. and K. Lundby (eds) (1997), *Rethinking Media, Religion and Culture*, Thousand Oaks, CA: Sage Publications.

Hull, J. (1991), *What Prevents Christian Adults from Learning?* Philadelphia, PA: Trinity International Press.

Johnson, E. (1992), *She Who Is: The Mystery of God in Feminist Theological Discourse*, New York: Crossroads.

LaCugna, C. (1991), *God for US: The Trinity and Christian Life*, San Francisco, CA: HarperSanFrancisco.

Lyon, D. (2000), *Jesus in Disneyland: Religion in Postmodern Times*, Cambridge: Polity Press (in association with Blackwell Publishers).

Mitchell, J. and S. Marriage (2003), *Mediating Religion: Conversations in Media, Religion and Culture*, Edinburgh: T&T Clark and New York: Continuum.

Palmer, P. (1998), *The Courage to Teach: Exploring the Inner Landscape of a Teacher's Life*, San Francisco, CA: Jossey-Bass.

Palmer, P. (1993), *To Know as We are Known*, San Francisco, CA: HarperSanFrancisco.

Roof, W. (1999), *Spiritual Marketplace: Baby Boomers and the Remaking of American Religion*, Princeton, NJ: Princeton University Press.

Senge, P. (1994), *The Fifth Discipline*, New York: Doubleday.

Tilley, T. (2000), *Inventing Catholic Tradition*, Maryknoll, NY: Orbis Books.

Vaill, P. (1996), *Learning as a Way of Being: Strategies for Survival in a World of Permanent White Water*, San Francisco, CA: Jossey-Bass.

Additional Resources

Anderson, H. and E. Foley (1997), *Mighty Stories, Dangerous Rituals*, San Francisco, CA: Jossey-Bass. This book is a wonderful description and critical analysis of the interwoven nature of ritual and narrative. In focusing on moments of birth, life covenant and death, it also provides an excellent introduction into Christian theological insight about baptism, marriage and anointing of the sick. The ways in which it talks about parabolic and mythic narratives and rituals provide crucial insight into our media culture immersion, too.

Kegan, R. and L. Lahey (2000), *How the Way We Talk Can Change the Way We Work*, San Francisco, CA: Jossey-Bass. For years I've been recommending Robert Kegan's work to people, particularly his books *The Evolving Self* and *In Over Our Heads: The Mental Demands of Modern Life*. Unfortunately, for many people his ideas are drawn in too complex and evocative a way in these books. I still think his books are important! But if you can't find your way through them, or you'd like an easier or more practical place to start, give this book a try. Kegan is a crucial scholar of adult learning and development, and in this small book he and Lisa Lahey walk people through a process of transformative learning.

McGann, M. (2002), *Exploring Music and Theology*, Collegeville, MN: Liturgical Press. Music shapes meaning in profoundly important ways, but seldom do media studies scholars who are considering popular culture and religion understand the liturgical and theological elements of that shaping process. Here's a lovely little book that suggests some ways to examine how music shapes meaning in religious communities.

Mitchell, J. (1999), *Visually Speaking, Radio and the Renaissance of Preaching*, Edinburgh, T & T Clark. This book is ostensibly 'about' radio preaching in Britain and America, but it is also deeply about conveying deep theological insights in ways that are attuned to the dynamics of media culture.

Tilley, T. (2000), *Inventing Catholic Tradition*, Maryknoll, NY: Orbis Books. This book considers Catholic tradition from the standpoint of practice. Focusing on Catholic intellectual tradition, rather than Catholic theological tradition, Tilley explains why catechesis has to focus on performative practice, has to work with orthopraxis not just orthodoxy.

Vella, J. (1994), *Learning to Listen, Learning to Teach*, San Francisco, CA: Jossey-Bass. This book is chock full of great stories about learning and teaching in a variety of contexts all over the world. Vella has organized it around a set of 12 principles that are great basic principles for all kinds of learning environments.

Weinberger, D. (2002), *Small Pieces, Loosely Joined*, New York: Perseus Books. The best book I've found for helping theologians and members of communities of faith begin to understand why the Net has had such an impact. This is a luminously written, accessible introduction that raises profoundly theological questions.

Chapter 12

Changes in the Thai Catholic Way of Life

Siriwan Santisakultarm

Stories about the Thai Catholic lifestyle are little known to most people around the world. I believe this is due to the fact that Thai Catholics are a minority in a mostly Buddhist country. In 2000, the population of Thailand was 62 million, but only 272,350 were Catholics (Thai Catholic Calendar, 2001). Furthermore, Thai Catholics have lived quietly and peacefully within the country, not creating any problems of media interest. Thus, the rich heritage of Thai Catholics is an untold story.

In this chapter I wish to share with you my experience and observations as a Thai Catholic. A number of significant shifts have occurred in the Thai cultural context over the past half-century. This chapter concerns the decline in Thai Catholic life as Catholic village communities changed for a number of reasons, including the migration of young people to urban, predominantly Buddhist communities. This trend has been compounded by the influence of materialism, consumerism, individualism and syncretism. My own experience growing up in a strong Catholic village community and migrating to the city offers an illustration of this cultural change.

Yet, I believe there are seeds of new hope emerging for fostering communities of faith through the new initiatives of the Catholic Bishops' Conference of Thailand and committed Thai Catholics of the twenty-first century.

The Community of Thai Catholics Fifty Years Ago

I was born in 1957 and grew up in a small Catholic village. The members of my family were parishioners of the Church of St Peter's Chair (Bansueknang) of the Talingchan district in the Thonburi province in the suburb of Bangkok. The village consisted of about 800 persons, of Thai, Chinese and mixed origins. This Thai Catholic way of life could be found in various provinces of Thailand. In the year 2000 there were about 447 such villages in Thailand (Thai Catholic Calendar, 2001).[1] The center of almost every Catholic village or community was the parish church with a Catholic school.

From my childhood I remember being a member of three different families: the first was that of my mother and father, the second that of my baptismal godparents, and the third that of my confirmation godparents. Each one directly influenced

165

my religious formation. The relationship and community we shared gave us an intimate sense of being one family. Larger Catholic families of eight or more children experienced more profoundly the sense of family or community, with more godparents engaging themselves in the lives of the natural family.

Godparents had a distinctive role to play in the upbringing of their godchildren. They not only participated in the baptismal ceremony in the church but also were expected to provide assistance to their godchild whenever possible. This was realized not only by giving gifts and money but also by the special care, attention and advice they offered regarding the faith and spirituality formation of their godchildren. People with many godchildren were respected as exemplary Christians and Catholics of profound faith.

The Communication-rich Environment of the Catholic Village

In our small Catholic village everyone knew every family and its story. This is how it was before the influence of today's modern communications that appear to distract us from the intimate intercommunication and sense of community that bonded us as one family in the past.

Throughout my childhood, storytelling – communicating by word of mouth – offered us not only a sense of our Catholic identity but also a mechanism of moral control that helped ensure our adherence to the teachings of the church. News spread quickly in our village. If you did a good deed, you were surely admired. One might have even been elected or appointed a village leader, president, or member of the parish council committee by the good deeds remembered. One might have been sought after to be godparents, and good married couples were invited to be witnesses at new weddings. Parents or godparents of children who entered religious life or the priesthood were greatly admired and respected by other villagers. Within this communication-rich environment, therefore, parents tried to behave well and teach their children to pray so that their children's and grandchildren's faith might blossom into religious vocations. According to the Catholic Bishops' Conference of Thailand (Thai Catholic Calendar, 2001), there are 660 priests, 1429 religious sisters and 122 religious brothers in Thailand. The ratio of Catholics to priests in Thailand is approximately 412 to 1.[2]

Those in the Catholic village who misbehaved or committed such crimes as gambling, adultery, cheating, not attending mass or not participating in communion and confession were resented by other members of the village. Furthermore, people who committed terrible sins – such as divorce, abandoning their family, never confessing or going to communion – were not allowed to be buried in the graveyard of the church. The communication-rich environment created the moral climate of our Catholic villages.

One of my most joyful moments and vivid memories is the sound of the bell every Sunday morning calling the faithful to church. Almost every member of the family went to church. Our parish had specially reserved seating for mothers with children, thus encouraging parents of newborn children to attend mass. Villagers looked forward to going to church every Sunday because they could dress up, children would play in front of the church, and beautiful pictures, newspapers and magazines were available for reading and bringing home. The church's bulletin, which was produced by the school, was also available to everybody.

The homily of the priest was exciting for those who attended mass; everyone was curious, wondering who would be found fault with *this* Sunday and who would be instructed and corrected by the priest during the homily. The priest mentioned the names of people who always came late to mass or left early. People were even more interested in listening to the priest's ranting and raving about those who the previous week had misbehaved by fighting, gambling, practicing witchcraft or joining another religion. The image of the family or person criticized would be undermined – they could lose face. They would be challenged by the priest to stop misbehaving and convert themselves to the accepted religious view. Occasionally, people resisted the priest's intonations of moral behavior and did not attend church or participate in community activities.

The involvement of priests in people's private lives created conflict in the villages, but their involvement decreased with changes in the Catholic Church itself. The sacrament of reconciliation and holy communion are examples. Before the 1960s, the church taught that one could not receive communion without also taking the sacrament of reconciliation. As a result, few received communion, some because they did not want to deal with the priest for the sacrament of reconciliation. As transportation became more readily available, some went to churches outside their village. In 1965, the Catholic Church of Thailand began to teach that Catholics could receive communion without undergoing the sacrament of reconciliation with the priest, provided their sin was minor. As a result, the number of people receiving communion rose. Today few approach the sacrament of reconciliation but many receive communion.

Still, in the 1950s and 1960s, the priest was the center of village life. If a person were sick and unable to go to church, the priest would bring the holy communion to that person in the afternoon when he visited the Catholic houses in the village. After the mass everyone had the opportunity to talk; young men and women engaged in conversation and adults would not find fault with them. Parents conversed spontaneously and creatively exchanged the family and village news of the week.

Catholics were dependent on the Catholic community and believed in the priests. The policy of the Catholic Church in Thailand, following faithfully the ways of the missionaries who spread Catholicism since 1567, was that the priest was the head of the community (Chumsripan, 1994, pp. 63–85).[3] In this role, he controlled village land, a tradition that dates back to the sixteenth century when the king gave land to the first missionaries, who organized the first Thai Catholic villages. Priests continued the tradition of buying land and arranging for Catholics to live together, giving the village priest powerful control over the village.[4] Today, priests do not have such absolute power, as they must answer to an elected pastoral council in each church, and land reform is done by a department of the church. Likewise, in the past the priest controlled the village school, but today the schools are run by the religious congregation. Village Catholics still respect the priest, but only in religious matters; the priest is not part of their daily lives as he was in the past.

These changes were in the context of gradual but profound changes in the means of communication and transportation in my village during the 1960s and early 1970s. In 1967, electricity arrived, replacing lamps and candles. Wealthy families installed television sets in their houses, and their neighbors gathered to watch with them after church on Sundays and sometimes in the evenings. The means of transportation along the canal also gradually changed, as engine boats replaced paddle boats. Little by little, the governor of Bangkok built a road around the village. And in 1974, the first telephone line came to the village, although only one or two families could afford to connect the line to their houses.

Living Together: The Foundation of Love and Sharing

As a child, I studied the catechism every morning at school. The Sisters of the Sacred Heart of Jesus of Bangkok taught us the basic truths of the Catholic faith, preparing us for the sacraments and introducing us to sacred music and prayers. A variety of rich liturgical year activities, such as Christmas, Corpus Christi and Easter, were brought to life through biblical dramas, dance and choral presentations. Everyone in the village participated in the planning and execution of these celebrations. Men built the stage and scenes for our shows, women prepared special dishes to contribute to the community meal and the leader of the village was ever present to supervise the entire process. By sharing and working together during these celebrations, our community became stronger and more unified in our faith.

One particular parish celebration was especially meaningful to me. Each year on the anniversary of our parish's patron saint, St Peter's Chair, families would decorate their boats with flowers and banners and join a 'floating procession' around the village. We incorporated much festivity, pageantry and joyfulness in this celebration. In one sense this was a great demonstration of how we communicated, passed on and preserved our rich Catholic heritage.

Often in nearby Buddhist villages there were also grand celebrations around their religious holidays and commemorative religious events. There were fascinating entertainment shows that would draw the attention of a few Catholics who joined in the events. The elders of the village said that because the priest did not allow Catholics to join in the Buddhist activities, the Catholic numbers were always low.

There were times following evening prayer and before children retired that mothers would re-tell animating stories about the school and church in the village. They could capture the imagination of the children by poetically describing how the men from the village traveled to the northern forests to cut wood and carry it down south along the Chao Praya River. One of the elderly men, the head of carpentry in the village, and his assistant helped build the local church. The women helped by preparing food for the workers.

Another important activity that helped ground our Catholic identity and enrich our bonds of community was the tradition of praying for the dead for seven consecutive nights following a person's death. All of the villagers would come to the home of the deceased after their daily work to pray. There was no discrimination in these times of sorrow. Food was served after our prayer, and, as it always did, food played an important role in holding our community together. Occasionally more than one person died within the same period of time and the community would come together daily for two or three weeks to pray and eat.

I recall one more religious event that seemed to bond our faith community together. There was a special statue of our Blessed Virgin that the parish priest would bring around the village in procession. The statue would be enthroned in a different house each night during a particular period of time. Every member of the family would pray together when the statue was present in their home.

These are a few examples of how our Catholic faith helped bring our village together better than any other social institution could. Those who shared the same beliefs found a variety of religious reasons to come together and celebrate their common bond. This bond became a source of inspiration for ongoing education and creative religious expression within our culture. Here was fertile ground for molding our moral character and sending the deep roots of our Catholic heritage into every fiber of our being.

Today, many of these practices have changed, and although the Catholic villages still exist, the community spirit in them is very different. Today, when someone dies, the body might be taken to a well-known church more convenient to mourners who do not live in the village. The practice of bringing the icon of the Virgin into the home for evening prayers is now rare. Television has contributed to the decline in this ritual, as people prefer to watch favorite evening programs. In addition, villagers who work outside the village often return home too late for the prayers.

The Three Main Means of Religious Media in the Community

I hope to have conveyed something of the importance of relationships in the Thai Catholic communities fifty years ago. In terms of communication, I believe there were three major ways in which people in our villages communicated faith.

The first was human or personal media. Our fathers, mothers, relatives, neighbors, priests, sisters and teachers were the key communicators. This type of communication was very powerful and its influence was felt in many of the inter-actions we had with one another in the community. The communication-rich environment was a control mechanism of the community of religious faith.

Knowledge of the faith and religious experience was instilled in us through the human and personal media and stayed with us throughout our lives.

The second way of communicating faith was through religious activities that were embedded in our lives. We might refer to these as traditional media. In our Catholic community, these religious activities were the ceremonies we celebrated as a community that nurtured faith within ourselves and bonded the community into a unified and solid community of faith.

The third way was through materials produced by the Catholic Social Communications of Thailand, now known as UCIP (l'Union catholique internationale de la presse, or the Commission for Mass Media). At first, the organization produced only printed material such as newspapers, magazines, leaflets, posters and calendars. In 1968, the work was extended to electronic media, the video and audio sector, and is now called SIGNIS Thailand (The World Catholic Association for Communication). This association began with the production of cassettes, prayers and Church songs. These products could not compete with commercial media, with some exceptions. For example, the Catholic Office of Communication took movies such as *Ben Hur* and *The Ten Commandments* to Catholic villages, where they were popular with both Catholics and Buddhists. The practice largely ended in 1978 with the arrival of modern transportation to take people to the city and its new movie theaters. In 1977, the organization began to produce radio and television programs.

Life Outside the Catholic Community

The rich sense of community that we once experienced began to fade when we left the village. Young people left every day to attend the university, as I did in 1974 when I enrolled at Thammasart University in the heart of Bangkok. As we looked toward the future, we had to travel to find good positions with high salaries in the city, in hopes of securing comfort and security for ourselves. Fifty years ago, Thais would attend school for only four to seven years before they turned to farming. Instead of leaving after elementary school to work in the field, I traveled from my village to high school each day, then to the university, where I got a master's degree. My family was the first in the village to have someone attend a university. When I went to work at a government-owned television station, the largest communication organization in Thailand, everyone in my village talked about it. When I became a television news reporter, people talked about it even more. Little by little after that, young people in my village made their way into higher education.

Young educated Catholics left the villages because there was little work, except in the schools, for educated people. When they moved to the city, they were surrounded by Buddhist society. At first, many found it difficult to preserve their Catholic identity. This was due to the fact that Catholic instructions had forbidden them to join other religious activities. In contrast, religious ceremonies were integrated into the daily working lives of Buddhists, as new building projects, company anniversaries and receptions for guests were all celebrated. Catholic employees who attended found it difficult because church law at the time forbade participation. Some Catholics who were promoted to high positions in companies were careful not to reveal that they were Catholic.

The Powerful Means of Communication no Longer Exist

As time passed, many of us intermarried and started families with people of other religious faiths. Thus, we lived further away from the fundamental Catholic context, which originally nurtured our profound experience and identity as Catholics. A recent survey found that 66 to 75 percent of Catholic families in Bangkok are families with only one Catholic parent (Muangrat, 1998, p. 105). That number has increased in the past two decades, from 368 Catholics married to non-Catholics in the Bangkok diocese in 1985, to 495 in 2002 (Saengtham College Thailand, 2001).

Communication research states that communication between persons, which is firmly grounded from the beginning, has a definite effect on attitudes, faith and opinions. The integrated and foundational communications in the Catholic society 40 to 50 years ago had a profound impact on how fervently Catholics lived their faith later in lives. The research of Nipa Muangrat (1998) confirms that Thai Catholics who receive religious messages early in life have a higher level of Catholic knowledge, faith and engagement in fervent religious activities.

Both families and individuals in Bangkok are challenged by the changing profile of neighborhoods and the lack of religious conversation and experience on a regular basis. Today we seldom have Catholic neighbors. We no longer hear the sound of the church bells on Sunday morning inviting us to church. Modernization brought about an increase in families in which one parent is Catholic and the other is of another religious tradition. Modern families have no time to care for and educate their children in the traditional ways. The more critical factor facing them today is that they are not prepared to impart knowledge and communicate faith and religion within the family. Thus, our once fertile ground has lost the means for nurturing strong communities of faith in the postmodern world. Yet, we discover that some families do not always go to church. Sunday worship or the liturgical life of the church seems to have lost meaning for some. People seem to accept the rituals of religious practice as a routine without participating in them as a means of nurturing faith and strengthening the community of faith, as was the goal in Catholic Thai villages of years gone by. Furthermore, we find that Catholics in the city have many different Catholic parishes to choose from, and as a result, people no longer have a close bond with any particular parish. People escape quickly after the mass. They return home and do not linger to chat and share news of the faith community because they hardly even know who their co-worshippers are. The powerful moral chastisement that once at least animated conversation among the villagers no longer exists. People no longer live on church land and under the ever-present gaze of the parish priest; the power of the priest as a means of human media (communication) has been lost. Thus, the interest and curiosity of a bonded faith community has weakened in the twenty-first century.

Self-adjustment to Survive in Society

As Catholics who emerged from a strong traditional Catholic community, we are discovering that the new cultural context of the twenty-first century demands that we reevaluate the world in which we live in the light of gospel values. However, the new Asian context offers us profound challenges influenced by the convergence of new social economic factors and new political arenas and environments.

Thailand's economy declined dramatically in the mid to late 1990s. As a result, Thailand's government borrowed money from foreign countries, which intensified the insecurity problems in the political arena and lead to cheating, corruption and bribery. Social problems related to drugs, unemployment and injustices further stimulated the expanding crises we face. Competition has justified an attitude of selfishness and possessiveness to the detriment of community. The movement toward globalization has only intensified a growing sense of insecurity and loss of identity that amplifies our problems.

Each of these factors, I believe, has a direct negative influence on faith and religious behavior. The fertile ground from which we originally emerged is being washed away by individualism and capitalism. Muangrat's study (1998) of the relationship of modernization to Catholic beliefs, faith and religious practice in Bangkok indicated that Thai Catholics in Bangkok are 'medium' in modernization and religious beliefs. This contrasts with an earlier study by Joseph A. Kahl (1968), who argued that modernized people would be more rational in religious belief, and the level of belief would decrease. However, Muangrat's research also indicated that religious practice, such as family prayer, is very low. The only religious practice then left to them is going to church on special religious holidays such as Christmas, Ash Wednesday and Easter. Currently in Bangkok only 61 percent of Catholics go to church every Sunday (Muangrat, 1998, p. 108).

These questions and concerns continue to haunt us. Thus, as Thai Catholics we are faced with finding new ways to handle with care and preserve the faith in the modern society of Bangkok. Being able to influence the expanding new negative realities and attitudes toward faith and religion is the challenge that faces us. What are we to do? How can we do it? My own answer was to work in communications with the Catholic Church in Asia. As president of SIGNIS Asia, I hope to encourage the growth of faith in modern urban contexts in Thailand and elsewhere in Asia through the media.

Does Catholic Communication Help Delayed Faith?

Somprasong (1994, p. 84) surveyed the efficiency of using the media of the Catholic Social Communications of Thailand (now the Commission for Mass Media) for communicating faith and news about the church. Somprasong stated that the activities of the Catholic media office brought about movement of news and information, knowledge and understanding about the church. However, questions persist: is the communication inspirational? Does it bring faith into the lives of its hearers and/or viewers? Furthermore, Thai Catholics receive information from many parts of the world, distracting their attention from church initiatives. Often the church cannot compete.

The role of the Catholic media in the past 20 to 30 years is a remarkable story. When the Catholic media office established its radio and television sector, the audiences were Catholic but later expanded to other religious groups as well. Radio and television catered to all. The Catholic Church organized a religious event for the Bangkok bicentennial celebration in 1982 and bought airtime from the government television station, Channel 9, and broadcast live throughout the country. At the same time, the assembly of the Federation of Asian Bishops met for the first time in Bangkok, with bishops from other countries in attendance, including 100 from elsewhere in Asia. The live broadcast had a large audience, as the government-owned station went to virtually every house in Thailand. For the first time, the Catholic Church of Thailand paid for a wide broadcast of inner activities of the church. In the past, the church had live broadcasts of such things as a special mass on the King or Queen's birthday, but this conference had nothing to do with non-Catholics. Thus it was considered a major event.

After that, the Catholic leader Bishop Michael Kitbunchu was appointed cardinal in a ceremony covered live from Rome and downlinked locally. At that time the Thai government prohibited all live television broadcasts in order to conserve energy. But Catholic Social Communications of Thailand obtained permission from General Prem Tinnasulanon, then the Prime Minister. The live broadcast event became big news in Thailand.

As a result of this major television advance, a small group of Thai Buddhists attacked Christian religions and Christians in an official statement. The event moved the Catholic media to review its use of television and to conclude that Catholic news should emphasize love, service and sharing more than religious ceremonies that might bring about division in society.

A New Approach to Thai Society

While Catholic villages declined in the ways I have described, Catholic education became more popular in Thai society. As the value of education grew with modernization, the reputation of Catholic schools became widespread. They had long been considered elite schools, and in fact the first Catholic school, established in 1665, was intended for male members of the royal family as well as for Catholics. In Bangkok, the Catholic education system is comprehensive, with educational opportunities available from pre-school through universities. Modern Catholic families depend upon this system. As Bangkok's population continues to grow, with well over 12 million people in the year 2000, there are approximately 79,015 Catholics who state they plan to pass on their Catholic values and traditions to the next generation in this way (Muangrat, 1998, p. 110).

Catholic educational institutions also try to strengthen values and traditions. The Jesuits first arrived in Thailand in 1954. The Catholic Bishops' Conference of Thailand entrusted the care of university students to the Jesuits and in 1976 the Catholic Youth Council was established to look after Catholic youth in the education system and after they leave school. In each university, Catholic students are organized into an association, the Federation of Thai Catholic University Students. A priest chaplain visits the students, organizes prayers, masses and recollections, seminars, workshops on relevant topics and the like. During the summer vacation, Catholic students organize joint activities for community outreach programs in which students construct schools or teach. These projects take place in non-Catholic communities and in communities of hill tribe minorities as well among Catholics.

Another significant approach to Thai society is the Thai Catholic Church's role in refugee relief. In the 1970s and 1980s when people in Vietnam, Cambodia and Laos suffered from a cruel and devastating war, large numbers of refugees entered Thai territory to escape war, hunger, hatred, sickness and persecution. In 1978, the Catholic Bishops' Conference of Thailand established The Catholic Office for Emergency Relief and Refugees (COERR) to provide emergency relief for victims of natural disasters, render assistance to refugees and displaced persons and to help Thai nationals and their communities affected by forced migration into Thailand. COERR's activities were and are based on a humanitarian ethos and the principle of Christian charity and solidarity regardless of benefits, color, creed, sex, or political beliefs. Hundreds of volunteers from about thirty countries came to work with COERR. The organization also worked with the United Nations, Thai authorities and about one hundred NGOs and foundations concerned with refugees.

There are other aspects of the Thai Church that should be considered in this process of change. For example, there is a renewed spirit of evangelizing the hill tribe people or 'Thai People of the Mountains', as the King calls them. In addition, there are advances in the road map towards inculturation in the sense that all bishops are Thai, and the liturgy and music is Thai. The Catholic Church today has a major seminary in Thailand for the training candidates to the priesthood, while before we sent them abroad. In civil society, Catholics are more active, along with Buddhists, Muslims and other Christians, in non-governmental organizations (NGOs) than in the past. It has been a long journey for Thailand, from a military dictatorship surrounded by Communist countries to a democratically elected government with ASEAN partnership.

With these changes have come other social problems, such as the AIDS epidemic, increased drug use, gambling and commercial sex. The Catholic Church is doing something about these problems within its own limited resources of personnel and means. The church sponsors AIDS shelters and drug rehabilitation centers in Thailand, and several Catholic NGOs are working against the abuse of women and children. So to be 'Thai Catholic' today is to be 'more Thai' and 'more civic' minded, more inserted into the social, political, and economic life of Thailand than in the 1950s and 1960s, when being a good Thai Catholic meant going to church, practicing religion and being a good person. It also meant obeying the priest, sharing life among other Catholics, marrying a Catholic and not taking part in Buddhist ceremonies. Today, to be a good Catholic in Thailand means being concerned about society and not discriminating between Catholics and other religious groups. The idea is to help one other to have a better life without boundaries and to live together in unity.

Thai Catholics are United with Thai Society

The social activities mentioned above are channels for Catholics to lead a good Catholic life and witness to their faith without separating themselves from the local culture. While the strong traditional means of human communication mentioned before might not exist, we are finding that social participation in these Catholic groups helps Catholics be less isolated from society, as they work with Buddhist society and Buddhism, the national religion and base of our Thai culture.

Since the Catholic lifestyle of Thai people has shifted as a result of the new cultural context within which we live, we need to find new ways of being and becoming dedicated Catholics. We can begin by responding to the needs of people by working for peace and manifesting this peace through our own approach to communication in our everyday lives. We can introduce meaningful content that stimulates the religious imagination of our viewers and hearers. We can prepare women and men to become effective leaders witnessing to the faith in their ordinary lives.

Conclusion

Catholics in Thai culture have experienced radical shifts in the cultivation of their faith. As we have seen, the past offers a solid ground of formation that penetrated the environments of our lives. We could not but think 'being and living' Catholic. Rapid cultural change has influenced a movement away from the traditional media for faith communication. As we have seen, this resulted in weakening the fundamental grounding in faith, creating a diaspora of Catholics in our urban communities and distracting Catholics from their faith commitment. The ultimate impact is the lessening of one's Catholic identity and understanding one's role as a Catholic in a Buddhist culture.

The Catholic Bishops' Conference of Thailand in collaboration with Thai Catholics has energetically accepted the challenge to find a practical solution to our dilemma. The formation of new Catholic lay associations of groups of all interests, ages and professions, to bond together to be a bridge of unity and healing within the church and our Thai culture for working toward justice and peace is one possible solution. Thus, we are finding that human media continue to be the fundamental means for communicating and nurturing strong communities of faith in shifting times.

Notes

1   There are no records of how many Thai Catholic villages existed in the 1950s, but it is likely that this number has not changed. The villages today are different because their Catholic identity and spirit of unity are not as strong, a point I will discuss later in the chapter.
2   There are no comparable figures for the 1950s.
3   For the most part, missionaries came from France, but some also came from Portugal and Italy.
4   One had to be baptized a Catholic to live on this land. Originally only Catholics married to Catholics had the right to live on the Church's land, but later an exception was made for those who married non-Catholics with the permission of the Bishop. Thai Catholic families did not own the land but had a right to live on the land by virtue of their commitment to the faith.

References

Chumsripan, S. (1994), 'The history of the Catholic Church of Thailand', in *Twenty-five Years of Thai Vatican*, Bangkok: Assumption Printing Press.

Kahl, J. A. (1968), *The Measurement of Modernism*, Austin, TX and London: The University of Texas Press.

Muangrat, N. (1998), 'The relationship of communication behavior, modernization and the people's beliefs, faith, religious practice among Catholics', Bangkok: Department of Public Relations, Chulalongkorn University.

Saengtham College Thailand (2001), 'The research of marriage between different religions', Nakhornprathom Province, Thailand: Saengtham Printing.

Somprasong, C. (1994), 'Media role and strategy for evangelism: Mass media usage for evangelism distribution by Catholic Social Communications Center of Thailand, 1966–1993', Bangkok: Department of Mass Communication, Chulalongkorn University.

Thai Catholic Calendar (2001), Thai Catholic Office of Communication, Bangkok: Assumption Printing Press.

Additional Resources

Adiwatanasit, C. and P. Kanchavamonai (1979), 'Can Buddhism survive modernization?' Bangkok: Department of Social Science, Kasetsart University.

Saint John's University, Bangkok, Thailand, 'History of The Catholic Churches in Thailand', http://www.stjohn.ac.th/Department/info/ch_history.html. Text in English.

UCIP World Congress (2004), 'Religion in Thailand: Buddhism Plays a Profound Role in People's Reactions to Events', http://www.ucip.ch/cong/ath#2, Bangkok, Thailand. Background for World Congress 2004 in Bangkok. Text in German, English, Spanish and French.

Catholic Media in Thailand

Catholic Internet network in Thailand, http://lox2.loxinfo.co.th/~thcatcom. In English and Thai.

Information and Technology Section of The Archdiocese of Bangkok, in Thai: http://www.catholic.or.th.

ISSARA, Catholic Magazine online, in Thai: http://www.issara.com.

UDOMSARN, Catholic Weekly Newspaper and Monthly Magazine, in Thai: http://www.udomsarn.com.

Catholic Productions in Context of Thai society

(For all items, contact Catholic Social Communications of Thailand by email: thcatcom@loxinfo.co.th or http://www.udomsarn.com)

Choice for a Better Life, video, 23 minutes. Presents facts on the drug situation in Thailand based on data from 1997. A co-production of many Catholic Commissions in Thai Society. VHS–PAL in Thai and English.

The Cry of My Appeal, video, 25 minutes. Filmed and produced in Thailand, the first to trace child prostitution back to its root causes and masked myths. Based on data from 1993. VHS–PAL in Thai, English and Spanish.

His Foot Speaks … in Painting, video, 21 minutes. The life story of Lonson Loh-Come, a young man born with no arms, and a self-taught artist. A production for the Society in the economic crisis in Asia, 1998. VHS and VCD–PAL, in Thai and English.

The Moment of Life, video, 21 minutes. Produced as a video campaign for a social collaboration. Produced in 2002. VHS and VCD–PAL, in Thai.

Chapter 13

The US Catholic Church Sexual Abuse Scandal: A Media/Religion Case Study

Frances Forde Plude

Most of the Roman Catholic priests alive in the United States today have witnessed much change within their church. They have seen Catholics become major players in American culture. They have seen the church reinvent itself in relation to the modern world, in conformance with other heady revolutions of the 1960s. They have watched a culture of dissent descend upon the church as theologians and others disagreed strongly about how to implement Vatican II.

And today the Roman Catholic Church is in the midst of one of its most serious crises since the Reformation. It is now clear that a significant number of priests and some lay persons within the Catholic Church have imposed sexual experiences on vulnerable individuals (male and female), many of them youth. This involves a relatively small percentage of all priests and a small percentage of sexual abuse cases among the total population. Still, the harsh reality of this scandal and, even more significantly, the failure of church leadership to deal appropriately with problem priests, are now eating away at the heart of Catholic culture in the United States. This commentary reviews the role media have played and are playing in this continuing drama, and how churches should respond to a new media environment.

I will attempt to analyze the situation from a lay perspective rather than focusing on the perspective and the policies of the institutional church and its leadership. This analysis is based upon my own personal knowledge of the Catholic Church and a significant number of priests, several of whom have been unmasked as sexual abusers. My intent is to view these scandals in the light of a changed media context. My analysis consists of a review of some US newspapers, TV coverage, some Catholic periodicals and Internet sites. I have also called upon several decades of study of Catholic Church communication practices. As sexual abuse media coverage accumulated, certain trends emerged. I have attempted to identify these patterns and ask appropriate questions. To what extent have the media played a pivotal role in uncovering a long and well-hidden secret? Have media reported the issue thoroughly and without bias? How has the Catholic Church responded to media coverage? What role has the Internet played as a media forum? And, perhaps most importantly, how should the leadership in this church, and in other churches, alter their media practices and their own internal communication flows in the light of a competitive global mediated environment with its new 'talk-back' culture?

In reviewing the media context we must ask how dialog or a dialectical process ought to permeate church communication realities. What conflicts seem inherent in this talk-back environment? How can these tensions be dealt with if the Catholic Church is to heal itself and emerge once again as a major moral force in a postmodern world?

The Transformed Media Environment

Today's media environment has three characteristics of direct relevance to our discussion:

1. We have new insight into how people mediate their individualized religious experiences through media.

Stewart Hoover has articulated clearly that media and religion intersect more and more as people today seek meaning in their lives (Hoover, 2003). As we build a self-identity, we seek personal autonomy in matters of faith. Wade Clark Roof calls this 'a spiritual marketplace' (Roof, 1999). These realities create challenges for the Catholic Church.

While modern culture appears to be secular, in fact research interviews show that many people do much meaning-making through media narratives which they interpret and apply to their own development of a self-identity. Called *mediation*, religious seeking occurs within and is altered by media stories: news stories, entertainment stories and advertising narratives. Apparently, this is one way people can identify their media use as significant; their own interpretative interaction adds meaning and purpose to their lives.

This audience-reception view of media use is absolutely foreign to most church authorities, who continue to stress media content as instruments to be used to evangelize. This neglects the whole area of media *use* by audiences. *Catholic Church officials need to be aware that the scandal narrative is mediated by audiences and not just by newsrooms.* Church communicators need to update their very limited understanding of media use; the field of communication studies now offers a whole new view of media and culture and how audiences mediate or interpret media narratives rather than being totally manipulated by program content.

2. We must acknowledge the dialogic or interactive (talk-back) nature of communication media.

As I have studied the development of interactive communication from feudal society to our postmodern culture, I have examined the relationship of media formats to cultural structures and social/religious thought. Clearly a unified medieval Christendom was altered by the medium of printing which empowered individual voices. Much later telephone and computer technologies enabled interactivity. Finally, increasing diversity of media channels – especially those media formats allowing talk-back – seems to facilitate decentralization, economic, political, and religious liberation, and the decline of hierarchical authority structures, including that of churches.

Unless churches today truly value feedback and two-way communication, religious authority will remain under siege just when global problems cry out for prophetic wisdom. American Catholics, especially females, are demanding to interact more directly in church administration and organizational decision-making. This is also being negotiated on a theological level within the Catholic Church. In an issue of *Theological Studies*, Bradford Hinze (2000) speaks of two approaches to dialog. 'One approach accentuates the role of obedience in the dialogue of revelation and the Church.' Hinze notes that the official theology of the Catholic Church 'is representative of this teaching'. An alternative approach emphasizes 'the need for open, collegial, consultative dialogue ... with creative, critical, and dissenting opinions, long-suppressed voices, especially among women and non-Western communities, other Christian churches (and) other religions and philosophies...' (Hinze, 2000, p. 213). The larger drama of the sexual abuse crisis is about the construction of a dialogical Catholic Church.

3. *When scandals are revealed, church groups and media institutions have differing interests and professional inclinations. The two groups do not share communication patterns, institutional rhetoric, scandal exposition and resolutions sought.*

Paul Soukup (1997) has written about the different approaches to scandal taken by religious communities and media organizations. His analysis, although written before the current Catholic Church scandals, can assist us in understanding why religious groups fear scandal and why media organizations find the scandal story particularly attractive. Using biblical references about giving scandal, Soukup shows that for religious groups 'scandal emerges as a tool for establishing identity and social control within the religious community' (p. 224). One key reason for avoiding scandal lies in preserving the community. Another reason for avoiding scandal, however, may lie in the attempt by men to preserve their patriarchal power and privilege.

Soukup notes that news media approach scandal in a very different way. To media organizations, scandal is 'a means to extend their own power to define society and situate other institutions within it. Thus, the news media tend to regard scandal as an instance of moral hypocrisy and employ public exposure, even ridicule, to develop the story. In addition, of course, many media outlets make use of scandal as a commodity' (p. 225) to enhance media sales. This analysis, however, avoids the fact that a major function of news media in democracies as the Fourth Estate is to actively pursue contradictions in areas of public concern and to bring these contradictions into the open, even or especially against the wishes of the institution in which these contradictions are to be exposed. *Churches and media institutions need to be aware of these conflicting ideologies as each responds to media coverage of church scandals.*

The US Catholic Church Infrastructure

The Roman Catholic Church has represented one of the largest religious and social service global systems throughout much of its history. The current Catholic population is 1.045 billion and there are 62.2 million Catholics in the United States – 22 percent of the nation's population.[1] There are 19,093 Catholic parishes or congregational units in the United States (Froehle and Gautier 2000) and the Catholic Church sponsors 1,110 US hospitals and health care facilities, 1,085 residential care facilities, 8,170 schools and 233 colleges and universities. In addition, there are 1,406 affiliated social service agencies known as Catholic Charities USA. This clearly is a potent force for faith and service in US culture.

Staff figures within the US Catholic Church show significant trends. There are currently almost 45,000 priests, but this number is down from 58,632 in 1965. There are 74,177 vowed religious Sisters, a 100,000 decrease from their 1965 figure. However, there are 30,000 lay persons or religious in various church ministries and another 30,000 in training. There are 13,000 lay deacons, 150,000 Catholic-school teachers, and 25,000 lay associates of religious orders. So the decline in vowed priests and religious is somewhat offset by a growing population of certified and committed lay ministers.

Within the integration of Catholic institutions and the Catholic population into US culture, we discover three interesting factors. First, a dialectic exists between the American character and Roman Catholicism in the US. The church membership reflects the individualism, the enthusiasm and the consumerism of Americans in general. And, like others, Catholics do much of their meaning-making in response to media stories. Second, a continuing dialectic reflects the broad changes within Catholicism identified in a recent sociological study by Richard A. Schoenherr entitled *Goodbye Father* (2002). He mentions the following: a movement from dogmatism to pluralism; a tension between the celibacy rule and a growing personalism of human sexuality; a strong feminist movement; and growing empowerment of the laity. These factors are part of the matrix of church teaching and US culture.

A third factor, which may affect the context of the Catholic Church sex scandal, has been identified as 'the new anti-Catholicism' by scholar Philip Jenkins in a book of that title (2003). Jenkins notes that racist and anti-minority attitudes and comments are branded unacceptable in US culture. However, he claims that even before the sexual abuse scandal it had been possible to indulge in anti-Catholic bias and rhetoric – beyond what could be legitimate critique. Any critical response to such prejudice is branded as Catholic Church censorship. Some analysts, like Peter Steinfels mentioned below, see some anti-Catholic bias in some of the media coverage. While Jenkins praises *The Boston Globe* for its work, footnotes throughout his book cite many examples of news stories and headlines that are grossly slanted.

The Scope of Ministerial Sexual Abuse

The first thing to be said about sexual abuse is that it is evil, it does life-long damage to those on whom it is perpetrated, and every effort needs to be made to ensure that it is halted, victims are given justice and caring, and perpetrators are stopped and brought to account. We do not presently have solid data about the extent of the problem in the Catholic Church, in other religious groups, in schools, or in the population at large. The very nature of the problem makes solid data difficult to establish. The Rev. Dr Marie Fortune is founder and director of the Center for the Prevention of Sexual and Domestic Violence (http://www.cpsdv.org). In an article in *Christian Century*, Fortune cites a Fuller Theological Seminary dissertation suggesting that as many as 38 per cent of ministers or clergy are inappropriately sexually involved with their congregants (Fortune, 1991). While there may be questions about this shockingly high number, there clearly are abuses of pastoral power.

Concerning youth abuse in general *The Economist* (Anonymous, 2002, pp. 27–28) notes: 'Sex offenders who prey on children go where children are ... They teach in schools, coach sports teams, run scout troops and day-care centres.' *The Economist* cites researcher Charol Shakeshaft's findings that 15 percent of pupils in schools are sexually abused by a teacher or staff member between kindergarten and high-school graduation. Many of these institutions make private settlements and move abusers out with letters of recommendation, known as 'passing the trash'. Clearly sexual abuse of youth and related cover-up exist in many different institutional settings and also within families.

The extent of sexual abuse cases involving US Roman Catholic priests is hard to quantify. Reasons for this include:

- the culture of confidentiality and secrecy in the Catholic Church;
- the lack, until recently, of available court records; and
- the hesitancy of many victims to come forward.

The New York Times assembled a Catholic priest abuse database by examining newspaper accounts and court records, along with church documents and statements (Goodstein, 2003). This information was checked against lists of priests assembled by victim advocacy groups and dioceses were called for further clarification. These data covered cases reported in the first year after *The Boston Globe* broke the sexual abuse story in January 2002. The numbers below have increased since January 2003, but they provide a snapshot of available data at that time.

The New York Times database indicates:

- 1,205 US priests had been accused;
- 4,268 victims had made public claims;
- most of the abuse occurred in the 1970s and 1980s;
- every region of the country was seriously affected;
- more than a dozen dioceses reported more than 20 cases each.

It needs to be noted that *The New York Times* database included 'only ordained priests who faced specific accusations of abuse of a child' (Goodstein, 2003, p. 1, 20–21). Their figures excluded deacons, brothers, nuns or lay persons working for the Catholic Church. Cases involving adult parishioners were also excluded. The newspaper noted that *most of the abuse cases had happened many years ago and did not involve pedophilia* (adults interested in pre-pubescent children), but was abuse perpetrated on post-pubescent youth.

Church leaders have continually tried to make the point that the number of cases began to drop markedly by the 1990s because the bishops *did* begin to address the problem. Also seminary-training programs began more sophisticated psychological screening of candidates by this time and human sexuality instruction had been inserted into the seminary curriculum. These facts have often been ignored by media coverage. John Jay College of Criminal Justice of the City College of New York has been commissioned to do a definitive study to obtain more authoritative figures, but the researchers' need for extensive data has alarmed many bishops. There is reasonable skepticism about how open the church will be about its records unless pressured by criminal prosecution. During a meeting of US bishops in St Louis in June 2003, the bishops met with John Jay College researchers to clarify goals and procedures.

Richard Sipe, a former priest and psychotherapist, has counseled hundreds of clergy and victims of abuse and he expresses great respect for those who attempt to live out the celibacy charism. Sipe suggests the need for a special study of sexuality within the cult of clerical celibacy.[2] He estimates that 6 percent of all US Catholic priests have committed youth sexual abuse. Sipe's figures are not the result of a scientific survey and are questioned by many. However, *The New York Times* database shows that 6.2 percent of priests ordained in the Archdiocese of Baltimore in the last half-century have been implicated in the abuse of minors. In Manchester, New Hampshire the percentage is 7.7 and in Boston it is 5.3. It may be this percentage is somewhat representative of some other dioceses (although not all) if church leadership were more open and if other victims stepped forward. There may even be more victims from the decade of the nineties, but many victims have not yet reached an age of maturity where they can find the courage to speak up. However, in an earlier study within the Archdiocese of Chicago, 2.6 percent of the priests were subject to complaints and a Review Board with solid credentials decreased the total to 1.7 percent.

Media Coverage and Response to the Coverage

Although there has been media coverage in the past about several high-profile clergy sexual abuse cases, a systematic investigative report about clergy sexual abuse and cover-up in the Archdiocese of Boston was released by *The Boston Globe* (Globe Spotlight Team, 2002, p. 1). From the very beginning of this media coverage there was shock and rage, along with great relief on the part of many victims who felt their pain was finally being acknowledged. On the *Globe*'s web site, it is easy to access all the information obtained by the *Globe* investigative team, along with many other helpful resources and links. Due to the extent of the problem and easy online access, this story was immediately featured on major news outlets across the US and throughout the world. With multiple channels of cable news in the United States, the story was literally trumpeted 24 hours a day.[3]

Steinfels, a noted Catholic layman and one-time religion editor for *The New York Times*, noted that 'between 6 Jan and mid-April (100 days) the Boston newspaper published over 250 stories, many on page one, about the sexual abuse of minors by Catholic priests' (Steinfels, 2002, p. 9). All this and more continues to be available at the *Globe* web site.

It is of interest to reflect upon what Catholic media did with the story. There are three major biweekly Catholic organs. *America* (http://www.americapress.org), a Jesuit publication, is read regularly by many bishops and Catholic leaders, along with *Commonweal* (http://www.commonwealmagazine.org), a respected journal published for many decades by lay persons. Both contained thoughtful and widely varied articles on the sexual abuse issue: on the 'clerical club' among Catholic clergy; on the issue of homosexuality within the Catholic priesthood; and on what the laity can do to provide more leadership within the church. The biweekly newspaper *National Catholic Reporter* (*NCR*) (http://www.natcath.com) also offered comprehensive coverage.[4] Other more moderate or conservative Catholic newspapers include *Our Sunday Visitor* and *The Wanderer*. The latter contained an interview with Philip Jenkins, mentioned above, about anti-Catholic bias. *The Wanderer* also argued that media coverage neglected a major part of the problem – the 'sexualization' of American culture. All of these publications have web sites and their archives provide a rich and easily accessible record of their coverage.

One of the most effective commentaries has been offered by Steinfels. His (London) *Tablet* article cited above notes several problems:

- coverage gave a skewed or imprecise understanding of the issue;
- coverage of the Catholic bishops was often distorted;
- the 'blizzard' effect of the coverage included almost no thoughtful analysis;
- extracting patterns from all the data was almost impossible;
- 'the church' was covered as a monolith, rather than as 194 different dioceses; and
- awareness and response to abuse grew slowly in the culture as well as in the church.

While not referring specifically to the *Globe*, Steinfels concludes: 'columnists settled numerous scores with the Catholic Church: from the way they were treated in parochial school to the Church's opposition to abortion and refusal to ordain women' (p. 11). He adds there was virtually no counterbalancing commentary. Steinfels also noted when addressing Catholic media personnel in Los Angeles that easy access to the *Globe* web site meant the Boston story was echoed continually around the country by local reporters, becoming a template, even though many diocesan situations were vastly different.

Another well-known Catholic sociologist and novelist, the Rev. Andrew Greeley, writing in the 20 February 2003 issue of *America* magazine, called the coverage of *The New York Times* 'virulent anti-Catholicism'. The *National Catholic Reporter* disagreed in a lengthy editorial entitled 'Greeley aims at the wrong target' (2003, p. 24). If a reporter or a news organization was inclined toward anti-Catholic prejudice this story certainly provided the perfect opportunity to vent it. It is not unreasonable to assume this did sometimes happen. Most would agree, however, that the Catholic Church was clearly guilty of a self-inflicted wound and any attempt to control the news, as it had in the past, only made it look worse. And there was widespread recognition that the media had done a singular service to society and to the church by providing extensive coverage of the problem. The Pulitzer Prize awarded to *The Boston Globe* for the sexual abuse coverage confirmed this.

The media did occasionally point out the steps taken by church leadership to deal with the problem. These include development of:

- a charter for the protection of children and young people;
- essential norms for dioceses in dealing with allegations;
- an office of child and youth protection at the bishops' headquarters;
- an independent national review board; and
- a national audit to confirm that diocesan policies are implemented.

Documentation on all of these issues, along with other helpful items (statements, presentations, press releases, Vatican interaction, articles and church policy background) is available at the web site of the United States Conference of Catholic Bishops (http://www.nccbuscc.org/comm/restoretrust.htm). The extensive resources available there indicate that the bishops' national office understands the importance of having a web presence that provides information and even some self-criticism.

The Impact of the Internet as Forum

The Internet obviously represents a whole new resource for data gathering, study, analysis and talk-back. The Internet engine drove the church scandal story forward and continues to do so. Through archived material, it makes available with a mere 'point and click' a tracking of past media stories and an up-to-date monitoring of current coverage. Bill Mitchell, a Notre Dame University graduate and former journalist, began an interesting tracking service. He searched the Internet twice a day for the latest coverage on clerical sexual abuse, copied the headlines, added the name of the publication and some sentences and then linked each article to a web site he runs called the 'Clergy Abuse Tracker'. The site was hosted by the Poynter Institute, an ethics watchdog and training site for journalists in St. Petersburg, Florida (http://www.poynter.org/clergyabuse/ca.htm). Mitchell called this site 'part media experiment, part service to journalists and part service to the church'. Almost 1,000 users visited this clergy abuse site daily; 700 have signed up for daily email updates. Most are probably journalists. One mentioned that she tried to monitor smaller newspapers this way to get a sense of the impact on small towns and parishes. Mitchell, a former news editor, claims the scandal media coverage has been 'aggressive' and 'impressive'. He does not believe the media are 'out to get the church' but, rather, have done the church a service.[5]

The University of Southern California Annenberg School publishes an online journalism review (http://www.ojr.org/ojr/ethics/1028655580.php) that contains a commentary entitled 'A Tangled Web: New Media and the Catholic Scandals' by Stephen O'Leary. He suggests 'it is possible that the Internet has changed the power balance that formerly governed the reporting of religious news' (p. 1). O'Leary comments that the hard-hitting and detailed reporting of this crisis reflects a change in the news judgment of reporters and 'The Internet has fundamentally altered the balance that governed the relationship between media institutions and more traditional powers such as the Church. Journalists and bishops alike are now struggling with the new realities of covering religion in the wired world' (p. 2).

O'Leary's special research focus is religious communication, including a study of religion on the Internet. He notes the web has made detailed information and formerly secret documents from sex abuse cases available to millions of readers. Another significant change is that the web allows people to read news in cumulative batches, thus 'contributing to the perception of the problem as systemic and international in scope'. He cites the fact that the web site of a group of survivors of priests' sexual abuse now averages 1,000 visits per day – providing an online support group for such individuals. The web offers many forums for both wounded and hopeful-for-change Catholics.

Conclusion: The Changed Media Environment of Religious Practice

A few years ago one of America's leading Catholic figures, the late Cardinal Joseph Bernardin, of Chicago, was accused of sexual abuse. The day this news became public the Cardinal was on his way to a bishops' meeting in Washington DC. He made himself available to the press, answering their questions candidly under an intense media spotlight and in the face of extreme humiliation. One reporter asked him if he lived a celibate life and he answered the question. I recall he told the media he had to catch his plane to Washington, but he would be willing to continue the press conference when he got off the plane there. I will always remember this as an example of a church leader who respected the public's right to know and the role of the media in pursuit of the facts.

It turned out that the accusation was false and was subsequently withdrawn. Later, in a dramatic private meeting, the accuser and the Cardinal spoke of reconciliation and forgiveness. Some time later, Bernardin met with the media again to reveal that he was losing his battle with cancer and had a short time to live. It was reported at this meeting some members of the press wept openly. With Bernardin on its cover, *Time* magazine noted that after his diagnosis the Cardinal's work among cancer patients was giving all of us a lesson in how to face death.

This story presents a stark contrast to the Catholic Church's relationship with the media during the sexual abuse crisis. What accounts for this difference? First, there is the surprising scope of the matter. Most Catholics, even people who work closely with church officials and parish priests, had no idea of this problem or its size. We simply didn't suspect it; the church leadership had been very effective in suppressing the secret. And once the issue was revealed, many, many victims came forward to testify to the harm done to them. Incredible pain was present in almost every story of damaged lives. It seemed inconceivable that bishops could transfer priests around to many parishes, thereby putting more and more youth in danger. The Church appeared to have been more concerned with protecting its priests and avoiding scandal than in safeguarding its young people.

Another major component was the resulting financial impact. It became clear the Catholic Church would have to pay many, many millions of dollars as lawyers represented groups of victims. Many people decided to withhold contributions to Catholic charities, believing their donations would go into such huge settlement debts.[6] Some felt the church should sell off some of its extensive property holdings (especially large bishops' residences) to pay the debt.

As the issue heated up, and for many years before the scandal broke, bishops were guided by their attorneys and insurance companies in responding to the problem. Sometimes victims who were abused by priests faced more pressure from church attorneys who tried to intimidate them or buy their silence. Now victims were supported by the court system and the general public and received additional strength from victims' own support groups.

This pressure for the church to assume responsibility and to be accountable happened just as major US corporate scandals were exposed and government agencies and the stock market were facing similar scrutiny for negligence or misdeeds. *Time* magazine put three female whistleblowers on their persons-of-the-year cover. Americans were deeply concerned about an extensive American leadership failure. In the Catholic Church this pointed to the need for a better process for the selection of bishops.

There is no doubt that a new media culture contributed to the sense of crisis. Twenty-four-hour news outlets (cable news channels, radio and TV talk shows, the Internet) kept the story going. The drama unfolded: cardinals were called to Rome to talk with the Pope, bishops prepared to gather in Dallas and debate a 'zero tolerance' policy, and in many dioceses new cases came to light. The criminal court system became involved when prosecutors stepped up boldly to demand files from many bishops and to insist that some speak under oath about what had happened and how the church had handled cases. All this drama fed the media coverage as testimony taken under oath by bishops appeared on the Internet.

In all this coverage there was not enough nuance or systematic analysis. Overlooked often was the fact that some cases involved actions from many years ago. The situation was labeled a pedophile crisis when very few of the cases involved very young children (although some high-profile cases did). And there was little analysis of the difference between legitimate confidentiality and a vast culture of secrecy. It was hard to sort out the need for forgiveness while at the same time holding abusers accountable.

As the news coverage piled up and remained online for continual reference, it became clear that there were *systemic* problems in the church that needed to be confronted, analyzed and reformed. Among these issues were:

- seeing the role of priest and bishop as a fraternity beyond accountability;
- a climate of secrecy and protection supporting this lack of accountability;
- a lack of respect for the voices of lay persons (often mothers) who complained; and
- an ambivalence in the Catholic population about the church's sexual teaching.

Because of a culture of dissent within Catholicism between liberals and conservatives, the sexual abuse issue became entangled in various other agendas. Some said celibacy was the problem. Some urged the church to update its sexual theology, but some said Catholics had already absorbed too much of the sexual liberation of US culture and media.

Lay persons in the church, both male and female, began to see they needed to accept responsibility for *their* church, rather than submissively allowing 'the clerical club' to manage the institution's structure. Many acknowledged that – apart from any specific church teaching or dogma – much needed to be changed in the church's management system, including financial transparency and its structure of leadership and decision-making. In a thoughtful analysis in *Commonweal* magazine theologian Luke Timothy Johnson addressed changes within Catholic culture in recent decades in the United States (Johnson, 2003, p. 11). Johnson noted this is pertinent to how Catholics now view sex and sexual morality. He accused the Catholic Church of incoherence in its teaching on sexuality, along with corruptive abuse of power – refusing to discern its sexual morality by listening to views of women and other laity.

I have monitored this matter primarily from a communication perspective. Quite apart from the question of who should be priests and whether or not they should marry, the church seems to be a dysfunctional communication system with excessive secrecy, almost no transparency, and a somewhat arrogant lack of accountability. I have written before that interactive communication tools seem to be a metaphor for a more dialogic church (Plude, 1992, 1994, 1996). It now seems clear it is not simply a matter of dialog – of talking and listening more. Rather the Catholic Church and other churches must become more comfortable as a *dialectical system*. In the language of cybernetic theory, they must accept inputs and respond with appropriate outputs in order to keep their systems in balance. Again, we are not talking here primarily about doctrine, but about organizational communication structures.

It is vital for church authorities to truly listen. People continue to say about some of the bishops: 'They simply don't get it!' As bishops refuse to allow Voice of the Faithful groups and others to meet on church property, they are demonstrating their unwillingness to listen to their own people. In their approach to the media, church officials have sometimes scolded media personnel as if they were naughty children. There are legitimate concerns and criticism of the media role; these problems do need to be addressed. But many leading US media figures are caring and well-educated Catholics. They should be invited often to share their ideas and suggestions about how the church can be a better communicator. The bishops do have a Communication Committee but the current situation calls for more widespread input and expertise. The problem is trust and credibility, not just smooth public relations.[7]

The Catholic Church in the US can benefit from the cleansing that now must occur. Recognizing that the general public is media-savvy, all churches can utilize modern telecommunication tools to *be* communicative, rather than just controlling packaged messages. As mentioned above, churches need to study and be aware of the newer emphases on how audiences receive media narratives, how interactive the culture has become, and how churches and media organizations respond to scandal in vastly different ways.

I spoke earlier of the major impact of the Catholic Church throughout its 2000-year history. The previous two millennia, along with a divine presence within the church, constitute what my Orthodox Christian friend reminds me is 'the invisible church'. There is this other component: the prayers and sacrifices continually made over the centuries by individuals to help repair this institutional wound as well as a wounded world. All of this presence and prayer will continue to be part of the renewal process.

The late Cardinal Bernardin inspired a project entitled the Catholic Common Ground Initiative. The goal was to have a dialogic forum within the church. In a recent newsletter (3 December 2001) the group published an interview with Rev. Ladislas Örsy, a respected Jesuit canon law expert. He commented: 'Dialogue is, and must be, part and parcel of the life of a Christian community because no one person has the privilege to possess the divine mysteries in their fullness and to have the final words about them. The mysteries were given to the whole community' (p. 6).

Notes

1   All statistics are from the Center for Applied Research in the Apostolate (CARA) at Georgetown University and are 2002 figures.

2   Sipe's two volumes on the subject are: *A Secret World: Sexuality and the Search for Celibacy* (1990) and *Sex, Priests, and Power: Anatomy of a Crisis* (1995).

3   In Boston there were two additional factors feeding the frenzy. In its follow-up book *Betrayal* (2003), the *Boston Globe* staff note: '(Boston) is the only major archdiocese in the U.S. where Catholics account for more than half the population. In no other major American city are Catholics more represented in political precincts, in courtrooms, in boardrooms. Nowhere else has the impact of the scandal been more deeply felt. And nowhere else has the erosion of deference traditionally shown the Church been more dramatic' (p. 7). Thus, the newspaper faced the prospect of great pressure to suppress the story and the possibility of backlash by readers when it was released. Instead, Catholics generally felt gratitude for this exposure and the rage turned against church leadership. Many of the court officials and victims' lawyers who confronted the church in the case were prominent Catholics. The second unique aspect of the Boston situation was that Cardinal Bernard Law, the local church head, became a lightning rod around which the storm raged. Long a power broker in the US Catholic Church (and in Rome), Law's defiance enraged people within the media, among Catholics, and in the population at large. For the first time devoted Catholics took to the street in protests, priests began to speak out against their pastoral leader, and an organization called Voice of the Faithful (http://www.votf.org) began to provide a systematic way to organize for change in the church. Many people called for Cardinal Law's resignation and eventually he did resign from his post.

4   *NCR* has been a leader in covering sexual issues within the Church. It exclusively broke the story of sexual abuse of some nuns in Africa by Catholic clergy there when the church leadership in Rome continued to stall in acknowledging the problem. With correspondent John Allen Jr on site in Rome, *NCR* provides Vatican commentary regularly in the newspaper and on its web site.

5   If one examines *The Boston Globe* Web site (http://www.boston.com/globe/spotlight/abuse) one becomes aware of the extent of a virtual resource library. The site offers a complete archive of *Globe* coverage and various categories of information are organized for web visitors. Categories include: the fall of Cardinal Law; the text of court depositions; the victims; the financial cost; the church's response; investigations and lawsuits. In addition the site provides an extensive list of resources – providing direct links to media outlets, official church sites, church reform groups, victims' groups, the Catholic press, and so on. Message boards are provided so individuals can post comments and an interactive map allows anyone to see exactly where accused priests have been stationed. Video documentary material is provided. This and other web sites provide a new kind of nonlinear environment for individuals to move within. Such a site is available at any time, so even months after the fact one can keep current on the issue. Another Internet phenomenon is the web log, where individuals provide journal reflections and others can respond. One such 'blogspot' is entitled 'Catholic and Enjoying It!' (http://markshea.blogspot.com). The Voice of the Faithful web site (http://www.votf.org) provides a continuing forum for individuals who seek a supportive group for change in the church. VOTF goals include: to support those who have been abused; to support priests of integrity; and to shape structural change with the Catholic Church. Its site provides a list of '15 Things Any Catholic Can Do'.

Another aspect of the Internet is the work being done by colleges and universities to renew the Catholic Church in the light of the scandal. Major Catholic institutions, such as the University of Notre Dame and Boston College, are undertaking major research and development projects to tap into the expertise at their institutions. The Boston College project is entitled 'The Church in the 21st Century: From Crisis to Renewal'. At its web site (http://www.bc.edu/church21) one can connect with audio and video (speeches), with seminar announcements, and occasional papers. Also included is an extensive research bibliography on topics such as: roles of lay men and women, priests and bishops; sexuality in the Catholic tradition and contemporary culture; handing on the faith to the next generation; and web sites for research in religion and the social sciences.

6   The Louisville and Boston dioceses have settled for 25 million and 85 million, respectively.

7   In 1997 two research studies analyzed how Catholics of England and Wales obtained their religious information, the relative impact of various information sources, and the perception of the Catholic Church by Catholics and non-Catholics. Both studies showed personal experience was a key factor in an individual's perception of the church. (Catholic school experience was almost without exception a positive factor.) See McDonnell (2003).

References

Anonymous (2002), 'Passing the Trash', *The Economist*, 6 April, 27–28.

Boston Globe investigative staff (2003), *Betrayal: The Crisis in the Catholic Church*, Boston: Back Bay Books.

Catholic Common Ground Initiative Report (2001), 3 December, pp. 3–6.

Fortune, M. (1991), 'How the Church Should Imitate the Navy', *Christian Century*, 23 January, p. 765.

Froehle, B. and M. Gautier (2000), *Catholicism USA: A Portrait of the Catholic Church in the United States*, Maryknoll, NY: Orbis Books.

Globe Spotlight Team (2002), 'Scores of Priests Involved in Sex Abuse Cases', *The Boston Globe*, 31 January, p. 1.

Goodstein, L. (2003), 'Train of Pain in Church Crisis Leads to Nearly Every Diocese', *The New York Times*, 12 January, pp. 1, 20–21.

Greeley, A. (2003), 'The Times and Sexual Abuse by Priests', *America*, 10 February.

Hinze, B. (forthcoming), *The Practices of Dialogue in the Church: Aims, Struggles, Prospects*.

Hinze, B. (2000), 'Ecclesial Repentance and the Demands of Dialogue', *Theological Studies*, **61**, 207–38.

Hoover, S. M. (2003), 'Religion, Media and Identity: Theory and Method in Audience Research on Religion and Media', in Jolyon Mitchell, Jolyon and Sophia Marriage (eds), *Mediating Religion: Conversation in Media, Religion and Culture*, London and New York: T & T Clark.

Hoover, S. M. (1998), *Religion in the News: Faith and Journalism in American Public Discourse*, Thousand Oaks, CA, London: Sage.

Horsfield, P. (2003), 'Electronic Media and the Past-Future of Christianity', in J. Mitchell and S. Marriage (eds), *Mediating Religion: Conversations in Media, Religion and Culture*, London and New York: T & T Clark.

Jenkins, P. (2003), *The New Anti-Catholicism: The Last Acceptable Prejudice*, Oxford, UK: Oxford University Press.

Johnson, L. T. (2003), 'Sex, Women and the Church', *Commonweal*, 20 June, p. 11.

Lakeland, P. (2003), *The Liberation of the Laity: In Search of an Accountable Church*, New York and London: Continuum.

Lull, J. and S. Hinerman (eds) (1997), *Media Scandals*, Cambridge, UK: Polity Press.

McDonnell, J. (2003), 'Desperately Seeking Credibility: English Catholics, the News Media and the Church', in Jolyon Mitchell and Sophia Marriage (eds), *Mediating Religion: Conversations in Media, Religion and Culture*', London and New York: T & T Clark.

O'Leary, S. (n.d.), 'A Tangled Web: New Media and the Catholic Scandals', *USC Annenberg Online Journalism Review* (http://www.ojr.org/ojr/ethics/1028655580.php).

Plude, F. (1996), 'Forums for Dialogue: Teleconferencing and the American Catholic Church', in P. A. Soukup, *Media, Culture and Catholicism*, Kansas City, MO: Sheed and Ward, pp. 191–200.

Plude, F. (1994), 'Interactive Communication in the Church', in P. Granfield (ed.), *The Church and Communication*, Kansas City, MO: Sheed and Ward, pp. 179–95.

Plude, F. (1992), 'Modern communications vs. centralized power', *The Syracuse Record*, 13 April, p. 9.

Roof, W. C. (1999), *Spiritual Marketplace: Baby Boomers and the Remaking of American Religion*, Princeton, NJ: Princeton University Press.

Schoenherr, R. A. (2002), *Goodbye Father: The Celibate Male Priesthood and the Future of the Catholic Church*, Oxford, UK: Oxford University Press.

Sipe, A. W. R. (1995), *Sex, Priests, and Power: Anatomy of a Crisis*, New York: Brunner/Mazel.

Sipe, A. W. R. (1990), *A Secret World: Sexuality and the Search for Celibacy*, New York: Brunner/Mazel.

Soukup, P. A. (1997), 'Church, Media and Scandal', in James Lull and Stephen Hinerman (eds), *Media Scandals*, Cambridge, UK: Polity Press.

Steinfels, P. (2003), *A People Adrift: The Crisis of the Roman Catholic Church in America*, New York and London: Simon and Schuster.

Steinfels, P. (2002), 'Abused by the Media', *The Tablet*, 14 September.

PART IV
AN OVERVIEW

Chapter 14

Major Issues in the Study of Media, Religion and Culture

Robert A. White

Over the last ten to fifteen years the study of media and religion has changed profoundly. In the early 1990s researchers were still concerned with the 'impact' of the televangelists or other institutional religious media. Were the audiences as large and diverse as the primetime preachers claimed? Were televangelists becoming a major political force in the US or in Latin America? These were not far from the administrative, effects research of parish sociology. Although these might have been valid questions, they were still side issues. This research was relatively unrelated to the central concerns of the sociology of religion and were not informed by theories of religion or of media. No major theorist in these fields was giving the relationship of media and religion much attention (Hoover, 2002c).

The changes in the study of media and religion can be traced, in part, to the major shifts in the sociology of religion that appeared in the work of Robert Bellah and colleagues' *Habits of the Heart* (1985) and Wade Clark Roof's books (1993, 1999) documenting the new religious cultures. British sociologist Beckford (1989) was among the many who signaled growing doubts about many of the truisms in the sociology of religion such as the inevitable disappearance of religion, progressive secularization and the essentially conservative nature of religion. The functionalist focuses on institutional religion had failed to notice that, while institutional religion was declining, religion as movements and as cultural practice was growing in importance.

More significant, perhaps, has been the tendency to redefine religion as a cultural category and at the heart of the formation of cultural identities. Durkheim, Weber and Marx had all seen religion as important in the modernization process, but as a specific institutional sector that had to disappear with increasing social differentiation, rationalization and new social class formations. Sociologists such as Giddens observed the continued relevance of religion in cultural development as a sign of the incapacity of modernization as theory and as practice, with its emphasis on functionalist automatic responses, to provide a moral foundation for society. Social theorists, such as Habermas, have also stressed that public discourse and media, shorn of the purely instrumentalist connotations and interpreted as public discourse, are central in the formation of cultures.

As Lynn Schofield Clark notes in her chapter (Chapter 1), underlying much of the shift is a new form of cultural analysis that owed much to the rise of various traditions of cultural studies. Particularly important were the British critical tradition represented by Stuart Hall, the American consensual approach represented by James W. Carey and the important Latin American tradition represented by Columbian Jesús Martín-Barbero and Venezuelan Antonio Pasquali. All of these traditions have roots in Gramsci, the Frankfurt School and in the French thinkers such as Bourdieu, Foucault, de Certeau, Lacan and Ricoeur. What all of these approaches have in common is the perception that social actors are not simply part of historical forces but are constructing cultural meaning around personal identities in a context of concentration of social power. Methodologies of research focus much more on how individuals and local movements create a cultural discourse around their sense of identity. Typically, meaning-construction is revealed through life histories, histories of movements, discourse analysis and other methods of uncovering a *process* of creating a cultural 'logic'.

In the following pages I would like to discuss ten of the particularly debated issues in the current research on media, religion and culture. Many of the chapters in this book go into greater detail on one or another of these issues.

1. Why and to What Extent Are the Media a Source of Symbols for Constructing Religious Identities?

The classical explanation of the formation of belief systems and religious identities is that one is born into or converted into a religious tradition and that the tradition impresses its worldview and norms on to the personality of the individual. As recent as the early 1970s the landmark study of what Americans believe carried out by sociologists Stark and Glock (1968) assumed that religious beliefs and practices are defined largely by denominational membership. Religious media of each denomination or national religious tradition – oral, print or electronic – with their powerful rhetoric were assumed to be the major instruments for impressing the group identity on the individual. If individual members came in contact with alternative views, this was largely filtered through the explanations of one's religious denomination.

Sociologists of religion in the 1970s and 1980s revealed that, in fact, most persons construct their own belief systems out of a repertoire of symbols offered by the context of religious affiliation but also by many other sources. Individuals perhaps always did this, but new research methodologies tended to focus on what *individuals* believe. The personalist belief systems were in part due to the impact of globalization which tended to set in during the 1960s and 1970s: higher levels of education, more mobility and travel, the pluralist images of television, and the increased incomes and leisure to explore other lifestyles. Also, in the 1970s and 1980s the development of reception analysis in media studies showed that individuals in audiences actively select material from media presentations according to their identities. All individuals are a complex mixture of personal and social identities, and each person has many codes for understanding a media presentation. Furthermore, each person actively seeks symbols that will be relevant to his or her identity questions at any given moment. Every media user selects, rejects, allows himself or herself to be seduced, questions or relishes with others and also undertakes a potentially endless series of other decoding activities.

One of the first major studies of religious media reception strategies was conducted by Stewart Hoover with followers of Pat Robertson's '700 Club' (1988). The interviews revealed that Robertson was a source of meanings that came as answers to a process of identity construction that started far back in childhood religious experiences and continued from life crisis to life crisis. Prior to their acquaintance with the prophet-like figure of Robertson, many had a kind of unhappy 'split' in their identity: a middle-class lifestyle but origins in an evangelical religiosity. Robertson, a Yale University graduate with Pentecostal religiosity, provided the symbols that allowed the followers to identify deeply with the televangelist. The conversion experience was not a result of the 'impact' of the television programs but the total involvement with a movement. The movement provided a multi-media cultural environment – TV programs, books, small group discussions, involvement with ministries to youth, new friend groups – a culture with a satisfying belief system from all of these symbolic resources. Although most of the people interviewed continued to be affiliated to the congregations of their religious denominations and had other sources of religious inspiration by far the most salient reference point was the world of the Pat Robertson movement. Hoover's study provided an insight into the *interrelation* of beliefs and practices of people involved in the 'electronic' para-church, but more important it showed how the religious identity of the persons studied evolved through a lifetime and how the *movement* of a televangelist helped to define religious identities at this point in their lives.

Similar studies of other movements, for example, the intensely devoted followers of the *Radio Maria* movement in Italy, Poland and elsewhere in the Catholic Church, show that the strongest attachment of personal identities to religious beliefs occurs in rallies and revitalizations within churches and denominations, and that the radio or television program is often the focal point of the identification (Horsfield, 1984). The biographical approach used in the study of the members of Robertson's '700 Club' evolved into the research project of Hoover and his associates at the University of Colorado, a project which came to be known as the 'Symbolism, Media and Life Course' (Hoover, 2002a, 2002b, 2002c).

A central question for this research program is how people use media to construct meaning in their lives. The conception of culture places great emphasis on 'meaning', the interrelation of perceptions of reality. To use the word 'constructs' implies that every individual is an active subject, trying to create a coherent world in everyday life so that the or she can interact with this environment and with other people with a higher degree of certainty. It is assumed that the most central meaning-construction is the continual definition and redefinition of self-identity across the life span. Thus the core question is how people use the media to construct a self-identity.

The Media, Symbolism and the Life Course project defends its constructivist approach to media and religion in part because major social theorists such as Anthony Giddens affirm that the emphasis of late modern societies on the adaptation to nature has receded. Contemporary cultures are more aware that nature is itself a human construction and that we can change and develop as we wish. Similarly, sociologists of religion have documented that religion for most is not taking on the institutional belief system, but selecting symbols and meanings from a wide variety of religious and secular systems to build their own belief systems. For a variety of reasons, the media are an important means of getting in contact with the available systems of symbolic materials with which to build identity (Hoover, 2003).

For example, Lynn Clark (2003) in her study of the role of media use by teenagers in the adolescent culture in the western US, describes in great detail how one teenager, Elizabeth, uses a great variety of media – the telephone, Internet, television, and so on – to continually explore the meaning systems of a great variety of people to arrive at her own definition of the meaning of a situation. On the telephone, Elizabeth queries her friends as to what they think about people and situations in the school environment in order to get some point of reference for her own opinions. She uses the Internet as a 'safe' way to explore intimate relations without having to commit herself to any one type of relationship. The media enable her to reach far beyond her own small world, 'zapping' along rapidly to 'try on' the greatest possible number of meanings to finally assemble the set that is most consonant with her perception of her own identity.

The research reveals the aloneness of people with their own identities, and how the media relations are the closest thing to personal consciousness. This is true not only of American adolescents such as Elizabeth, but of young and old in many parts of the world. A quiet, somewhat retiring adolescent girl from Chile living with her family in Rome feels relatively estranged from her family, but comes alive when she describes her world of *telenovelas* (Yevenes, 2002). A study of how women in the Netherlands interpreted the then popular TV series, *Dallas*, some twenty years ago revealed that the most salient part of the lives of many was entering into Sue Ellen and other female characters of this American serial drama (Ang, 1993). The research of Clark reveals great diversity in the coherence and security of adolescent religious meaning systems, from the quite closed and secure systems of Muslims, traditional Catholics, or Mormons to the open and much more fragile belief systems of those who do not live in any particularly strong context of belief system. Increasingly most live in a world of great social mobility and have no strong attachments to community, institutions or overarching ideologies.

Indeed, the postmodern context makes many television viewers, especially in more self-conscious cultures such as are found in Europe, deeply suspicious of all historical projects. The neoliberal political-economic policies tend to throw people more and more into the insecurities of the marketplace. The 'real world' is increasingly harsh for young people trying to get into schools, find jobs, find stable friends and stable life mates. A more stable world is found in the media and those who share similar interests as media fans (Jenkins, 1992).

The studies also reveal the attempt to use the media to cope with a much more pluralistic, multicultural world. Younger people especially know that they must live in a world in which they have to deal empathetically with people of greatly differing religious and cultural backgrounds. The ability to get along with everybody demands a high level of tolerance, low levels of fundamentalistic attachments and lower levels of visible symbols of any personal belief system. People jump from channel to channel in order to know something of a great variety of cultural discourses in order to deal smoothly with these subcultural contacts. This need to live between many different cultural worlds leads to a kind of 'flattening' of the symbols of cultural belief systems that may have had their remote origin in the hostilities and rigid differences of *cujus regio, eius religio* (the religion of the ruler determines the religion of the territory).

This approach moves away from 'administrative' media research which focuses on the effects of a given religious institution because that approach presents the false view that the institutional formula of religion is the only thing that is meaningful to persons. This effects perception of the media led to the distorted view that the televangelists had a major influence on the political values of Americans when, in fact, these media figures represented just one of many sources of political meaning. Rather the focus is on the life world of a person across space and biographical time. Elizabeth, in the example above, is somewhat active in a Lutheran Church, but the meaning of this for her bears little relation to the Lutheran belief system. Although Elizabeth is much more open to religious institutions as a source of meaning than seemingly many young people her age, she takes from a variety of religious meaning systems without any full realization that these are 'religious'. In an increasingly complex and pluralistic world, most people are hesitant to restrict their identity to any one religious belief system and tend to avoid 'religion' because it is perceived as more constrictive.

The Media, Symbolism and the Life Course group encountered a variety of ways that individuals and families establish identities and relate to media, all in a process of negotiating with media and culture in modern life. The group's book, *Media, Home and Family* (Hoover et al., 2004) describes a process of negotiation of family identity as parents and children reflected on their own experiences and certain widely held beliefs about media in the US. This negotiation helped locate the families on 'larger maps of morality, religion, gender, social location, individual purpose and other parameters of modern life' (ibid., pp. 5–6). These 'accounts of media' often included religious beliefs, which were cited in a variety of frameworks and sensibilities. The authors describe their move from a focus on individual agency (an emphasis of some audience research) to a more contextualized, social approach (ibid., pp. 35–50).

Some might argue that the emphasis of some reception research on the use of media in personal identity construction has tended to neglect context. As Klaus Bruhn Jensen (2002) stresses, reception analysis must take into consideration factors of context. 'Statements and actions must always be interpreted with reference to their context(s)' (p. 238). The observation of reception attempts to locate this with the 'normal' routine of the home, family, and friend groups, but at times relatively little of how these 'mediations' influence the interpretation seems to come through. There may be a danger of focusing religious reception too much on the individual, consciousness of self-identity and relating to specific cultural symbols. It is important to locate the individual within cultural movements. We need to ask not only what kind of identity individuals are creating but what kind of culture we are creating and whether this is the kind of culture we want.

What this analysis of total life situations reveals particularly well is the relationship between the macro socio-economic conditions of life and the strategies of identity construction that people adopt. Classical ethnographic studies tended to present a rather neatly organized system of harmonious meanings that individuals are socialized into. When the focus is on the life space of the individual, it becomes more apparent how fragmentary a cultural environment is and how difficult it is to construct an identity. An economy of short-term contracts and great uncertainty breeds a strategy of low commitment, high tolerance and loose, open belief systems. These teenagers in the study of Clark are also rather detached from the media except for some momentary enjoyment and some brief 'snatching' of symbols for their own life story. Many of the US adolescents do not seem to be deeply immersed in any one medium or genre such as popular music.

Again, what seems to be needed is more research on persons in different contextual situations, the significance of the mediations. It is also important to see the use of media in the context of a fairly complete life story. How do people gather different symbols from different media to construct over time a personal identity.

2. In What Sense Are the Belief Systems Constructed with Media Symbols 'Religious'?

As studies of media and religion and social scientists in general take as their reference point individual constructions of meaning systems, regardless of whether this fits with any form of institutional religion, this has created an intense debate about what religion is (Greil and Robbins, 1994). There have been several stages in the debate. The early research on media and religion was unselfconsciously concerned only with whether the institutional symbols were transmitted to members, and religion was understood unambiguously as institutional religion. The social sciences also used religion in the institutional sense or as some primitive form of this. Sociologists of religion began to invent new categories insofar as people became less involved with institutional religion, but still considered themselves religious. Some sociologists have maintained that there are *substantive* areas of human behavior that are to be called religious and others profane or secular. *Functionalists* have argued that any kind of behavior can be termed religious by analysts if it has the function of religion in a person's life. Others observe that both substantive and functional definitions assume 'definitional essentialism', that is, that religious behavior is a distinct part of human behaviors and that any given practice can be labeled religious or non-religious according to the definition.

Greil and Robbins argue (leaving behind the definitions of social science) that:

> religion is not an entity but rather a *category of discourse* whose precise meaning and implications are continually being negotiated in the course of social interaction. Religion from this perspective is not a concrete 'thing' which may be either present or absent in a society, but rather an idiom, a way of speaking about and categorizing actors' experience. (Greil and Robbins, 1994, p. 6)

This definition tends to designate as religious what a particular cultural group considers religious. The social scientist may follow the discipline in designating something as religious in order to get to a phenomenon that the discipline is analyzing, but then use terms which describe what the group sees, thinks and does. The important thing is that the terms of analysis enable the researcher to see and describe the phenomenon as it is. All societies have ways of drawing a map describing different categories in order to make sense of reality and communicate with each other about this reality. It is important to 'get inside' this sense-making and see the world from that perspective.

If studies of media and religion, in a first stage, defined religion in institutional terms, in a second stage, many who were critiquing film, television and journalism from a theological perspective argued that media do not have to be an echo of dogma to be religious if they reveal the form and logic of religion. God is present in all creation and in all creativity. This perception of what is God's presence or not is, of course, a theological definition of a particular religious tradition.

Hoover specifically objects that this is still a distorting 'essentialism' because it is based on a fixed prior conception of what is or is not religious and does not allow the observer to let the cultural group say what it thinks is religious. Hoover (2002a) follows R. S. Warner in affirming that, in order to capture the breadth and complexity of the contemporary religious experience, the definition of what religion is must be based on what is expressed and experienced, not what is ascribed by hegemonic cultures (Warner, 1993).

Lynn Schofield Clark, using this approach in her studies of how adolescents construct their identities using media symbols, went to a cultural site that the culture and her discipline call religious. That is, she presented to teenagers a television program, *Touched by an Angel*, something clearly from an institutional religious tradition, but with a rather general, 'tolerant' angel image. One adolescent boy remarked that one reason he liked it was that it was *not religious*, suggesting a frequently noted observation that young people's identity is not informed by institutional religion. Most of the teenagers generally were entertained by the program and identified with the benevolent actions of the 'angels'. What they especially identified with was the morally positive action of helping young people find the right path in life. A similar observation came from the Chilean adolescent in Rome who has no strong institutional religious inclination (the family does not identify with institutional religion), but is inspired by the heroines of the *telenovelas* and is attracted to this genre so strongly (Yevenes, 2002). The attractiveness of the moral goodness of media personalities was the central conclusion of the large study of British viewers of *Dallas* and *Eastenders* conducted by Sonia Livingstone (1990). She found that the most salient experience was identifying the 'good' characters and rejecting the 'bad'. Is this identification with the moral orientation of media a religious expression and experience? Gregory Peterson (2001) thinks that religion is best defined as a worldview which acts as an orientation and normative reference for moral conduct and goal-setting in life. This may be a definition that sums up the sense-making maps and categories that people use to communicate with each other. It may be a definition that includes the various approaches to the subject of religion today.

The challenge seems to be to find a discourse about religion that avoids the tendency to make particular essentialistic conceptions of religion a self-serving ideology and at the same time does not reduce religion to a purely functional residual category that has no meaning in itself. It may be that the development of the concepts of symbol, narrative and identity in the cultural studies tradition can provide a discourse about religion that responds to this challenge.

3. How Are Mass-produced Popular Religious Images Used in the Construction of Personal Identity?

As David Morgan points out, the more 'official' view of the role of popular media, especially religious images, is that it caters to the lowest taste and fosters superstition and silly emotionalism. One of the major shifts in the study of religion and media is the gradual acceptance of the important role of popular media.

Morgan's studies of *Visual Piety* (1998) focus on the use of material culture to create and sustain a self-identity over a biographical lifetime and in cultural space. His studies focus on what historically has been a central 'pool of symbols', the cultural industry of religious images. These studies focus on the social practice of 'looking'.

The role of images in religious piety and commitment has been widely discussed, but the data presented in *Visual Piety* (1998) are among the most solid and richly differentiated. The methodology of soliciting letters (531 were received) has been quite successful in some studies of television reception because it stimulates those who are particularly interested to spontaneously describe the subjective meaning of the text for them.

The major conclusions could serve as the points of reference for the research of others studying the interplay of media, religion and culture:

- 'The repeated and routine usage of and ritualized interaction with devotional images generates a stability or baseline against which to measure one's well-being' (Morgan, 1998, p. 204). Morgan's theoretical approach and data tend to confirm that people use images to gain solidity and 'objectivity' for their religious life space. The users of images seek consistency in their own character over a lifetime and assurance that the world has not changed radically. This tends to confirm the earlier research of Hoover, who found that people identified with their selection of a given televangelist because it helped them to 'come back' to deeper strata in their life-identity, especially after going through experiences which shattered outer layers of roles. Televangelists communicate not so much in terms of transporting information but rather as icons of a certain permanency that enable people to make transitions in their religious life world in a way that preserves the deepest layers of identity.

  One might ask whether the concept of 'habitus' taken from Bourdieu that is applied here might also be useful in explaining the significance of repeatedly used genres of television, including religious genres, in the lives of people. The use of media genre theory tends to be relatively absent from the Media, Symbolism and the Life Course projects while in my own research and that of my students, the repeated use of a genre is an important locus of sustaining what a person considers to be religious. The devotion of fans to a particular genre tends to bring out particularly deep strata of identity and what is seen to be religious. Young people in Chile, who are less close to the institutional church, tend to take the imagery to form their religious discourse from a specific genre: *telenovelas*.

- The images which an individual brings into the life space become the anchor around which awareness of self develops through a lifetime. 'The self ... is a vast repertoire (of roles) cohering around a tightly knit core, itself a historical formation but one whose origin occurred so early in life that it is unavailable to memory and, in its earliest phases, hardly distinguishable from the biology of pleasure and pain, that makes up an infant's life' (Morgan, 1998, pp. 204–5). We might say that these visual symbols are the point of negotiation between the roles that the culture holds out to a person and the internal awareness of the self-seeking pleasure, realization and integration. Many of the authors in this book see the media as a repertoire of symbols for the progressive definition of identity. Again, I think that this conception of the interaction of the self and images describes well this process of definition of identity.

- Morgan found that different denominations – Catholics, Lutherans, and others – tended to have different interpretations of the same images. What some backgrounds saw as an inspiringly religious icon was anti-religious to others. Visual material tends to help different religious groups establish their collective identities with different interpretations of the meaning of the same image. This echoes the finding of Lynn Clark that young age cohorts, obviously with an identity and self-concept formed in the US of the 1990s, tended to have their own rather 'unorthodox' interpretation of religious symbols such as angels. This suggests fertile areas of research such as exploring how objects or images that seemingly have little relationship to religion can be invested with religious meaning by some groups.

- The *Visual Piety* research has also shown how images can objectify and legitimate a given social order and structure of power. Images help a given structure of reality gain legitimacy and passive acceptance. Roberto Goizueta's research comes to mind (also that of Germán Rey) as an example of critical analysis of the role of particular iconic figures in sustaining a given structure of power. People's self-identity seems reassured by the symbols that sustain a particular just or unjust order. Peter Horsfield, who seems to be one of the few who is thinking about media from an ecclesial and pastoral perspective, is also concerned about media and ecclesial power structures.

- Still another important line of thinking in Morgan's generative analysis is the role of images as self-representation, that is, as the articulation and symbolization of roles to be performed, as summaries of personal narratives (partial and complete), and as reference points in personal religious autobiography. Here I see a connection with Horsfield's interest in the variety of emerging religious cultures within ecclesial traditions. The decline of the text-based religious institution makes it far more difficult for these institutions to 'coerce' one meaning of the religious symbols. The rise of the visual image – that so many religious leaders fear – enables many to return to a more medieval 'village-based' religiosity; that is, each village or group creates its own religious icons as symbols of its belief systems.

4. What is the Role of Popular Culture in Religious Education?

One of the major issues is that the typical young person finds the major life interests in the world of popular culture and popular media. Traditionally, the best religious youth programs have realized this and built a series of activities around sports, music, drama and other major interests of young people. The objectives have been to build interpersonal skills for family, community and nation. Church, school, family, community and popular culture are interlinked in a youthful 'liminal experience', and all is sacralized by a kind of mixture of civic religion and denominational versions of the civic religion. Today, much of the community interlinking has come apart and the political–economic structures have colonized the life space of family, community, school, church and popular culture. Young people know that the community space is far less important for their survival than popular culture. What there is of community, myth and discovery of identity is in popular culture. The challenge is to rebuild the linkages between communities and popular culture and at the same time to generate more capacity for discernment for freedom. Given the general weakness of the family to cope with this today, the school and extra-curricular religious education contexts may be much more important. How to bridge the gap?

Mary Hess (2004) provides a syntheses of relationship of religious education and popular culture, or, more specifically, how religions identity is shaped in part by culture. She deals with methodologies of religious education and is convinced that we must help people to build their faith commitment out of their cultural habitat and their life context, which is popular culture. She shares the concern that the institutional church, theological education and religious education, by misunderstanding and rejecting popular culture, reject young people.

I think, however, that there is a deeper theme in her writings, namely, that the young especially are living in another world of connectedness. The implicit foundation of much of religious education was the connectedness of building a *modern nation*. Much of religion was bound up with helping people become rationally modern and entering into the national myth. In the postmodern, post-national context, popular culture may be a more real foundation of connectedness, the real basis for building community. I found the draft of her chapter on 'The Bible and popular culture: Engaging sacred text in a world of "others"' (2004) particularly interesting because of her use of Richard Shweder's analysis of how people (particularly anthropologists) can enter into the cultural worlds of others. Hess would argue that most people today learn to comprehend and deal with the complex cultural diversity of today's pluralism through the mass popular media. They do this by entering into the narrative organization of culture. Even the 'sex and violence' (or perhaps, most of all because of the sex and violence) of popular culture is a way of our understanding the murky realities of sex and violence in our cultures. The premise here is that of much current reception theory, namely, that the impact of the media is not a process of simply imitation but a search for narratives that 'fit' the implicit narrative in our own core identity, as Morgan discusses above.

She follows through the four steps of Shweder to see how the use of popular culture can possibly lead toward greater connectedness in religious education.

1　Recognize the other as having greater insight into some aspect of human experience that could be used to reveal hidden dimensions of ourselves.
2　Getting the other straight, that is, entering into the internal logic of the intentional world constructed by the other to understand the strategies of 'meaning-making' that are provided.
3　Deconstructing and going beyond the other, that is, having understood the world of others we then begin to experience how it is to explore the world through the way others perceive it. We attempt to see the rationality of the world of the other, given their circumstances.

4   Witnessing in the context of engagement with the other in order to understand
    ourselves better in the process. I think what this implies is that we begin to see
    both the similarities and the differences with others to be able to rise to a higher
    level of commonalities in which we share similar values. We can thus not only
    tolerate other cultures but we can see their positive value for those of my culture
    group and for our common good.

A central question for those in religious education is how to help people find God
in the media. The pastoral implications are great if we realize that the agrarian
symbolism no longer has relevance for many people. Without falling into the
'essentialism' characteristic of some religious film or TV criticism, it is important to
understand better the relationship of formal aspects of media and the awareness of
how narrative, symbolism or archetypes awaken an awareness of personal
spirituality. Those who live in a world of popular media have a spirituality that is
attuned to that kind of symbolism.

Methods of teaching popular culture in a religious context still face major
hurdles. As Hess suggests, we also need to understand the world of those in the
churches who have reservations about popular culture and why so many emphasize
that we need to have tools of discernment in using popular culture.

Particularly important for the approach of Hess in religious education is Roberto
Goizueta's approach to theology and popular culture seeing the community's lived
religious faith as the fundamental 'text' for the theologian, for it is here – in the
concrete lives of the people – that the theologian directly encounters the God about
whom he or she dares to speak. 'As the primary expressions of religious faith,
symbols and rituals demand theological explanation and critique, but theology can
never forget its roots in the symbols and rituals that embody the lived faith
(Goizueta, 2002, p. 19). And, as Goizueta emphasizes, we must go into the faith
communities of the marginal and oppressed to discover this faith in its more pure,
non-ideologized form. The *mass, popular* media are produced for these groups and
are often an articulation of the tastes and aspirations of these groups. Religious
education would seek both to critically examine this popular culture, but also to
discover popular spirituality in this media culture. Our Latino theology and the
theologies of other faith communities would be greatly enriched by a theology of
their use and misuse of the popular media.

5. How to Bridge the Hostile Gap between Church Leadership and the World of Popular Culture?

The gap that is taken up here is part of a larger series of culture wars that has grown
more hostile since the late 1960s. Virtually all who are doing research in the area of
media, religion and culture touch on this at some point. This may manifest itself as a
clash with authority, but it is something much deeper, at the level of cultures. The

camps defend themselves and attempt to destroy the other with distorting ideologies that cover over ambitions for power and make dialogue at times almost impossible. The consequences of this breakdown of dialogue are shown in the inability to confront the most pressing human problems in most societies because of the inability to come up with some solutions that are acceptable to all. The moral claims of those who live more in the realm of popular culture go unrecognized.

The clash between the cultures is manifested in a series of antinomies that one hears constantly repeated:

- Popular culture is at best trivial, a waste, degrading our academic standards and at worst seductive, corrupting and destroying many of the main institutions such as family and church, versus popular culture is life, freedom, creativity, forging a new culture, responding to personal identities.
- The salvation of our civilization lies in the ability to hold universal principles, read the classics of our history, uphold the culture of the book, cultivate an aesthetic which is disinterested and uplifting, versus popular culture unites the person, body and spirit, is expressive, responds to the needs of the moment, employs all of the senses, upholds the poetic and the lyric in our cultures.
- Our societies need more authority, control, communication among those who are truly wise, versus they need a culture of participation, transparency, horizontal communication.
- Emphasis on linear communication, the maintenance of hierarchy and patriarchy, maintaining the purity of cultures, ethnicities, races, religions, justification of hegemonic cultural groups, versus emphasis on more dialogical, communitarian communication, breaking down exclusions of all kinds, finding common symbols.
- Fundamentalist and conserving, hostile to cultural change, cultural pluralism and cultural dialogue, versus promotes cultural dialogue, sees the advantage of interreligious and multicultural communities.
- Sees solutions through instrumental rationality and technology, espouses a hard-science approach, versus sees solutions through dialogue, empathy into other's positions and problems, the qualitative and the subjective.

These cultural antinomies are so well known – and so taken for granted – that they seem almost trite. All work through religious orthodoxies and through the media. The young now see the church as a highly ideological institution and the church leaders see the young as aggressive.

A central issue is whether those working in the area of religion, media and culture have the resources to bring these antagonistic groups together in dialogue. Part of the problem of the Catholic Church that Frances Forde Plude describes in her analysis of the sexual abuse revelations is due to a certain contempt for the media by the church. Has the Catholic Church or other churches that aspire to be part of the hegemonic culture learned that the church must respect and live with and in the media?

6. What is the Role of the 'New Movements' in the Research and Discussions of Media, Religion and Culture?

The late nineteenth and twentieth centuries were ones of great movements of workers and peasants, an epoque of forming national organizations to build and to take control of the nation-state. At times these movements were able to negotiate a redistribution of power. Often after great sacrifices and bloodshed, the structure of power remained virtually unchanged. The new movements are small and local, often protesting local issues and claiming at best only small victories that few notice.

The protagonists of the new movements are not economically but culturally defined. That is, their 'natural' condition – as women, youth, racial and ethnic groups, gender orientation, the elderly – are defined culturally as 'naturally inferior'. Everywhere these movements are fighting an *apartheid* of cultural ideologies. The movements rise spontaneously in the context of the everyday over seemingly incidental events, with a strong emotional outburst. The underlying conflict is over the value of the cultural definition of the group, a problem of cultural capital that does often translate into better economic conditions. Often the movements validate the knowledge of women or of ethnic/racial and other marginal groups as more valuable than 'expert' knowledge.

The main impact is that the community recognizes the group as 'empowered', as having resources that must now be respected. The 'natural condition' considered inferior now is seen as something essential and important for the community. The main impact on the community is clearly cultural. The primary goal is at the cultural level and, through this, transformations at the political-economic level.

Clemencia Rodriguez (2001) compares the new movements to 'swamp bubbles' that come to the surface and then disappear. The significance is enormous when one considers the multitude of these little movements around the world. They are the tactics of the weak, and their greatest power is the ability to bring about cultural change.

The objective is not to create a great dichotomous movement of us against them in order to take the power of the nation-state, but rather to undermine the legitimacy of concentrations of power. By unmasking the ideologies of exclusion, people cease to believe in them. They do not try to get control of the media to re-educate the public in their views, but to share among all the few media resources that are available. They seek rather to quietly change the local structure of communication in patterns that are more participatory and dialogical, like the communication structures of the small movements. Because the movements remain small, they are less likely to develop hierarchical structures. Often, such movements seek validation in a religious worldview because they are questioning the foundations of our social construction of reality (Beckford, 1989, pp. 170–71).

The new movements speak a language of rights – the right to communicate, the right to participate – because that is the only way they can overcome the exclusionary culture that is imposed on them. The new movements seek what Jolyon Mitchell has termed 'communicative justice'. The new media in Africa, discussed by Kwabena Asamoah-Gyadu (Chapter 5), seek explicitly to confront the West on the cultural level by dismantling the ideologies that continue to undergird the neo-colonialism of the West. Religion is implicit in the culture and in the media, and the message is that salvation for the degenerate West comes from Africa.

7. What is the Role of the Discussion of Spirituality and Theology in the Discourse of Media, Religion and Culture?

Classical social science eliminated the discourses of theology and spirituality from interdisciplinary dialogue because these phenomena seemed to have no reality in themselves. Religion seemed to be reducible to characteristics of a social system according to Durkheim or a projection of our personalities according to Freud. This began to change with the development of the cultural sciences, which focused on meaning, symbolism, ritual and myth. Social constructions of reality are real, indeed, the most real because we could eventually see that everything, including nature, is a cultural construction. Clifford Geertz's *Interpretation of Cultures* (1975) has been important because it made clear the procedures of the cultural sciences. Geertz describes religion as a system of symbols and defines a religious symbol as an outward sign that awakens the awareness of an interior experience. The cultural sciences began to speak of symbolic realism, emphasizing that the symbol is a real relationship to the 'experience' in my consciousness, however I might want to define that experience.

At this point, in my estimation, the cultural sciences began to draw near to the theological sciences and to offer the possibility of interdisciplinary dialogue. Theology also, perhaps because of a dialogue with cultural anthropology, began to focus on symbols. Indeed, with the renewal of theology and the relinking to its historical, biblical and liturgical roots, theology began to see itself as a 'science of symbols'. More precisely, perhaps, theology has increasingly begun to see itself as the science of the explanation of symbols, that is, to explain what this symbol signifies in the experience of the particular religious group. Cultural sciences may state the relationship of symbols to ritual and experience, but theology is able to go into the subjective experience of the person to explain why this symbol is generated by this personal or group experience. Spirituality, as I understand it, is the description and discernment of interior experience. This 'symbolic theology' becomes the point of intersection with the cultural sciences, spirituality (description of the interior experiences) and theology, the explanation of why this symbol is understood to be related to this experience.

To take Christian theology as an example, the key symbol, the crucifixion of Jesus, has as a referent the experience of the Christian community. They began to see their suffering as part of the suffering of Jesus, the sacrificial Lamb of God. Theology gets inside of the experience as an experience of 'faith' to explain this experience in a language that is intelligible to public discourses and intelligible to other cultures.

8. What are the Tasks of Reflection on Media, Religion and Culture in the Context of Globalization?

Globalization has brought together the great religions in direct confrontation. The growing presence of Christianity in Africa and Asia has brought a militant reaction in some parts of these continents. For Europeans the realization that Muslims may well be a solid religious majority in some European countries fills some Europeans with panic. Europe has struggled for hundreds of years to have a relative religious tolerance and pluralism, but many wonder if a Muslim majority would not impose its logic of domination. All religions seem to be less cultural and much more aggressive.

How to solve this problem is not clear. Europe, for example, was able, after hundreds of years, to move its religious conflict to the cultural level but it did so at the cost of excluding religion from the public, cultural sphere. For some, the result has been a moral vacuum in the public sphere.

What resources for cultural dialogue and consensus can the cultural studies tradition bring to the issues of religious and cultural conflict that globalization is causing? Reception theory, insofar as it focuses on individuals in a family or group context, is far too narrow for this. British cultural studies did take into consideration cultural hegemony and the struggle of cultural movements to defend their own identity in this societal context. There is much less help in this, however, for understanding how different major cultural groups come to recognize the mutual benefit of each group for each other and for the benefit of the whole society. Can those of a Christian or secular tradition in Europe come to realize that the Muslim presence is a very significant contribution not only to the cultural development of Europe but also to religious and political development? Can the Hindu tradition in India come to recognize that the Christian, Muslim and other religious presence is making a significant contribution to the cultural and political development in India?

As Lynn Schofield Clark points out in this book (Chapter 1), the political and economic institutions of the world have become so co-opted by global hegemony that only more marginal institutions, such as the *local* churches in their grass-roots constituencies, are able to appeal to national motivations in a way that is responsive to the people.

9. What Contribution Does the Reflection on Media, Religion and Culture Make to the Development of a Civil Society?

The concept of civil society as a guiding principle for the development of democracy has emerged in recent years in close relationship to cultural studies. Central to the notion of civil society is the attempt to move collective decision-making away from the dominance of the state bureaucracy into the sphere of citizens organized as cultural groups. This is even more important in countries which that have experienced recurring civil conflict. A goal is to move social conflict between social and cultural identities out of the vicious cycle of military and political force to the cultural level. The civil society moves away from the blind hand of economic competition as the guiding force in a society to a kind of public deliberation around some common social goals. The notion of civil society implies the presence of a 'middle zone' of cultural organizations between the privacy of the individual, family and local community and the coercive monopoly of the state. These cultural groups are not simply the classical contractually based interest-group organizations but communities of like values which are conscious of the worth of their cultural identities for the national community. These groups do have representative interests, but far more important is their self-conscious awareness that their cultural values are important for other communities and for the national community.

The deliberation between cultural communities regarding decisions takes place largely in the context of the media. Not only the news media, but also many other genres – especially fiction drama and comedy – enable one cultural community to know how their values and activities are perceived and evaluated by other cultural groups. Given the emphasis on the study of individuals' use of news and other programming, relatively little is known systematically about how cultural communities 'deliberate' and decide about the major public affairs.

The moral and cultural consistency of many cultural groups is influenced by their dominant religious identity. Also important is the capacity of these groups to dialogue and negotiate with other religious groups. Much depends on the ability of a given cultural group to project its value claims into the public debate and to grasp, as a cultural group, what are the claims of other groups. The internal media within the cultural group is important in terms of forming internal public opinion.

Some of the most significant research on the interaction of cultural communities in the process of public deliberation has been done by Robert Wuthnow (1992). Hoover's *Religion in the News: Faith and Journalism in American Public Discourse* (1998) carries the analysis into the mediated process of deliberation. The question of how religious identities work into the deliberation process and how effective they are in bringing to bear their moral identities in the formation of public decisions and public policy is much less studied.

10. The Contribution of the Media, Religion and Culture Research to Current Debates Regarding Communication Ethics

Over the last twenty years a communitarian normative paradigm has begun to have significant influence on normative theory, balancing somewhat the influence of the individualistic libertarian ethic which has dominated the normative theory of public discourse in western societies for some four hundred years. The libertarian tradition that the ownership of the media gives the proprietor undisputed control over the content has been tempered by the existence of the social responsibility and public service paradigms. The communitarian proposal is challenging all of them.

At the practical level the growing influence of the communitarian paradigm is indicated by the growing number of community radio and television stations throughout the world. The spread of the Freirian and similar animation methods at the level of groups and communities is another indicator. The 'public journalism' movement in the US is an indicator. The drive toward the democratization of communication which began as part of the NWICO[1] continues to be an important theme. The spread of the groups associated with the 'new movements' referred to above also stress a dialogical, participatory communication.

Much of the inspiration for this new paradigm is clearly associated with the rise of the cultural studies tradition. Central to cultural studies is the notion of the public as the active user and interpreter of the media. The neo-Marxist origins of cultural studies stressed the capacity of the working class to create its own culture. In the US, James Carey's espousal of the ritual, communion model of communication emerges out of his long-term interest in John Dewey and the belief in the right to communication of the people.

Scholars associated with media, culture and religion research are important contributors to the development of communitarian paradigm. One of the most important documents defining the communitarian paradigm is the Christians et al.'s, *Good News: Social Ethics and the Press* (1993). A central question is the degree to which the religious cultural communities in a given country contribute to the development of a strong ethics of public discourse.

So Why Worry About these Issues?

There is increasing awareness that one of the tragedies in the western intellectual tradition is reducing religion to a disappearing, residual category. The same is true of mass popular media culture. Two of the most deeply constituent areas of human experience have remained outside of serious reflection. The effort to build a science around univocal, universalist categories ruled out something so deeply personal and intimate as religious experience or our 'secret enjoyment' of something so vulgar as popular culture.

The chapters in this book are, perhaps, reflective of very personal and deeply felt experiences. They take seriously a series of seemingly unimportant experiences ranging from horror films in Ghana to Latino fiestas in Texas. This book would argue that the religious and the popular are the sites where we are building our cultures, including our religious cultures. We need to ask what kind of culture we are creating in these experiences, whether these are the kinds of cultures we want to create, and who is involved in the creation process.

Note

1 The movement among Third World countries in the 1970s which sought 'The New World Information and Communication Order' (NWICO) was an attempt to gain an explicit commitment of the developed nations to respect the political, economic, communication and cultural autonomy of the new nations through international policy agreements. The movement used, as its principal forum, the meetings and policy-making mechanisms of the United Nations, and UNESCO in particular. One of the major goals was an attempt to introduce communication policies in Third World nations which would bring transnational communication corporations to respect local development priorities rather than global marketing campaigns. The movement failed largely due to the pressure that transnational economic interests placed on the governments in the major industrial powers and the pressures these governments brought on the UN and UNESCO to abandon this issue.

References

Ang, I. (1993), *Watching Dallas: Soap Opera and the Melodramatic Imagination*, London: Routledge.

Beckford, J. A. (1989), *Religion and Advanced Industrial Society*, London: Unwin Hyman.

Bellah, R., R. Madsen, W. M. Sullivan, A. Swidler and S. M. Tipton (1985), *Habits of the Heart: Individualism and Commitment in American Life*, Berkeley, CA: University of California Press.

Christians, C. G., J. P. Ferré and P. M. Fackler (1993), *Good News: Social Ethics and the Press,* New York: Oxford University Press.

Clark, L. S. (2003), *From Angels to Aliens: Teenagers, the Media and the Supernatural*, New York: Oxford University Press.

Geertz, C. (1975), *The Interpretation of Cultures*, London: Hutchinson.

Goizueta, R. (2002), 'Theology and Popular Culture', unpublished paper presented at the meeting of the International Commission on Media, Religion and Culture, Vancouver.

Greil, A. and T. Robbins (1994), 'Introduction: Exploring the Boundaries of The Sacred', in A. Greil and T. Robbins (eds), *Religion and the Social Order*, London: Jai Press, pp. 1–26.

Hess, M. E. (2004), 'The Bible and Popular Culture: Engaging Sacred Text in a World of "Others"', in Robert Fowler (ed.), *New Paradigms in Bible Study*, Philadelphia, PA: Trinity Press Internatrional.

Hess, M. E. (2002), 'Rescripting Christian Education for Performative Practice', plenary address, Luther Seminary Convocation, St Paul, MN.

Hoover, S. M. (2003), 'Religion, Media and Identity: Theory and Method in Audience Research on Religion and Media', in Jolyon Mitchell and Sophia Marriage (eds), *Mediating Religion: Conversations in Media, Religion and Culture*, London: Continuum, pp. 9–20.

Hoover, S. M. (2002a), 'The Culturalist Turn in Scholarship on Media and Religion', *The Journal of Media and Religion*, **1**(1), 25–36.

Hoover, S. M. (2002b), 'Religion in the Media Age', *Expository Times*, **113** (9), 300–305.

Hoover, S. M. (2002c), 'The Culturalist Construction of Religion in the Media Age', in S. M. Hoover and L. S. Clark (eds), *Practicing Religion in the Age of the Media*, New York: Columbia University Press, pp. 1–6.

Hoover, S. M. (1999a), 'Rethinking Form and Content: Religion on Television or Television Religion', paper given at the Conference on Religious Function of Television, University of Heidelberg, Germany.

Hoover, S. M. (1999b), 'The Converging Worlds of Religion and the Media', address delivered at Edinburgh Conference on Media, Religion and Culture.

Hoover, S. M. (1998), *Religion in the News: Faith and Journalism in American Public Discourse*, London: Sage.

Hoover, S. M. (1988), *Mass Media Religion: The Social Sources of the Electronic Church*, Newbury Park, CA: Sage.

Hoover, S. M., L. S. Clark, D. F. Alters, with J. G. Champ and L. Hood (2004), *Media, Home and Family*, New York and London: Routledge.

Horsfield, P. (1999), 'Electronic Media and the Past-Future of Christianity', address delivered at Edinburgh Conference on Media, Religion and Culture.

Horsfield, P. (1984), *Religious Television: The American Experience*, New York: Longman.

Jenkins, H. (1992), *Textual Poachers: Television fans and participatory culture*, London: Routledge.

Jensen, K. B. (2002), *A Handbook of Media and Communication Research: Qualitative and Quantitative Methodologies*, London: Routledge.

Livingstone, S. (1990), *Making Sense of Television: The Psychology of Audience Interpretation*, Oxford: Pergamon Press.

Morgan, D. (1998), *Visual Piety: A History and Theory of Popular Religious Images*, Berkeley, CA: University of California Press.

Peterson, G. (2001), 'Religion as Orienting World View', *Zygon*, **36** (1) (March), 5–20.

Rodriguez, C. (2001), *Fissures in the Mediascape: An International Study of Citizen's Media*, Cresskill, NJ: Hampton Press.

Roof, W. C. (1999), *Spiritual Marketplace: Baby Boomers and the Remaking of American Religion*, Princeton, NJ: Princeton University Press.

Roof, W. C. (1993), *A Generation of Seekers: The Spiritual Journeys of the Baby Boom Generation*, San Francisco, CA: Harper.

Warner, R. S. (1993), 'Work in Progress Toward a New Paradigm for the Sociological Study of Religion in the United States', *American Journal of Sociology*, **98** (5), 1044–93.

Wuthnow, R. (1992), *Rediscovering the Sacred: Perspectives on Religion in Contemporary Society*, Grand Rapids, MI: William B. Eerdmans.

Yevenes, A. M. (2002), 'La Telenovela Chilena como fuente de simbolismo religioso para los jovenes Chilenos', unpublished paper presented to the doctoral commission, Faculty of Social Science and Communication, The Gregorian University, Rome.

Additional Resources: Most Recommended Books in the Area of Media, Religion and Culture

Clark, L. S. (2003), *From Angels to Aliens: Teenagers, the Media and the Supernatural*, New York: Oxford University Press.

Granfield, P. (ed.) (1994), *The Church and Communication*, Kansas City, MO: Sheed and Ward.

Greil, A. and T. Robbins (eds) (1994), *Between Sacred and Secular: Research and Theory on Quasi-Religion*, Greenwich, CT: JAI Press.

Hoover, S. M. (1988), *Mass Media Religion: The Social Sources of the Electronic Church*, London: Sage.

Hoover, S. M. and L. S. Clark (2002), *Practicing Religion in the Age of the Media*, New York: Columbia University Press.

Martin, D. (1980), *The Breaking of the Image: A Sociology of Christian Theory and Practice*, Oxford: Basil Blackwell.

Martin, J. W. and C. E. Ostwalt, Jr (eds) (1995), *Screening the Sacred: Religion, Myth and Ideology in Popular American Film*, Boulder, CO: Westview Press.

May, J. R. and M. Bird (eds) (1982), *Religion in Film*, Chicago, IL: The University of Chicago Press.

Melady, M. (1999), *The Rhetoric of John Paul II: The Pastoral Visit as a New Vocabulary of the Sacred*, Westport, CT: Praeger.

Rossi, P. J. and P. Soukup (eds) (1994), *Mass Media and the Moral Imagination*, Kansas City, MO: Sheed and Ward.

Schrader, P. (1972), *Transcendental Style in Film*, Berkeley, CA: University of California Press.

Stark, R. and C. Y. Glock (1968), *Patterns of Religious Commitment*, Berkeley, CA: University of California Press.

Wuthnow, R. (1992), *Rediscovering the Sacred: Perspectives on Religion in Contemporary Society*, Grand Rapids, MI: William B. Eerdmans.

Bibliography

Addae-Mensah, M. (2000), *Walking in the Power of God: Thrilling Testimonies about Supernatural Encounters with God*, Ontario, Canada: Guardian Books.

Adiwatanasit, C. and P. Kanchavamonai (1979), 'Can Buddhism Survive Modernization?', Bangkok: Department of Social Science, Kasetsart University.

Adorno, T. (1972/1991), *The Culture Industry*, London: Routledge.

Agyin Asare, C. (2001), *Power in Prayer: Taking Your Blessings by Force,* Hoonar, Netherlands: His Printing.

—— (1999), *Rooted and Built Up in Him: Things Which Make Sound Doctrine*, Accra, Ghana: Miracle Publications.

Anderson, B. (1991), *Imagined Communities: Reflections on the Origins and Spread of Nationalism* (rev. edn), London: Verso.

Anderson, H. and E. Foley (1997), *Mighty Stories, Dangerous Rituals*, San Francisco, CA: Jossey-Bass.

Ang, I. (1993), *Watching Dallas: Soap Opera and the Melodramatic Imagination*, London: Routledge.

Anonymous (2002), 'Passing the Trash', *The Economist*, 6 April, 27–28.

Appadurai, A. (1996), *Modernity at Large: Cultural Dimensions of Globalization,* Minneapolis, MN and London: University of Minnesota Press.

Arén, G. (1978), *Evangelical Pioneers in Ethiopia: Origins of the Evangelical Church Mekane Yesus*, Stockholm: EFS and Addis Ababa: Mekane Yesus.

Arhinful, D. K. (2002), '"We Think of Them": Money Transfers from the Netherlands to Ghana', in I. Van Kessel (ed.), *Merchants, Missionaries and Migrants: 300 Years of Dutch–Ghanaian Relations*, Accra, Ghana: Sub-Saharan Publishers.

Arnold, M. (1869/1994), *Culture and Anarchy*, New Haven, CT: Yale University Press.

Arredondo, P. (2000), 'Televisión Mexicana en Estados Unidos: ¿Extinción o Reconversión?' http://www.felafacs.org/dialogs/pdf21/arredondo.pdf.

Babin, P. (1991), *The New Era in Religious Communication*, Minneapolis, MN: Fortress Press.

Bakke, J. (1987), *Christian Ministry: Patterns and Functions within the Ethiopian Evangelical Church Mekane Yesus*, Oslo: Solum Forlag A.S. and Atlantic Highlands, NY: Humanities Press.

Banks, M. (2001), *Visual Methods in Social Research*, London: Sage.

Bar-Haim, G. (1997), 'The Dispersed Sacred: Anomie and the Crisis of Ritual', in S. M. Hoover and K. Lundby (eds), *Rethinking Media, Religion and Culture*, Thousand Oaks, CA: Sage.

Barnard, M. (2001), *Approaches to Understanding Visual Culture*, New York: Palgrave.

Bartra, R. (1987), *La Jaula de la Melancolía*, México: Grijalbo.

Baugh, L. (1997), *Imaging the Divine: Jesus and Christ-Figures in Film*, Kansas City, MO: Sheed and Ward.

Bauman, Z. (2000), *Globalization: The Human Consequences*, New York: Columbia University Press.

BBC World Service (2002), 'Western African Popular Video Film', *Omnibus*, radio documentary (producer and presenter, Jolyon Mitchell, 28 May).

Beaune, J.-C. (1980), *La Technologie Introuvable – Recherche sur la Définition et l'unité de la Technologie à Partir de Quelques Modèles du XVII et XIX Siècles*, Paris: Librarie Philosophique J. Vrin.

Beckford, J. A. (1989), *Religion and Advanced Industrial Society*, London: Unwin Hyman.

Bediako, K. (2000), 'Africa and Christianity on the Threshold of the Third Millennium: The Religious Dimension,' *African Affairs*, **99**, 303–23.

Bell, C. (1992), *Ritual Thinking, Ritual Practice*, New York: Oxford University Press.

Bellah, R., R. Madsen, W. M. Sullivan, A. Swidler and S. M. Tipton (1985), *Habits of the Heart: Individualism and Commitment in American Life*, Berkeley, CA: University of California Press.

Benjamin, W. (1969), *Illuminations*, New York: Shocken.

Bergeson, A. and A. Greeley (2000), *God in the Movies*, New Brunswick, NJ: Transaction Press.

Besançon, A. (2000), *The Forbidden Image: An Intellectual History of Iconoclasm*, trans. J. M. Todd, Chicago, IL: University of Chicago Press.

Blumhofer, E. (1993), *Aimee Semple McPherson: Everybody's Sister*, Grand Rapids, MI: William B. Eerdmans.

Blumler, J. G. and E. Katz (1974), *The Uses of Mass Communication: Current Perspectives on Gratifications Research*, Beverly Hills, CA: Sage.

Bolman, L. and T. Deal (1997), *Reframing Organizations: Artistry, Choice and Leadership*, San Francisco, CA: Jossey-Bass.

Boomershine, T. E. (1991), 'Doing Theology in the Electronic age: the Meeting of Orality and Electricity', *Journal of Theology*, **95**, 4–14.

—— (1987), 'Biblical Megatrends: Towards a Paradigm for the Interpretation of the Bible in Electronic Media', in H. R. Kent (ed.), *Society of Biblical Literature Seminar Papers*, Atlanta, GA: Scholars Press, pp. 144–57.

Boorstin, D. (1972), *The Image: A Guide to Pseudo-events in America*, New York: Atheneum.

Boston Globe investigative staff (2003), *Betrayal: The Crisis in the Catholic Church*, Boston, MA: Back Bay Books.

Boys, M. (1989), *Educating in Faith: Maps and Visions*, San Francisco, CA: Harper & Row.

Braman, S. and A. Sreberny-Mohammadi (1996), *Globalization, Communication, and Transnational Civil Society*, Cresskill, NJ: Hampton Press.

Brasher, B. (2001), *Give Me That Online Religion*, San Francisco, CA: Jossey-Bass.

Brown, D., S. Davaney and K. Tanner (eds) (2001), *Converging on Culture: Theologians in Dialogue with Cultural Analysis and Criticism*, New York: Oxford University Press.

Bruce, S. (1996), *Religion in the Modern World: From Cathedrals to Cults*, Oxford: Oxford University Press.

—— (1990), *Pray TV: Televangelism in America*, London: Routledge.

Brugger SJ, W. (1958), *Diccionario de Filosofía*, Bacelona: Editorial Herder.

Bruner, J. (1996), *Actual Minds, Possible Worlds*, Cambridge, MA: Harvard University Press.

Bucher, K. von (1893), *Die Entstehung der Volkswirtschaft: Vorträge und Versuche*, Tübingen:Verlag der H. Laupp'shen Buchhandlung.

Buddenbaum, J. (1998), *Reporting News about Religion: An Introduction for Journalists*, Ames, IA: Iowa State University Press.

—— (1990), 'Religion News Coverage in Commercial Network Newscasts', in R. Abelman and S. M. Hoover (eds), *Religious Television: Controversies and Conclusions*, Norwood, NJ: Ablex, pp. 249–63.

—— (1988), 'The Religion Beat at Daily Newspapers', *Newspaper Research Journal*, **9** (4), 57–69.

—— and D. Stout (1996), *Religion and Mass Media: Audiences and Adaptation*, Thousand Oaks, CA: Sage.

Burns, A. (1989), *The Power of the Written Word: The Role of Literacy in the History of Western Civilization*, New York: Peter Lang.

Bynum, C. W. (1999), 'Why All the Fuss About the Body? A Medievalist's Perspective', in V. E. Bunnell and L. A. Hunt (eds), *Beyond the Cultural Turn: New Directions in the Study of Society and Culture,* Berkeley, CA: University of California Press, pp. 251–52.

Calabrese, A. and J. Burgelman (eds) (1999), *Communication, Citizenship, and Social Policy: Rethinking the Limits of the Welfare State*, Lanham, MD: Rowman & Littlefield.

Campbell, J. (1949), *The Hero With a Thousand Faces*, New York: Pantheon.

Carey, J. (2002), Preface to the First Edition of the *Journal of Media and Religion*, *Journal of Media and Religion*, **1** (1), 1–3.

Carroll, N. (1990), *The Philosophy of Horror, or, Paradoxes of the Heart,* London and New York: Routledge.

Castells, M. (1997), *The Information Age: Economy, Society, and Culture, Vol. 2: The Power of Identity*, Oxford, UK: Blackwell.

—— (1996), *The Information Age: Economy, Society and Culture, Vol. 1: The Rise of the Network Society*. Oxford, UK: Blackwell.

—— (1989), *The Informational City: Information Technology, Economic Restructuring, and the Urban-Regional Process*, Oxford, UK: Blackwell.

Catholic Internet network in Thailand, http://lox2.loxinfo.co.th/~thcatcom.

Catholic Social Communications of Thailand, *Choice for a Better Life*, video, http://www.udomsarn.com.

——, *The Cry of My Appeal*, video, http://www.udomsarn.com.

——, *His Foot Speaks ... in Painting*, video, http://www.udomsarn.com.

——, *The Moment of Life*, video, http://www.udomsarn.com.

Christian, W. (1998), 'Spain in Latino Religiosity', in P. Casarella and R. Gómez (eds), *El Cuerpo de Cristo: The Hispanic Presence in the US Catholic Church*, New York: Crossroad Books, pp. 326–27.

Christians, C. G., J. P. Ferré and P. M. Fackler (1993), *Good News: Social Ethics and the News*, New York: Oxford University Press.

Chumsripan, S. (1994), 'The History of the Catholic Church of Thailand', in *Twenty-five Years of Thai Vatican*, Bangkok: Assumption Printing Press.

Ciecko, A. (2001), 'Superhit Hunk Heroes for Sale: Globalization and Bollywood's Gender Politics', *Asian Journal of Communication*, **11** (2), 121–43.

Cimino, R. and D. Lattin (1998), *Shopping for Faith: American Religion in the New Millenium*, San Francisco, CA: Jossey-Bass.

Clark, L. S. (2003), *From Angels to Aliens: Teenagers, the Media, and the Supernatural*, New York: Oxford University Press.

—— (2002), 'Young Peoples' Internet Practices and Spirituality: Preliminary Findings from the Teens and the New Media@Home Project', presented to the first meeting of the Pew Internet and American Life Advisory Board, Chicago, April.

—— and S. M. Hoover (1997), 'At the Intersection of Media, Culture, and Religion: A Bibliographic Essay', in S. M. Hoover and K. Lundby (eds), *Rethinking Media, Religion, and Culture*, Thousand Oaks, CA: Sage, pp. 15–36.

Clarke, A. C. (1999), *Greetings, Carbon-Based Bipeds!* New York: St Martin's Press.

Collins, R., N. Garnham and G. Lockley (1987), *The Economics of Television: The UK Case*, London: Sage.

Comaroff, J. and Comaroff, J. (1991), *Of Revelation and Revolution: Christianity, Colonialism, and Consciousness in South Africa*, Vol. I, Chicago: University of Chicago Press.

Cormode, S. (2002), 'Multi-layered Leadership: The Christian Leader as Builder, Shepherd, and Gardener', *Journal of Religious Leadership* (2), 69–104.

Davis, S. and C. Meyer (1999), *Blur: The Speed of Change in the Connected Economy*, New York: Little, Brown and Company.

Dewey, J. (1927/1957), *The Public and its Problems*, New York: H. Holt and Company.

De Witte, M. (2003), 'Altar Media's *Living Word:* Televised Charismatic Christianity in Ghana', *Journal of Religion in Africa*, **33** (2), 172–202.

Donham, D. L. (1999), *Marxist Modern: An Ethnographic History of the Ethiopian Revolution*, Berkeley, CA: University of California Press.

Droogers, A. (1994), 'The Normalisation of Religious Experience: Healing, Prophecy, Dreams, and Visions', in Karla Poewe (ed.), *Charismatic Christianity as a Global Culture*, Columbia, SC: University of South Carolina Press.

Drury, J. (1999), *Painting the Word: Christian Pictures and Their Meanings*, New Haven, CT: Yale University Press.

Duncan-Williams, N. (1990), *You are Destined to Succeed*, Accra, Ghana: Action Faith Publications.

Dupré, L. (1993), *Passage to Modernity: An Essay in the Hermeneutics of Nature and Culture*, New Haven, CT: Yale University Press.

Edwards, M. U., Jr (1994), *Printing, Propaganda and Martin Luther*, Berkeley, CA: University of California Press.

Eickelman, D. F. and J. W. Anderson (1999), *New Media in the Muslim World*, Bloomington, IN: Indiana University Press.

Eide, Ø.M. (1996), *Revolution and Religion in Ethiopia: A Study of Church and Politics with Special Reference to the Ethiopian Evangelical Church Mekane Yesus 1974–1985*, Studiea Missionalie Upsaliensia, no. 66, Stavanger: Misjonshøgskolens Forlag and Uppsala Universitet.

Eisenstein, E. L. (1983), *The Printing Revolution in Early Modern Europe*, Cambridge, UK and New York: Cambridge University Press.

—— (1979), *The Printing Press as an Agent of Change*, Cambridge, UK and New York: Cambridge University Press.

Ellul, J. (1985), *The Humiliation of the Word*, Grand Rapids, MI: William B. Eerdmans.

Engel, J. F. (1988), *How to Communicate the Gospel Effectively*, Achimota, Ghana: Africa Christian Press.

Espín, O. (1997), *Faith of the People: Theological Reflections on Popular Catholicism*, Maryknoll, NY: Orbis Books.

—— (1995), 'Pentecostalism and Popular Catholicism: The Poor and Traditio', *Journal of Hispanic/Latino Theology*, 3 (November), 14–43.

Evangelical Lutheran Church in America (1998), Board of the Division for Global Mission (March 20–22) Appendix 3, page 2, 'Membership Statistics of Companion Churches'.

Ewen, S. (1976), *Captains of Consciousness: Advertising and the Social Roots of the Consumer Culture*, New York: McGraw-Hill.

Fargher, B. L. (1988), 'The Charismatic Movement in Ethiopia, 1960–1980,' *Evangelical Review of Theology* (12), 344–58.

Febvre, L. and H.-J. Martin (1957), *The Coming of the Book: The Impact of Printing, 1450–1800* (D. Gerard, trans.), London: NLB.

Ferrater Mora, J. (1980), *Diccionario de Filosofía*, Madrid: Alianza Editorial.

Ferro, G. (2001), 'El Divino Niño: ícono para una nación', in *Belleza, Fútbol y Religiosidad Popular*, Bogotá: Cuadernos de Nación, Ministerio de Cultura.

Forbes, B. and J. Mahan (2000), *Religion and Popular Culture in America*, Berkeley, CA: University of California Press.

Forbes, R. J. (1965), *Studies in Ancient Technology*, vol. 2, 2nd edn, Leiden: E. J. Brill.

Fortune, M. (1991), 'How the Church Should Imitate the Navy', *Christian Century*, 23 January, p. 765.

Francis, M. (1995), 'Popular Piety and Liturgical Reform in a Hispanic Context', in A. M. Pineda and R. Schreiter (eds), *Dialogue Rejoined: Theology and Ministry in the United States Hispanic Reality,* Collegeville, MN: The Liturgical Press, pp. 165–66.

Freedberg, D. (1989), *The Power of Images: Studies in the History and Theory of Response*, Chicago: University of Chicago Press.

Freire, P. (1970), *Pedagogy of the Oppressed*, New York: Herder and Herder.

Froehle, B. and M. Gautier (2000), *Catholicism USA: A Portrait of the Catholic Church in the United States*, Maryknoll, NY: Orbis Books.

Gamboni, D. (1997), *The Destruction of Art: Iconoclasm and Vandalism since the French Revolution*, New Haven, CT: Yale University Press.

Gans, H. (1979), *Deciding What's News: A Study of CBS Evening News, NBC Nightly News, Newsweek, and Time*, New York: Pantheon Books.

García Canclini, N. (1995), *Consumidores y Ciudadanos*, México: Grijalbo.

—— (1989), *Culturas Híbridas*, México: Grijalbo.

García-Rivera, A. (1999), *The Community of the Beautiful: A Theological Aesthetics,* Collegeville, MN: The Liturgical Press.

Geertz, C. (1975), *The Interpretation of Cultures*, London: Hutchinson.

Gelder, K. (ed.) (2000), *The Horror Reader*, London and New York: Routledge.

Giddens, A. (1991), *Modernity and Self-Identity: Self and Society in the Late Modern Age*, Stanford, CA: Stanford University Press.

Gifford, P. (1998), *African Christianity, Its Public Role*, London: Hurst and Co.

Gillespie, M. (1995), *Television, Ethnicity and Cultural Change*, London and New York: Routledge.

Ginsburg, F. D., L. Abu-Lughod and B. Larkin (eds) (2002), *Media Worlds: Anthropology on New Terrain*, Berkeley, CA: University of California Press.

Gitlin, T. (1983), *Inside Prime Time*, New York: Pantheon Books.

—— (1980), *The Whole World is Watching*, Berkeley, CA: University of California Press.

Globe Spotlight Team (2002), 'Scores of Priests Involved in Sex Abuse Cases', *The Boston Globe*, 31 January, p. 1.

Goethals, G. (1981), *The TV Ritual: Worship at the Video Altar*, Boston, MA: Beacon Press.

Goizueta, R. (2002), 'Theology and Popular Culture', unpublished paper presented at the meeting of the International Commission on Media, Religion and Culture, Vancouver.

—— (1995), *Caminemos con Jesús: Toward a Hispanic/Latino Theology of Accompaniment*, Maryknoll, NY: Orbis Press.

González, J. (1990), *Mañana: Christian Theology from a Hispanic Perspective*, Nashville, TN: Abingdon Press.

—— (1990), *Las Vetas del Encanto. Por los Veneros de la Producción Mexicana de telenovelas*, Universidad de Colima, México.

Goodstein, L. (2003), 'Train of Pain in Church Crisis Leads to Nearly Every Diocese', *The New York Times*, 12 January, pp. 1, 20–21.

Gorski, P. (2000), 'Historicizing the Secularization Debate: Church, State, and Society in Late Medieval and Early Modern Europe, CA. 1300 to 1700', *American Sociological Review*, **65** (1), 138–67.

Granfield, P. (ed.) (1994), *The Church and Communication*, Kansas City, MO: Sheed and Ward.

Greeley, A. (2003), 'The Times and Sexual Abuse by Priests', *America*, 10 February.

Greil, A. and T. Robbins (eds) (1994), *Between Sacred and Secular: Research and Theory on Quasi-Religion*, Greenwich, CT: JAI Press.

—— (1994), 'Introduction: Exploring the Boundaries of The Sacred' in A. Greil and T. Robbins (eds), *Religion and the Social Order*, London: JAI Press, pp. 1–26.

Grundy, M. (1999), Colonization and Christianity in Zimbabwe, *The Literature and Culture of Zimbabwe*, available online at: http://www.scholars.nus.edu.sg/landow/post/zimbabwe/religion/grundy2.html.

Gruzinski, S. (2001), *Images at War: Mexico from Columbus to Blade Runner (1492–2019)*, trans. H. MacLean, Durham, NC and London: Duke University Press.

—— (1995), *La Guerra de las Imágene: De Cristóbal Colón a Blade Runner*, México: Fondo de Cultura Económica.

Hackett, R. (1998), 'Charismatic/Pentecostal Appropriation of Media Technologies in Nigeria and Ghana', *Journal of Religion in Africa*, **28** (3), 1–19.

Hadden, J. and A. Shupe (1988), *Televangelism, Power, and the Politics of God's Frontier*, New York: H. Holt.

Hallin, D. (1986), *The Uncensored War: The Media and Vietnam*, New York: Oxford University Press.

Hamilton, N. and A. Rubin (1992), 'The Influence of Religiosity on Television Viewing', *Journalism Quarterly*, **69** (3): 667–78.

Hangen, T. (2002), *Redeeming the Dial: Radio, Religion, and Popular Culture in America*, Chapel Hill, NC: University of North Carolina Press.

Harvey, D. (1990), *The Condition of Postmodernity*, Cambridge: Blackwell.

Heifetz, R. (1994), *Leadership Without Easy Answers*, Cambridge, MA: Harvard University Press.

—— and M. Linsky (2002), *Leadership on the Line: Staying Alive Through the Dangers of Leading*, Cambridge, MA: Harvard Business School Press.

Helland, C. (2000), 'Online-Religion/ Religion-Online and Virtual Communitas', in J. K. Hadden and D. E. Cowan (eds), *Religion on the Internet: Research Prospects and Promises*, New York: Elsevier Science Press, pp. 205–23.

Hertog, H. (1941), 'On Borrowed Experience. An Analysis of Listening to Daytime Sketches', *Studies in Philosophy and Social Science*, IX (1), 65–95.

Hess, M. E. (2004), 'The Bible and Popular Culture: Engaging Sacred Text in a World of "Others"', in Robert Fowler (ed.), *New Paradigms in Bible Study*, Philadelphia, PA: Trinity Press International.

—— (2002), 'Rescripting Christian Education for Performative Practice', plenary address, Luther Seminary Convocation, St Paul, MN.

—— (1999), 'From Trucks Carrying Messages to Ritualized Identities: Implications of the Postmodern Paradigm Shift in Media Studies for Religious Educators', *Religious Education*, **94** (3), Summer, 273–88.

Heward-Mills, D. (2000), *Catch the Anointing*, Accra, Ghana: Dag's Tapes and Publications.

Hexham, I. and K. Poewe (1994), 'Charismatic Churches in South Africa: A Critique of Criticisms and Problems of Bias', in K. Poewe (ed.), *Charismatic Christianity as a Global Culture*, Columbia, SC: University of South Carolina Press.

Hiebert, R. E., D. F. Ungurait and T. W. Bohn (1985), *Mass Media IV: An Introduction to Modern Communication,* New York and London: Longman.

Hinze, B. (forthcoming), *The Practices of Dialogue in the Church: Aims, Struggles, Prospects.*

—— (2000), 'Ecclesial Repentance and the Demands of Dialogue,' *Theological Studies*, 61, 207–38.

Hoover, S. M. (forthcoming), *Religion in the Media Age*, London: Routledge.

—— (2003), 'Religion, Media and Identity: Theory and Method in Audience Research on Religion and Media', in J. Mitchell and S. Marriage (eds), *Mediating Religion: Conversation in Media, Religion and Culture*, London, New York: T & T Clark.

—— (2002a), 'The Culturalist Turn in Scholarship on Media and Religion', *The Journal of Media and Religion*, **1** (1), 25–36.

—— (2002b), 'Religion in the Media Age', *Expository Times*, **113** (9), 300–305.

—— (2002), 'Religion, Media and Identity: Theory and Method in Audience Research on Religion and Media', paper presented to the Annual Meeting of the International Communication Association, Seoul, Korea, July.

—— (2001), 'Religion, Media, and the Cultural Center of Gravity', in D. Stout and J. Buddenbaum (eds), *Religion and Popular Culture: Studies on the Interactions of Worldviews*, Ames, IA: Iowa State University Press.

—— (1999a), 'Rethinking Form and Content: Religion on Television or Television Religion', paper given at the Conference on Religious Function of Television, University of Heidelberg, Germany.

—— (1999b), 'The Converging Worlds of Religion and the Media', address, Edinburgh Conference on Media, Religion, and Culture.

—— (1998), *Religion in the News*, Thousand Oaks, CA: Sage.

—— (1988), *Mass Media Religion: The Social Sources of the Electronic Church*, Newbury Park, CA: Sage.

—— (1985), *Mass Media Religion*, Thousand Oaks, CA: Sage.

——, L. S. Clark and D. F. Alters, with J. G. Champ and L. Hood (2004), *Media, Home and Family*, New York and London: Routledge.

—— and K. Lundby (eds) (1997), *Rethinking Media, Religion, and Culture*, California, London and New Delhi: Sage.

—— and A. M. Russo (2002), 'Understanding Modes of Engagement in Research on Media and Meaning-Making', paper presented to the Conference of the International Association for Mass Communication Research, Barcelona, July.

—— and S. Venturelli (1996), 'The Category of "The Religious": The Blind Spot of Contemporary Media Theory', *Critical Studies in Mass Communication*, **13** (September), 251–65.

—— and L. S. Clark (eds) (2002), *Practicing Religion in an Age of Media*, New York: Columbia University Press.

Horsfield, P. (2003), 'Electronic Media and the Past-Future of Christianity', in J. Mitchell and S. Marriage (eds), *Mediating Religion: Conversations in Media, Religion and Culture*, London and New York: T & T Clark.

—— (2002), *The Mediated Spirit*, Melbourne: Commission for Mission, Uniting Church in Australia.

—— (1989), 'Teaching Theology in a New Cultural Environment', *Media Development*, 6–9.

—— (1988), 'Evangelism by Mail: Letters from Broadcasters', *Journal of Communication*, **35** (1) (Winter), 89–97.

—— (1986), *Taming the Television: A Parent's Guide to Children and Television*, Sydney: Albatross.

—— (1984), *Religious Television: The American Experience*, New York: Longman.

—— (1981), 'Religious Television Broadcasting: An Analysis of the Theological Debate in Light of the Empirical Research', unpublished PhD dissertation, Boston University, Boston.

Hull, J. (1991), *What Prevents Christian Adults from Learning?* Philadelphia, PA: Trinity International Press.

Information and Technology Section of The Archdiocese of Bangkok, in Thai: http://www.catholic.or.th.

ISSARA Catholic Magazine online, in Thai: http://www.issara.com.

Jenkins, H. (1992), *Textual Poachers: Television Fans and Participatory Culture*, London: Routledge.

Jenkins, P. (2003), *The New Anti-Catholicism: The Last Acceptable Prejudice*, Oxford, UK: Oxford University Press.

—— (2002), *The Next Christendom*, New York: Oxford University Press.

—— (2002a), 'The Next Christianity', *Atlantic Monthly*, October, 53–68.

Jensen, K. B. (2002), *A Handbook of Media and Communication Research: Qualitative and Quantitative Methodologies*, London: Routledge.

Jewett, R. (1999), *Saint Paul Returns to the Movies: Triumph over Shame*, Grand Rapids, MI: William B. Eerdmans.

John Paul II (1999), *Ecclesia in America*.

Johnson, E. (1992), *She Who Is: The Mystery of God in Feminist Theological Discourse*, New York: Crossroads.

Johnson, L. T. (2003), 'Sex, Women and the Church', *Commonweal*, 20 June, p. 11.

Johnston, R. (2000), *Reel Spirituality: Theology and Film in Dialogue*, Grand Rapids, MI: Baker Academic.

Jones, S. (1999), 'Studying the Net: Intracacies and Issues', in S. Jones (ed.), *Doing Internet Research: Critical Issues and Methods for Examining the Net*, Thousand Oaks, CA: Sage.

Jørgensen, K. (1995), *Communication Means People: Manual on Communication in Society and Church*, Addis Ababa: Mekane Yesus Seminary.

Kahl, J. A. (1968), *The Measurement of Modernism*, Austin, TX and London: The University of Texas Press.

Kaur, R. (2000), 'Rethinking the Public Sphere: The Ganapait Festival and Media Competitions in Mumbai', *Polygraph* 12. Available online at http://www.lehigh.edu/~amsp/poly12.htm.

Kegan, R. and L. Lahey (2000), *How the Way We Talk Can Change the Way We Work*, San Francisco, CA: Jossey-Bass.

Kintz, L. and J. Lesage (1998), *Media, Culture, and the Religious Right*, Minneapolis, MN: University of Minnesota Press.

Kristeva, J. (1982), *Powers of Horror: An Essay on Abjection*, New York: Columbia University Press.

Lakeland, P. (2003), *The Liberation of the Laity: In Search of an Accountable Church*, New York and London: Continuum.

Landow, G. P. (2002), 'A Clash of Religions: Kaguvi Encounters the Christian Conception of the Afterlife', *The Literature and Culture of Zimbabwe*, available online at: http://www.scholars.nus.edu.sg/landow/post/zimbabwe/vera/afterlife.html.

Lang, K. (1964), 'Communications Research: Origins and Development', *International Encyclopedia of Communication*, 369–74.

Larkin, B. (2002), 'The Materiality of Cinema Spaces in Northern Nigeria', in Faye Ginsburg, Lila Abu-Lughod and Brian Larkin (eds), *Media Worlds: Anthropology on a New Terrain*, Berkeley, CA: University of California Press.

—— (2000), 'Hausa Dramas and the Rise of Video Culture in Nigeria', in Jonathan Haynes (ed.), *Nigerian Video Film,* Ohio: Ohio University Press.

Larry, J. K. (1999), *Pauline Images in Fiction and Film: On Reversing the Hermeneutical Flow*, Sheffield: Sheffield Academic Press.

Lasswell, H. (1938), *Propaganda Technique in the World War*, New York: P. Smith.

Lawrence, B. B. (2002), 'Allah On-line: the Practice of Global Islam in the Information Age', in S. Hoover and L. S. Clark (eds), *Practicing Religion in the Age of the Media:Explorations in Media, Religion, and Culture*, New York: Columbia University Press.

Lazarsfeld, P. and E. Katz (1964), *Personal Influence*, Glencoe, IL: Free Press.

Lehikoinen, T. (2003), *Religious Media Theory: Understanding Mediated Faith and Christian Applications of Modern Media*, Jyvaskyla, Finland: University of Jyvaskyla.

Levine, L. W. (1988), *Highbrow/Lowbrow: The Emergence of Cultural Hierarchy in America*, London and Cambridge, MA: Harvard University Press.

Lindlof, T. R. (1995), *Qualitative Communication Research Methods*, Thousand Oaks, CA: Sage.

Lippy, C. (1986), *Religious Periodicals of the United States*, Westport, CT: Greenwood Press.

Livingstone, S. (1990), *Making Sense of Television: The Psychology of Audience Interpretation*, Oxford: Pergamon Press.

Lowenthal, L. (1961), *Literature, Popular Culture and Society*, Englewood Cliffs, NJ: Prentice-Hall.

Lundby, K. (2002), 'Between American Evangelicalism and African Anglicanism', in S. M. Hoover and L. S. Clark (eds), *Practicing Religion in the Age of the Media*, New York: Columbia University Press.

Lyon, D. (2000), *Jesus in Disneyland: Religion in Postmodern Times*, Cambridge: Polity Press (in association with Blackwell Publishers).

Macy, G. (1995), 'Demythologizing "the Church" in the Middle Ages', *Journal of Hispanic/Latino Theology*, 3 (27), August, 23–41.

Magombe, P. V. (1996), 'The Cinemas of Sub-Saharan Africa', in Geoffrey Nowell-Smith (ed.), *The Oxford History of World Cinema*, Oxford: Oxford University Press.

Marcuse, H. (1941), 'Some Social Implications of Modern Technology', *Studies in Philosophy and Social Science*, **IX** (1), 414–39.

Marsh, C. and G. Ortiz (eds) (1997), *Explorations in Theology and Film*, Oxford: Blackwell Publishers.

Martin, D. (1980), *The Breaking of the Image: A Sociology of Christian Theory and Practice*, Oxford: Basil Blackwell.

Martin, J. and C. Ostwalt (1995), *Screening the Sacred: Religion, Myth, and Ideology in Popular American Film*, Boulder, CO: Westview Press.

Martín-Barbero, J. (1997), 'Mass Media as a Site of Resacralisation of Contemporary Culture', in S. M. Hoover and K. Lundby (eds), *Rethinking Media, Religion and Culture*. Thousand Oaks, CA: Sage.

—— (1987/1993), *Communication, Culture, and Hegemony: From the Media to Mediations*, trans. E. Fox and R. A. White, London: Sage (originally published as *De los Medios a las Mediaciones: Comunicación, Cultura y Hegemonia*).

—— and G. Rey (1999), *Los Ejercicios del Ver*, Barcelona, Spain: Gedisa Editorial.

Maxwell, D. (1998), 'Editorial', *Journal of Religion in Africa*, **28** (3), 255–57.

May, J. (ed.) (1997), *New Image of Religious Film*, Kansas City, MO: Sheed & Ward.

—— and M. Bird (1982), *Religion in Film*, Knoxville, TN: University of Tennessee Press.

Mazur, E. and K. McCarthy (eds) (2001), *God in the Details: American Religion in Popular Culture*, New York: Routledge.

Mazziotti, N. (1996), *La Industria de la Telenovela*, Buenos Aires: Paidós.

McDannell, C. (1995), *Material Christianity: Religion and Popular Culture in America*, New Haven, CT: Yale University Press.

McDonnell, J. (2003), 'Desperately Seeking Credibility: English Catholics, the News Media and the Church', in J. Mitchell and S. Marriage (eds), *Mediating Religion: Conversations in Media, Religion and Culture*, London and New York: T & T Clark.

McGann, M. (2002), *Exploring Music and Theology*, Collegeville, MN: Liturgical Press.

McLagan, M. (2000), 'Spectacles of Difference: Buddhism, Media Management, and Contemporary Tibet Activism', *Polygraph* 12. Available online at http://www.lehigh.edu/~amsp/poly12.htm.

McQuail, D. (1997), *Audience Analysis*, Thousand Oaks, CA and London: Sage.

Melady, M. (1999), *The Rhetoric of John Paul II: The Pastoral Visit as a New Vocabulary of the Sacred*, Westport, CT: Praeger.

Meyer, B. (2003), 'Impossible Representations: Pentecostalism, Vision and Video Technology in Ghana', presented to the annual meeting of the Society for the Anthropology of Religion, Providence, RI (April).

—— (2002), 'Prayers, Guns and Ritual Murder: Popular Cinema and Its New Figures of Power and Success', English translation of the French published text from *Politique Africaine*, **82**, 45–62. See: http://www2.fmg.uva.nl/media-religion/publications/prayers.htm.

—— (2001), *Modern Mass Media, Religion and the Imagination of Communities: Different Postcolonial Trajectories in West Africa, Brazil and India*, Research Proposal for NWO-PIONIER (grant received), available online at: http://www.pscw.uva.nl.media-religion.

—— (2001), 'Money, Power and Morality: Popular Ghanaian Cinema in the Fourth Republic', *Ghana Studies*, **4**, 65–84.

—— (1999), *Translating the Devil: Religion and Modernity Among the Ewe in Ghana*, Edinburgh: Edinburgh University Press.

—— (1998), 'The Power of Money, Politics, Occult Forces, and Pentecostalism in Ghana', *African Studies Review*, **41** (3), 15–38.

—— (1995), '"Delivered from the Powers of Darkness", Confessions about Satanic Riches in Christian Ghana', *Africa*, **65** (2), 236–55.

―――― and P. Pels (eds) (2003), *Magic and Modernity:Dialectics of Revelation and Concealment*, Stanford, CA: Stanford University Press.

Miles, M. (1996), *Seeing and Believing: Religion and Values in the Movies*, Boston, MA: Beacon Press.

Miller, D. E. (1997), *Reinventing American Protestantism: Christianity in the New Millennium*, Berkeley, Los Angeles and London: University of California Press.

Mitchell, J. (forthcoming) 'Film and Theology', in David Ford (ed.), *The Modern Theologians*, 3rd edn, Oxford: Blackwell.

―――― (2002), 'Western African Popular Video Film', *Omnibus,* radio documentary, BBC World Service, 28 May.

―――― (1999), *Visually Speaking, Radio and the Renaissance of Preaching*, Edinburgh, Scotland: T & T Clark.

―――― and S. Marriage (eds) (2003), *Mediating Religion: Conversations in Media, Religion and Culture,* London and New York: T & T Clark.

Monsivais, C. (2000), *Aires de Familia. Cultura y Sociedad en América Latina*, Barcelona: Anagrama.

―――― (1995), *Los Rituales del Caos*, México: Era.

Moore, R. L. (1994), *Selling God: American Religion in the Marketplace of Culture*, New York: Oxford University Press.

Morgan, D. (2005), *Religious Visual Culture in Theory and Practice*, Berkeley, CA: University of California Press.

―――― (2001), 'For Christ and the Republic: Protestant Illustration and the History of Literacy in Nineteenth-Century America', in D. Morgan and S. M. Promey (eds), *The Visual Culture of American Religions*, Berkeley, CA: University of California Press, pp. 49–67.

―――― (1999), *Protestants and Pictures: Religion, Visual Culture and the Age of American Mass Production*, New York: Oxford University Press.

―――― (1998a), 'Notes on Meaning and Medium in the Aesthetics of Visual Piety', unpublished email post to the media.faith listserve, http://monaro.adc.rmit.edu.au/mailman/listinfo/media.faith.

―――― (1998b), *Visual Piety: A History and Theory of Popular Religious Images,* Berkeley, CA: University of California Press.

―――― and S. Promey (eds) (2001), *The Visual Culture of American Religions*, Berkeley, CA: University of California Press.

Morley, D. and K. Robins (1996), *Spaces of Identity*, London and New York: Routledge.

Muangrat, N. (1998), 'The Relationship of Communication Behavior, Modernization and the People's Beliefs, Faith, Religious Practice among Catholics', Bangkok: Department of Public Relations, Chulalongkorn University.

Muniz, S. (1998), *Reinventado la cultura*, Barcelona: Gedisa.

Murdock, G. (1997), 'The Re-enchantment of the World: Religion and the Transformations of Modernity' in S. M. Hoover and K. Lundby (eds), *Rethinking Media, Religion and Culture*, Thousand Oaks, CA: Sage.

Naficy, H. (1993), *The Making of Exile Cultures: Iranian Television in Los Angeles.* Minneapolis, MN: University of Minnesota Press.

Negt, O. and A. Kluge (1974), *Öffentlichkeit und Erfahrung. Zur Organisations-analyse von bürgerlicher und proletarischer Öffentlichkeit*, Frankfurt am Main: Suhrkamp. Cited in B. Meyer (2003), 'Impossible Representations: Pentecostalism, Vision and Video Technology in Ghana', presented to the annual meeting of the Society for the Anthropology of Religion, Providence, RI.

Niebuhr, H. R. (1951), *Christ and Culture*, New York: Harper and Row.

Nord, D. (1984), 'The Evangelical Origins of Mass Media in America, 1815–1835', *Journalism Monographs*, **88**, 1–30.

O'Meara, T. F. (1999), *Theology of Ministry*, New York: Paulist Press.

Ong, W. (1982), *Orality and Literacy: The Technologising of the Word*, London: Methuen.

—— (1967), *The Presence of the Word*, New Haven, CT: Yale University Press.

Orsi, R. A. (1996), *Thank You, St. Jude: Women's Devotion to the Patron Saint of Hopeless Causes*, New Haven, CT: Yale University Press.

Ortiz, R. (1997), *Mundialización y Cultura*, Buenos Aires: Alianza.

—— (1985), *Telenovela: Historia e Producao*, São Paulo: Brasiliense.

Palmer, P. (1998), *The Courage to Teach: Exploring the Inner Landscape of a Teacher's Life*, San Francisco, CA: Jossey-Bass.

—— (1993), *To Know as We are Known*, San Francisco, CA: HarperSanFrancisco.

Pardun, C. and K. McKee (1995), 'Strange Bedfellows: Symbols of Religion and Sexuality on MTV', *Youth and Society*, **26** (4): 438–49.

Park, J. K. (2002), 'Constructing a Religion: Issues of the study of religion on the Internet,' paper presented to the International Communication Association, Seoul, July.

Park, R. E. (1925), 'Immigrant Community and Immigrant Press', *American Review*, **3**, 143–52.

Parker, E., D. Barry and D. Smythe (1955), *The Television-Radio Audience and Religion*, New York: Harper & Brothers.

Peck, J. (1993), *The Gods of Televangelism*, Cresskill, NJ: Hampton Press.

Peterson, G. (2001), 'Religion as Orienting World View', *Zygon*, **36** (1) (March).

Philip, T. V. (no date), 'The missionary impulse in the early Asian Christian tradition', *PTCA Bulletin*, 5–14.

Plude, F. (1996), 'Forums for Dialogue: Teleconferencing and the American Catholic Church', in P. A. Soukup, *Media, Culture and Catholicism*, Kansas City, MO: Sheed and Ward, pp. 191–200.

—— (1994), 'Interactive Communication in the Church', in P. Granfield (ed.), *The Church and Communication*, Kansas City, MO: Sheed and Ward, pp. 179–95.

—— (1992), 'Modern Communications vs. Centralized Power', *The Syracuse Record*, 13 April, p. 9.

Postman, N. (1987), *Amusing Ourselves to Death*, London: Methuen.

Rahner, K. (1966), 'The Theology of the Symbol', in *Theological Investigations, Vol. 4*, New York: Crossroad Books.

Rey, G. (unpublished), 'Polifemo entre Pucheros. La Telenovela Latinoamericana en el Fin de Siglo'.

—— (2002), 'La Historia de la Televisión Colombiana', in Guillermo Orozco (ed.), *Historia de la Televisión en América Latina*, Barcelona; Gedisa.

—— (2000), 'La telenovela en el fin de siglo: Cultura y melodrama en América Latina', in *Cultura y medios de comunicación*, Salamanca: Pontificia Universidad de Salamanca.

—— (1997), 'Os poros do rostro da vida', in José Tavares de Barros (ed.), *Imagens da America Latina*, São Paulo: Ediciones Loyola.

—— (1994), 'Los Matices de la Imaginación', in *La Realidad Imaginad: El Video en América Latina*, Bogotá: Ediciones Paulinas.

Rodriguez, A. (n.d.), 'Spanish International Network', http://www.museum.tv/archives/etv/S/htmlS/spanishinter/spanishinter.htm.

Rodriguez, C. (2001), *Fissures in the Mediascape: An International Study of Citizen's Media*, Cresskill, NJ: Hampton Press.

Romero, J. L. (1982), *Las Ideologias de la Cultural Nacional*, Buenos Aires: CEDAL. Cited in J. Martin-Barbero (1993), *Communication, Culture, and Hegemony: From the Media to Mediations*, trans. E. Fox and R. A. White, London: Sage.

Roof, W. C. (1999*), Spiritual Marketplace: Baby Boomers and the Re-Making of American Religion*, Princeton, NJ: Princeton University Press.

—— (1993), *A Generation of Seekers: The Spiritual Journeys of the Baby Boom Generation*, San Francisco, CA: Harper.

Rossi, P. J. and P. Soukup (eds) (1994), *Mass Media and the Moral Imagination*, Kansas City, MO: Sheed and Ward.

Roth, M. (1999), 'That's Where the Power Is: Identification and Ideology in the Construction of Contemporary Christian Music', unpublished thesis, The University of New Mexico.

Saint John's University (n.d.), 'History of The Catholic Churches in Thailand', http://www.stjohn.ac.th/Department/info/ch_history.html . Bangkok, Thailand.

Sawicki, M. (1994), *Seeing the Lord: Resurrection and Early Christian Practice*, Minneapolis, MN: Fortress Press.

Schmalzbauer, J. (2003), *People of Faith: Religious Conviction in American Journalism and Higher Education*, Ithaca, NY: Cornell University Press.

Schoenherr, R. A. (2002), *Goodbye Father: The Celibate Male Priesthood and the Future of the Catholic Church*, Oxford, UK: Oxford University Press.

Schrader, P. (1972), *Transcendental Style in Film*, Berkeley, CA: University of California Press.

Schultze, Q. (1991), *Televangelism and American Culture: The Business of Popular Religion*, Grand Rapids, MI: Baker Book House.

Scribner, R. W. (1994), *For the Sake of Simple Folk: Popular Propaganda for the German Reformation*, Oxford: Clarendon Press.

Senge, P. (1994), *The Fifth Discipline*, New York: Doubleday.

Silk, M. (1995), *Unsecular Media*, Urbana, IL: University of Illinois Press.

Singh, A. (2000), 'Preface to the Special Issue on World Religions and Media Culture', *Polygraph* 12. Available online at http://www.lehigh.edu/~amsp/poly12.htm.

Sipe, A. W. R. (1995), *Sex, Priests, and Power: Anatomy of a Crisis*, New York: Brunner/Mazel.

Sobrino, J. (1988), *Spirituality of Liberation*, Maryknoll, NY: Orbis Books.

Somprasong, C. (1994), 'Media Role and Strategy for Evangelism: Mass Media Usage for Evangelism Distribution by Catholic Social Communications Center of Thailand, 1966–1993', Bangkok: Department of Mass Communication, Chulalongkorn University.

Soukup, P. A. (1997), 'Church, Media and Scandal', in James Lull and Stephen Hinerman (eds), *Media Scandals*, Cambridge, UK: Polity Press.

Steinfels, P. (2003), *A People Adrift: The Crisis of the Roman Catholic Church in America*, New York and London: Simon and Schuster.

—— (2002), 'Abused by the Media', *The Tablet*, 14 September.

Steinglass, M. (2002), 'When There's Too Much of a Not-Very-Good Thing', in *The New York Times*, 26 May, Sunday, Late Edition, Final Section: Section 2, Page 16; Column 1.

Sunkel, G. (ed.) (1999), *El Consumo Cultural en América Latina*, Bogotá: Convenio Andrés Bello.

Sweet, L. (1993), *Communication and Change in American Religious History*, Grand Rapids, MI: William B. Eerdmans.

Tanner, K. (1997), *Theories of Culture: A New Agenda for Theology*, Minneapolis, MN: Fortress Press.

Tavares de Barros, J. (1997), *Imagens de América Latina*, São Paulo: Ocic-Brasil Edições Loyola.

—— (1994), *La Realidad Imaginada*, Santafé de Bogotá: Paulinas.

—— (ed.) (1992), *La Imagen Nuestra de Cada Día: Situación del Video Pastoral en América Latina,* Santa Fé de Bogotá, Colombia: Ediciones Paulinas.

Thai Catholic Calendar (2001), Thai Catholic Office of Communication, Bangkok: Assumption Printing Press.

Thomaselli, K. and A. Shepperson (2002), 'Speaking in Tongues, Writing in Vision: Orality and Literacy in Televangelistic Communication', in S. M. Hoover and L. S. Clark (eds), *Practicing Religion in the Age of the Media*, New York: Columbia University Press.

Thompson, E. P. (1963), *The Making of the English Working Class*, New York: Vintage Books.

Thompson, J. B. (1994), *Ideology and Modern Culture*, Stanford, CA: Stanford University Press.

Tilley, T. (2000), *Inventing Catholic Tradition*, Maryknoll, NY: Orbis Books.

Tocqueville, A. de (1835/2000), *Democracy in America*, trans. S. D. Grant, Indianapolis, IN: Hackett Publishing.

Tonnies, F. (1935/1957), *Gemeinschaft und Gesellschaft (Community and Society)*, trans. by C. P. Loomis (ed.), East Lansing, MI: Michigan State University Press.

Toulmin, S. (1990), *Cosmopolis: The Hidden Agenda of Modernity*, New York: The Free Press.

Tuchman, G. (1978), *Making News: A Study in The Construction of Reality*, New York: Free Press.

Turner, G. (1990), *British Cultural Studies: An Introduction*, London and New York: Routledge.

UCIP World Congress (2004), 'Religion in Thailand: Buddhism plays a profound role in people's reactions to events', http://www.ucip.ch/cong/ath#2, Bangkok, Thailand.

UDOMSARN Catholic Weekly Newspaper and Monthly Magazine, in Thai: http://www.udomsarn.com.

Ukadike, N. F. (1998), 'Critical Approaches to World Cinema: African Cinema', in John Hill, John and Pamela Church Gibson (eds), *The Oxford Guide to Film Studies*, Oxford: Oxford University Press.

Vaill, P. (1996), *Learning as a Way of Being: Strategies for Survival in a World of Permanent White Water*, San Francisco, CA: Jossey-Bass.

Valenzuela, N. (1986), 'Spanish Language TV in the Americas: From SIN to PANAMSAT', in J. Miller (ed.), *Telecommunications and Equity: Policy Research Issues*, New York: Elsevier, pp. 329–38.

Van Dijk, R. A. (1997), 'From Camp to Encompassment: Discourses of Transsubjectivity in the Ghanaian Pentecostal Diaspora', *Journal of Religion in Africa*, **28** (1), 135–59.

—— (1996), 'From Camp to Encompassment: Discourses of Transsubjectivity in the Ghanaian Pentecostal Diaspora, *Journal of Religion in Africa*, **26** (4), 1–25.

Veer, P. van der (2001), 'Transnational Religion', paper presented at the Conference on Transnational Migration: Comparative Perspectives, Princeton.

—— (1994), *Religious Nationalism: Hindus and Muslims in India*, Berkeley, CA: University of California Press.

—— (1993), *Orientalism and the Postcolonial Predicament: Perspectives on Southeast Asia*, Philadelphia, PA: University of Pennsylvania Press.

Vella, J. (1994), *Learning to Listen, Learning to Teach*, San Francisco, CA: Jossey-Bass.

Vera, Y. (1993), *Nehanda*, Harare: Baobab Books.

Veron, E. and L. Escudero (eds) (1997), *Telenovela. Ficción popular y mutaciones culturales*, Barcelona: Gedisa.

Wagner, B. A. (2003), '"Full Gospel" Radio: Revivaltime and the Pentecostal Uses of Mass Media, 1950–1979', *Fides et Historia*, **25** (1), 107–22.

Warner, R. S. (1993), 'Work in Progress Toward a New Paradigm for the Sociological Study of Religion in the United States', *American Journal of Sociology*, **98** (March), 1044–93.

Warren, H. (2001), 'Southern Baptists and Disney', in D. A. Stout and J. M. Buddenbaum (eds), *Religion and Popular Culture: Studies on the Interaction of Worldviews*, Ames, IA: Iowa State University Press.

—— (1998), 'Standing Against the Tide: Conservative Protestant Families, Mainstream and Christian Media', unpublished PhD dissertation, University of Texas at Austin.

Weber, M. (1919/1947), 'Science as a Vocation' (Wissenschaft als Beruf), in M. Weber, *From Max Weber: Essays in Sociology*, trans. H. H. Gerth and C. W. Mills (eds), London: Kegan Paul.

Weinberger, D. (2002), *Small Pieces, Loosely Joined*, New York: Perseus Books.

Wells, P. (2000), *The Horror Genre: From Beelzebub to Blair Witch*, London: Wallflower.

West, D. (1995), 'Filming the Chicano Family Saga: Interview with Director Gregory Nava', *Cineaste*, **21** (4), Fall, 26–28.

Williams, P. and L. Chrisman (1996), 'Introduction', *Colonial Discourse and Post-Colonial Theory*, New York: Columbia University Press, pp. 1–20.

Winston, D. (1999), *Red Hot and Righteous: The Urban Religion of the Salvation Army*, Cambridge, MA: Harvard University Press.

Wuthnow, R. (1992), *Rediscovering the Sacred: Perspectives on Religion in Contemporary Society*, Grand Rapids, MI: William B. Eerdmans.

Yevenes, A. M. (2002), 'La Telenovela Chilena Como Fuente de Simbolismo Religioso para los Jovenes Chilenos', unpublished paper presented to the doctoral commission, Faculty of Social Science and Communication, The Gregorian University, Rome.

Zaleski, J. (1997), *The Soul of Cyberspace: How New Technology is Changing our Spiritual Lives*, New York: HarperCollins.

Zubiri, X. (1993), *Intelligencia Sentiente*, Madrid: Alianza Editorial.

Zwick, R. (1997), 'The Problem of Evil in Contemporary Film', in John May (ed.), *New Image of Religious Film*, Kansas City, MO: Sheed & Ward.

Index

References to illustrations are in **bold**.